Model Construction with
GPSS-FORTRAN Version 3

The companion volume to this book is
The Simulator GPSS-FORTRAN Version 3
by Bernd Schmidt

Bernd Schmidt

Model Construction with GPSS-FORTRAN Version 3

With 41 Illustrations

Springer-Verlag
New York Berlin Heidelberg
London Paris Tokyo

Dr. Bernd Schmidt
Universität Erlangen Nürnberg
IMMD (IV)
Martensstrasse 3
D-8520 Erlangen
Federal Republic of Germany

CR Classification I.6

Library of Congress Cataloging in Publication Data
Schmidt, Bernd, 1940–
    Model construction with GPSS-FORTRAN version 3.
    (Advances in simulation)
    1. Digital computer simulation. 2. GPSS (Computer
program language) 3. FORTRAN (Computer program language)
I. Title. II. Series.
QA76.9.C65S3617   1987   001.4'34   87-4417

Printed and bound by R.R. Donnelley & Sons Harrisonburg, Virginia
Printed in the United States of America.

9 8 7 6 5 4 3 2 1

ISBN 0-387-96503-3 Springer-Verlag New York Berlin Heidelberg
ISBN 3-540-96503-3 Springer-Verlag Berlin Heidelberg New York

Contents

1 Continuous Models 1

  1.1 Host Parasite Model I 1
      1.1.1 Description of the Model............................ 1
      1.1.2 Implementation 2
      1.1.3 The Input Data... 4
      1.1.4 Results for the Simple Host Parasite Model 8
      1.1.5 Problems... 14

  1.2 Host Parasite Model II 15
      1.2.1 Description of the Model............................ 15
      1.2.2 The Results of the Host Parasite Model with
             Scheduled Events.................................... 16
      1.2.3 Problems... 18

  1.3 The Input of User Variables 20
      1.3.1 The Technique Used 20
      1.3.2 Problems... 21

  1.4 Host Parasite Model III 24
      1.4.1 Description of the Model............................ 24
      1.4.2 The Subroutine STATE 24
      1.4.3 Crossings and Conditions 25
      1.4.4 Events 25
      1.4.5 Checking of Conditions.............................. 26
      1.4.6 Summary of the Method Used........................ 28
      1.4.7 Results for Host Parasite Model III 28
      1.4.8 Problems... 30

  1.5 The Host Parasite Model IV 32
      1.5.1 Description of the Model............................ 32
      1.5.2 The Implementation 33
      1.5.3 The Results of the Host Parasite Model IV............ 34
      1.5.4 Problems... 36

2 Queued Systems 37

  2.1 Brewery Model I 37
      2.1.1 Descriptions of the Model............................ 37
      2.1.2 Implementation in Subroutine ACTIV 38
      2.1.3 Main Program 41
      2.1.4 The Subroutine ACTIV 42

2.1.5   Input Data Records 43
2.1.6   Example 44

2.2   Running of the Model 45
2.2.1   Example 45
2.2.2   Problems 50

2.3   Brewery Model II 51
2.3.1   Description of the Model 51
2.3.2   Calling the Random Number Generator 51
2.3.3   Collection and Processing of Statistical Data 52
2.3.4   The Subroutine ACTIV 53
2.3.5   The Results 54
2.3.6   Problems 57

2.4   Brewery Model III 58
2.4.1   Description of the Model 58
2.4.2   The Subroutine ACTIV 58
2.4.3   The Subroutine STATE 60
2.4.4   Crossings 60
2.4.5   Events 61
2.4.6   Checking of Conditions 62
2.4.7   Main Program 63
2.4.8   Summary of the Implementation 63
2.4.9   The Results 64
2.4.10 Problems 66

3   The Facilities 69

3.1   Model of a Squirrel 69
3.1.1   Structure of the Model 69
3.1.2   The Implementation 70
3.1.3   Main Program 70
3.1.4   The Subroutine ACTIV 71
3.1.5   Repetition of the Simulation 73
3.1.6   The Results 75
3.1.7   Problems 76

3.2   The Model of a Repair Workshop 77
3.2.1   Description of the Model 77
3.2.2   Implementation 77
3.2.3   The Results 79
3.2.4   Problems 81

3.3   Job Processing Model 82
3.3.1   Description of the Model 82
3.3.2   Implementation 82

          3.3.3   Main Program   84
          3.3.4   The Subroutine DYNVAL   85
          3.3.5   The Results..   86
          3.3.6   Problems...   89

    3.4   Group Practice Model   90
          3.4.1   Description of the Model.............................   90
          3.4.2   Implementation   90
          3.4.3   Main Program   91
          3.4.4   The Subroutine ACTIV   93
          3.4.5   The Results..   94
          3.4.6   Problems...   95

4   Pools and Storages   96

    4.1   Computer Model I   96
          4.1.1   Description of the Model.............................   96
          4.1.2   Implementation   97
          4.1.3   Settling Phase   99
          4.1.4   The Subroutine ACTIV   99
          4.1.5   Main Program 101
          4.1.6   The Results.. 102
          4.1.7   Problems... 105

    4.2   Computer Model II 106
          4.2.1   Alterations to Computer Model I.................... 106
          4.2.2   The Results.. 107
          4.2.3   Problems... 110

5   The Coordination of Transactions 112

    5.1   Model of Parcel Transport 112
          5.1.1   Description of the Model............................. 112
          5.1.2   The Implementation 112
          5.1.3   The Results.. 113
          5.1.4   Problems... 115

    5.2   Model of a Scenic Mountain 117
          5.2.1   Description of the Model............................. 117
          5.2.2   Implementation 117
          5.2.3   Problems... 121

    5.3   The Coordination of Simultaneous Activities 123
          5.3.1   Model of Car Telephones 124
          5.3.2   Structure of the Car Telephone Model................ 124
          5.3.3   The Results.. 126
          5.3.4   Problems... 127

6   Tanker Fleet Model 128

    6.1   Description of the Tanker Fleet Model 128

    6.2   The Structure of the Model 130
          6.2.1   State Variables.. 130
          6.2.2   The Events 131
          6.2.3   Setting the Flags 133
          6.2.4   The Conditions.. 134
          6.2.5   Testing the Conditions................................ 136
          6.2.6   The Subroutine ACTIV 137
          6.2.7   The Subroutine STATE 139
          6.2.8   Main Program....................................... 139
          6.2.9   Results of the Model of the Tanker Fleet............. 140
          6.2.10 Problems... 143

7   The Set Concept in GPSS-FORTRAN Version 3 144

    7.1   Host Parasite Model V 144

    7.2   Structure of the Model 146
          7.2.1   The Subroutine STATE 146
          7.2.2   The Events in Subroutine EVENT 146
          7.2.3   Setting of Flags 147
          7.2.4   The Conditions and Their Testing 148
          7.2.5   The Input Data.. 148

    7.3   The Results 149

    7.4   Problems 152

8   Specializations 155

    8.1   Variables and Their Graphical Representation 155
          8.1.1   The Cedar Bog Lake Model 155
          8.1.2   Construction of the Model 156
          8.1.3   The Results... 158
          8.1.4   Problems.. 160

    8.2   Combination of Model Components to Structure 161
          8.2.1   The Supermarket Model.............................. 161
          8.2.2   Structure of Model................................... 161
          8.2.3   The Results... 162
          8.2.4   Problems.. 164

8.3   The Representation of System Dynamics Models in GPSS-
      FORTRAN Version 3 166
      8.3.1 System Elements and System Functions of System
             Dynamics and Their Representation in GPSS-
             FORTRAN Version 3 166
      8.3.2 The Snowtire Supply Model 170
      8.3.3 The Results... 170
      8.3.4 Problems.. 172

8.4   Differential Equations of Higher Order 173
      8.4.1 Wheel Suspension Model I............................ 173
      8.4.2 Structure of the Model 174
      8.4.3 The Results... 174
      8.4.4 Problems.. 177

8.5   Stochastic, Continuous Systems 179
      8.5.1 The Wheel Suspension Model II....................... 179
      8.5.2 The Results... 179
      8.5.3 Problems.. 183

8.6   Delayed Variables 184
      8.6.1 The Host Parasite Model VI.......................... 184
      8.6.2 Implementation 184
      8.6.3 Combining the Data Areas for Delayed Variables..... 186
      8.6.4 Initialisation of the Delayed Variables 187
      8.6.5 The Results... 188
      8.6.6 Examples.. 188

References 191

Appendix 193

Index 286

1. Continuous Models

The host parasite model is used to demonstrate the simulation of continuous systems. Four versions of this model are used to show different techniques.

Host parasite model I   Description and simulation of the model

Host parasite model II   Scheduled events, combined model with continuous and event orientated components

Host parasite model III   Conditional events, definition and testing of conditions

Host parasite model IV   Dynamic alteration of the structure of the model

1.1 Host Parasite Model I

There are many examples in nature in which a species of parasite secures its continued existence by invading a species of host; the hosts are killed by the parasites which grow inside them. This type of breeding is done for example by parasitic wasps and eels.

Variations in population of both the hosts and the parasites can be observed. When the number of parasites increases, the number of invaded hosts increases and consequently the number of hosts declines. The decline of the number of hosts leads to a decline in the number of invaded hosts and therefore to a decline in the number of parasites. As a consequence the number of hosts can increase according to their normal growth rate.

1.1.1 Description of the Model

If one assumes the hosts have a natural excess of births over deaths equal to a, then the number of hosts x increases in the absence of parasites in accordance with the following differential equation:

$$dx/dt = a*x \qquad (1)$$

The rate of mortality depends on the natural mortality of the species and the number of encounters between hosts and parasites. In the model it is assumed that this is proportional to the product of the number of parasites and the number of hosts. This is based on the assumption that theoretically every parasite can invade every host; thus the number of possible invasions is x*y.

The number of actual invasions is a fraction c of the maximum number of possible invasions. Thus the actual rate of increase of the number of hosts is given by:

dx/dt = a*x - c*x*y   (2)

The rate of change of the number of parasites is given by the differential equation:

dy/dt = c*x*y - b*y   (3)

As a simplification, it is assumed that every invasion of a host leads to the birth of exactly one parasite and the parasites multiply only under such conditions.

The term b*y represents the mortality rate of the parasites. The number of hosts and number of parasites as a function of time is obtained by integrating the differential equations (2) and (3).

The constants are:

    a = 0.005
    b = 0.05
    c = 6.E-6

The initial conditions are:

    x(0) = 10000
    y(0) = 1000

Problem:

The behaviour of the system from T = 0. to T = 1000. is to be plotted.

1.1.2 Implementation

The differential equations (2) and (3) which describe the system are expressed in the subroutine STATE.

The two differential equations belong to a set. It follows that the model contains only the set NSET = 1.

For the hosts:

number of hosts x   = SV(1,1)
rate of change dx/dt   = DV(1,1)

For the parasites:

number of parasites y = SV(1,2)
rate of change dy/dt   = DV(1,2)

Thus the subroutine STATE is as follows:

```
C
C         Label selector
C         ==============
          GOTO(1),NSET
C
C         Equation for NSET = 1
C
1         DV(1,1) = 0.005*SV(1,1) - 0.000006*SV(1,2)*SV(1,1)
          DV(1,2) = -0.05*SV(1,2) + 0.000006*SV(1,2)*SV(1,1)
          RETURN
          END
```

The initial values are provided by the event NE = 1. The
subroutine EVENT is as follows:

```
C
C         Label selector
C         ==============
          GOTO(1),NE
C
C         Processing the event
C         ====================
1         SV(1,1) = 10000.
          SV(1,2) = 1000.
          CALL BEGIN(1,*9999)
          RETURN
```

Notes:

* Almost every event which assigns new values to continuous variables whose values are obtained by solving differential equations or alters them subsequently, should be
placed between two calls of the subroutine MONITR. In this way
the state of the system before and after the assignment is
recorded.

Exceptions are events which set initial conditions. The continuous variables have the value 0 before initialisation. If
this value is recorded by a call of the subroutine MONITR,
this leads to a distortion of the plot output.

* Every change of the continuous variables which occurs in the
subroutine STATE must be directly followed by the call of
the subroutine BEGIN.

Finally the subroutine ANNOUN is used to schedule the event NE =
1 in section 5 of the main program "Setting the initial
conditions".

Thus section 5 of the main program has the following form:

```
C
C         5. SETTING THE INITIAL CONDITIONS
C         =================================
C         SCHEDULE THE FIRST EVENTS
C         =========================
          CALL ANNOUN(1,0.,*9999)
C
```

```
C      SOURCE ACTIVATION
C      =================
C
C      PROCEED WITH THE SIMULATION
C
5500   IF(SVIN.NE.0) CALL SAVIN
C
```

It is wise to print the INTSTA array after every simulation. It contains statistical information about the integration. The output is performed by the subroutine REPRT6. It is called in section 7 "Terminating section" of the main program:

```
C
C      7. Terminating section
C      ======================
7000   CONTINUE
       CALL REPRT6
C
```

REPRT6 has no parameters.

The following actions are necessary for the implementation of the host parasite model:

* Define the differential equations in the subroutine STATE.

* Define the initial conditions in the subroutine EVENT

* Schedule the event NE = 1 in the main program

* Call REPRT6 in the main program

1.1.3 The Input Data

The required input data are read in section 3 of the main program "Input and assignment of variables" by the subroutine XINPUT from a file with a logical device number provided in UNIT1.
The input data is in free format, i.e. numbers can be input in I-, F- or E-format, and spaces are ignored.

The input file has the following layout:

```
TEXT;  HOST PARASITE MODEL I/
VARI;  TEND; 1000./
VARI;  EPS; 1.E-3/
VARI;  ICONT; 1/
INTI;  1; 1; 1.0; 2; 2; 0.01; 5.; 1.E-4; 10000/
PLO1;  1; 0.; 1000.; 10.; 21; 001001; 001002/
PLO3;  1;*W;HOST;*P;PARASIT/
END/
```

The input consists of 4 sections which are given the names TEXT, VARI, INTI and PLOT in the data records. The input is in free format. Values are separated by ";", and records are terminated by "/".

* TEXT

The text which follows the command TEXT appears as a heading at
the top of the results. In this example the heading is "Host
Parasite model I".

* VARI

The command VARI is followed by the name of a variable and its
value.

TEND; 1000.

The upper bound of the simulation time is assigned.   The
simulation run is ended at time 1000., the result are output, and
the program is stopped.

EPS; 1.E-3

EPS specifies the time difference required between   two
activities in order that they should not be regarded   as
simultaneous.

ICONT; 1
The model is continuous. This means that data for the integration
algorithm (INTI) and for plotting the results (PLOT) are
required.

The default setting applies to those input variables which are
not assigned values by a VARI command. This applies to TXMAX,
IPRINT, SVIN, and SVOUT.

TXMAX= 1.E+10

The host parasite model is continuous. Transactions are not used
and TXMAX is therefore meaningless.

IPRINT = 0

The trace of the individual state transitions is switched off.

SVIN = 0
SVOUT = 0

The saving and restoring of system variables does not take place.

* INTI

The two differential equations form a single set. Therefore only
one INTI record is necessary.

The command name INTI is followed by the index of the set. The
following values are placed in components 1 to 8 of the
integration array INTMA.

The integration array is described in volume 2, appendix A 3.2,
"Multidimensional Arrays".

The record for this example has the following layout:

```
INTI        Command name
1           Number of the set
1           Integration algorithm ( 1 = Runge Kutta Fehlberg)
1.          Initial step size
2           Number of continuous variables SV
2           Number of derivatives DV
            (Number of differential equations)
0.01        Minimum integration step size
5.          Maximum integration step size
1.E-4       Maximum relative error
10000       Maximum number of integration steps
```

* PLOT

There are three input records for each plot. The three plot records are placed in the three plot arrays PLOMA1, PLOMA2, PLOMA3. The plot arrays are described in volume 1, chapter 7.2.2 and in the volume 2, appendix A 3.2, "Multidimensional Arrays".

The second and third record can be omitted. In this case the default values are used. See volume 1, chapter 7.2, "Output of Plots".

Those fields of a record for which no values are provided are automatically assigned the value 0. Only the first and third records are needed in the host parasite model I. The first record defines the variables to be plotted.

```
PLO1        Command name
1           Index of plot
0.          Time of beginning of plot
1000.       Time of end of plot
10.         Time step size of monitor
21          Number of file to which plot data is written.
001001      Identification of the first variable to be plotted
001002      Identification of the second variable to be plotted
```

00n00m is the identification of variable m in set n.

If the derivative DV(n,m) is to be plotted then its identification in the record is -00n00m.

As only the two variables SV(1,1) and SV(1,2) are to be plotted, further information is not required. The fields for the other 4 variables are assigned the values 0 by the subroutine INPUT.

The second record provides the scale for the x- and y- axes. As the default setting is acceptable this record is not required.

The third record contains the plot symbols and gives a short description of the variables.

```
PLO3        Command name
1           Number of plot
*W          Plot symbol for the first variable
HOST        The eight characters of the short description
*P          Plot symbol for the second variable
PARASIT     The eight characters of the short description
```

Further information is not required and the values of the remaining variables are assigned default values by the subroutine INPUT.

The input data is ended by the record END/.

For convenience the structure of the PLO2 record is described here:

PLO2; number of plot; size of time step; print indicator; scale; minimum; maximum;

Size of time step

The parameter size of time step determines the scale of the x-axis.

0   x-axis unit = monitor step size (default setting)

value   an arbitrary value can be chosen for the unit of the x-axis.

Print indicator

The print indicator determines the extent of the output.

1   plot
2   plot and table of values (default setting)
3   plot, table of values, and phase diagram

Scaling

The scaling refers to the representation of the y-axis.

0   quick plot (default setting)
             The variables to be plotted are so scaled, that their range of values is not much less than the size of the plot. The scaling factors are chosen so that the scales of the y-axis are, as far as possible, round numbers. The scaling factors of the variables are independent of each other.

1   maximum scaling
             every variable is so scaled that it occupies the whole of the plot.

2   uniform representation with bound
             All variables are plotted with the same scale. This makes it easy to compare the variables. Particular regions can be selected and plotted. In this case the values of the minimum and maximum must be provided.

3   Uniform representation without bound.
             All variables are plotted with the same scale. Rounded values are selected for the bound.

4   Logarithmic representation of the absolute value of the functions.

Comments:

* The files which contain data to be plotted should be given numbers from 21 onwards.

* The print symbol is characterised by preceeding it by the character *. The character * is not printed. The combination ** is allowed.

* If the indicator for the scaling is not equal to 2, then the last two values, the minimum and maximum, can be omitted.

1.1.4 Results for the Simple Host Parasite Model

The results begin with the contents of the file containing the input data records.

All input data records are subjected to a plausibility check. If an error is found an error message is output and the simulation run is terminated. If the allowable relative error of an integration step is larger than 0.01, a warning is output but the simulation run is continued.

Then all values of the input data which control the simulation run are printed. The character string which was input in the TEXT record is used as a heading. The user should check very carefully the correctness of these values.

The third section of the output contains the integration statistics. It provides the following information:

* number of integration steps

The number of integration steps which actually occured during the simulation run is output.

* average step size
The average integration step size is output. This can be affected by a reduction of the step size caused by a discrete activity or a monitor call.

* number of crossings
The number of crossings which were detected and localised during the simulation run is output.

* Average number of steps per crossing.
The number of additional integration steps needed to localise a crossing is output.

Notes:

* The user should ensure that the maximum permissible relative error of the integration is compatible with the relative error of the representation of real numbers in the computer. If the average integration step size output by the subroutine REPRT6 is of the order of magnitude of the monitor step size, this is an indicator that the integration step size is bounded because of the monitor. The permissible relative error would allow a larger integration step size.

An initial step size of the order of magnitude of the average integration step size is recommended.

When testing the user should observe the first 100 integration steps using the trace IPRINT.

* The integration statistics are output by the subroutine REPRT6, contained in section 7 "Terminating section" of the main program.

The plots and tables of values of the required state variables are output after the integration statistics. This is done by the call of the subroutine ENDPLO in the main program. The parameter ISTAT in the parameter list controls the output of statistical information as follows:

ISTAT=0   no output of the confidence interval and the settling phase

ISTAT=1   output of the confidence interval and the settling phase.

The heading of every plot starts with a short summary for each variable plotted. This summary contains information about the minimum, the maximum, the mean, and statistical information.

The statistical information refers to stochastic systems. In such systems the mean must be estimated using the available samples. The centre of the confidence interval is the estimated sample mean. The probability that the actual mean is in this interval is 95 %.

If the system has a settling time, then its length is estimated. The amount by which the mean would change when samples made during the settling period are rejected is output.

Notes:

* The mean, confidence interval, and the change of the mean due to the exclusion of the settling period are only computed and printed when this is called for by setting ISTAT=1 in the parameter list of ENDPLO. This should only be done if it is really necessary, because the calculation of the statistical values requires many file accesses and therefore a lot of computation time.

* If the techniques implemented in GPSS-FORTRAN Version 3 cannot calculate the confidence interval or the settling time, then an appropriate message is output instead of the values of the confidence interval and the displacement of the mean due to the settling phase.
Text is associated with the X- and Y-axes via the string supplied by the user in the data record PLO2. If the record PLO2 has not been input, then the default value is used.

The Y-axis is labelled separately for each variable.

Example:

The Y-axis for the parasite population extendes from 0 to 2000. The complete Y-axis is divided into 100 rows of characters. Thus

a row of characters represents the value 20.
The scale of the X-axis is determined by the default values. If
no special value is provided a column of characters has the width
of a monitor step.

In the present example, the monitor step size has the value 10.
Accordingly, the step size of the X-axis is 10.
Duplicate symbols are defined at the top line along the plot.
These are used when 2 or more print symbols for different
variables are to be printed at the same position.

The events are also indicated by a * at the top. In the current
example there are no events.

Note:

    * The values of the state variables are recorded by the subrou-
    tine MONITR and written to a file. The subroutine MONITR is
    called by the subroutine FLOWC in the flow control at intervals
    of time given by the monitor step size.

The subroutine MONITR can also be called by the user. Every call
of MONITR by the user is regarded as an event, i.e. there is
always a * in the column EVENT at the time at which a user call
of MONITR has occurred.

The plot is followed by the table of values.

The table of values should be used for the analysis of the
results of the simulation. The plots only provide an
approximation to the values. In particular, important information
can be omitted as intermediate values cannot be output.

The analysis of the results for the simple host parasite model
shows the oscillation with a time delay which is typical of this
type of model. The increasing population of hosts with a corresponding delay leads to an increase in the population of parasites and vice versa.

It is significant that the dynamic behaviour of the number of
hosts and parasites depends also on the initial values. If the
initial values are altered the dynamic behaviour of the model can
be quite different. See volume 2, chapter 1.1.5, problem 1.

Notes:

    * It is to be noted in analysing the results that the curves
    for the host and parasite populations are plotted with dif-
    ferent scales. It is recommended that the output is specified
    so that the same scales are used for both curves. See volume
    2, chapter 1.1.5, problem 3.

    * The simulation run can take place either in batch mode or in
    interactive mode. The mode of operation is determined by the
    variable XMODUS assigned a value in section 1, "Selection of
    the mode of operation" of the main program. See Volume 1,
    chapter 7.4 "Modes of Operation". Then:

    XMODUS = 0   batch operation (default setting)
    XMODUS = 1   interactive mode

  *   The input data records are to be provided in a file with
name "DATAIN" with the logical device name UNIT1. Output is to
a file with the name "DATAOUT" with the logical device number
UNIT2. See volume 2, appendix A2, "Model Construction."

The default values are:

UNIT1 = 14
UNIT2 = 15

T = 1000.00   RT = 1000.00

INTEGRATION STATISTICS
=======================

SET	NUMBER INT.STEPS	MEAN STEP SIZE	NUMBER CROSSINGS	NUM.STEPS PER CROSSING
1	202.00	4.9505	0.	0.

.P L O T   NR 1

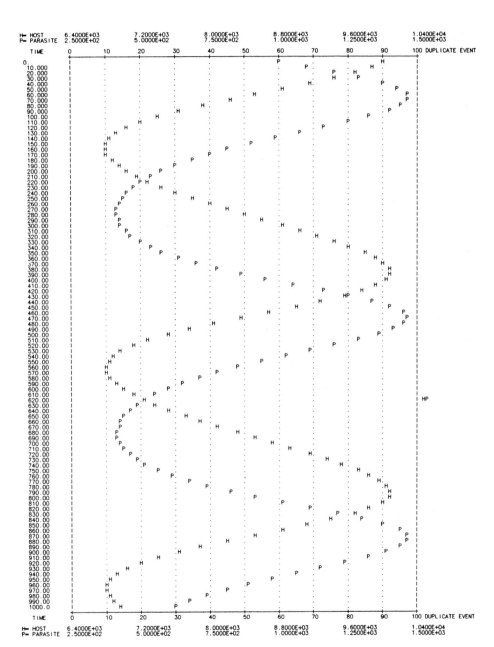

1.1.5 Problems:

The problems should make the user familiar with the use of GPSS-
FORTRAN Version 3.

* Problem 1

The simulation is to be repeated with the following initial
conditions:

x(0) = 5000.   x(0) = 10000.
y(0) = 1000.   y(0) = 2000.

Note:

   * The two assignments of SV (1,1) and SV (1,2) in the subroutine EVENT are to be altered.

* Problem 2

For the original problem a second plot is to be produced, which
shows the rates of change DV(1,1) and DV(1,2).

Note:

   * The number of plots is determined by the number of given plot
   data records. Each plotis produced by reading in the corresponding data records. If the derivative is to be plotted instead
   of the variable, then the characteristic of the variable is
   given a minus sign.

The two additional data records required in this problem have the
following form:

PLO1; 2; 0.; 1000.; 10.; 22;-001001;-001002/
PLO3; 2;*X;HOST;*Y;PARASIT/

* Problem 3

A plot is to be output in which the variables SV(1,1) and SV(1,2)
have the same scale.

Note:

   * PLO2 must be as follows:

   PLO2; 1; O; 2; 3/

1.2 Host Parasite Model II

Events belong to the discrete part of the simulator. They can be
used to represent discontinuities in the behaviour of a function
of time.

Scheduled and conditional events are distinguished.   The time at
which scheduled events will occur is known. Conditional events
occur when the state of the system is such that a particular
condition is true.

It is possible in GPSS-FORTRAN Version 3 to include events in a
continuous model. This leads to combined discrete and continuous
models.

In simulators which can only deal with continuous models and
cannot deal with discrete activities, it is necessary to
represent a discontinuity by a curve with a very steep slope.

This technique has the disadvantage that the integration step
size must be drastically reduced within a very short time
interval in order to take into account the sudden change of the
differential coefficient.

Discontinuities occur seldom in real systems. One often observes
a continuous change of a state variable with a steep slope rather
than a discontinuity.   It is however recommended that a
discontinuous change is used in the model to represent
occurrences in the system of large and sudden changes of value.

There are two reasons for this:

1. The processing of such a discontinuity is very simple in a
simulator which can deal with discrete events.

2. The error caused by representing a rapid but continuous change
in the system by a discontinuity in the model is normally small.

1.2.1 Description of the Model

First the representation of scheduled events are shown in an
example. The host parasite model from chapter 1.1 is slightly
extended for this purpose:

The number of parasites is to be reduced to half its value at
T = 300.

This is a scheduled event which alters the state variable
SV(1,2).   The event occurs in addition to the event which
assigns initial values. Thus the subroutine EVENT is as follows:

```
C
C       Label selector
C       ==============
        GOTO(1,2), NE
C
C       Event processing
C       ================
1       SV(1,1) = 10000.
        SV(1,2) = 1000.
        CALL BEGIN(1,*9999)
        RETURN

2       CALL MONITR(1)
        SV(1,2) = SV(1,2)/2.
        CALL BEGIN(1,*9999)
        CALL MONITR(1)
        RETURN
```

The event NE = 2, as the event NE = 1, is scheduled in the main program by the statement

```
        CALL ANNOUN(2,300.,*9999)
```

The flow control activates the event NE = 2 only once, at time T = 300.

It is recommended that events which alter the values of SV or DV during the simulation are monitored. This is done by placing calls of the subroutine MONITR immediately before and after the event. As a result the values of the continuous variables before and after the event are recorded and output. Thus the user can check the correct occurrence of the event.

1.2.2   The Results of the Host Parasite Model with Scheduled
        Events

One can see from the plot that the results for models I and II are identical until time T = 300.

The number of parasites is reduced at time T = 300. This event is shown by a * in the event column at the right hand edge of the plot.

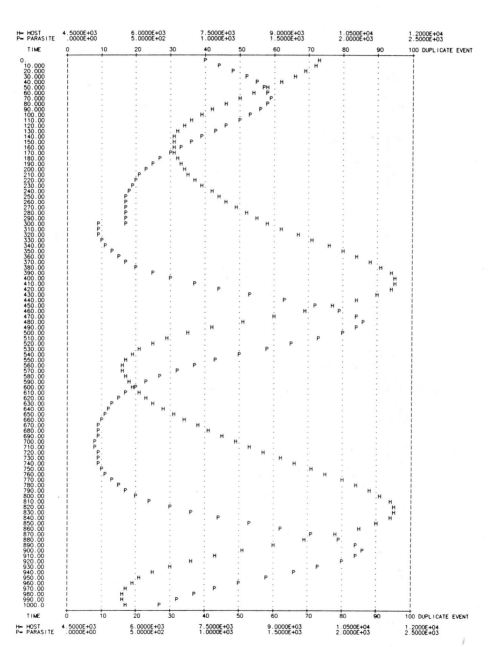

1.2.3 Problems

The problems show further possible applications of GPSS-FORTRAN Version 3.

* Problem 1
The number of parasites is to be halved at intervals of 300 units of time.

Note:

  * After the first occurrence of the event NE = 2, the succeed-
  ing event at time T + 300 must be scheduled. The second event
  is represented by the following code in the subroutine EVENT:

```
2      CALL MONITR(1)
       SV(1,2) = SV(1,2)/2.
       CALL BEGIN(1,*9999)
       CALL MONITR(1)
       CALL ANNOUN(2,T+300.,*9999)
       RETURN
```

* Problem 2

All state transitions between T = 280. and T = 310. are to be traced.

Note:

  * The trace of the execution of the model is controlled by the
  variable IPRINT. Itis initially set to IPRINT = 0. The trace is
  switched on by the event NE = 3 and switched off by the event
  NE = 4. Both events are scheduled in the main program:

```
       CALL ANNOUN(3,280.,*9999)
       CALL ANNOUN(4,310.,*9999)
```

The coding of the events is exceedingly simple:

```
3      IPRINT = 1
       RETURN
```

```
4      IPRINT = 0
       RETURN
```

Since IPRINT is a control variable rather than a state variable,
it is not necessary to call MONITR or BEGIN.

It is possible to schedule the event NE = 4 during the occurrence
of event NE = 3. In this case the call

```
       CALL ANNOUN(4,310.,*9999)
```

does not occur in the main program.

The event NE = 3 is now as follows:

```
3      IPRINT =1
       CALL ANNOUN(4,T+30.,*9999)
       RETURN
```

This has the same effect as:

```
3       IPRINT = 1
        CALL ANNOUN(4,310.,*9999)
        RETURN
```

* Problem 3

An event is to be coded which will set JPRINT(20) = 2 in the
interval from T = 280. to T = 310.   See Volume 1, chapter 5.3.2
"The Trace Indicators IPRINT and JPRINT".

1.3 The Input of User Variables

GPSS-FORTRAN Version 3 supports the free format input of the variables IPRINT, ICONT, SVIN, SVOUT, TEND, and TXMAX. The user can input in free format the values of user variables in the main program.

1.3.1 The Technique Used

The following steps must be taken for free format input:

The identifiers of variables which are to be input in free format are placed in the variables VNAMEI or VNAMER in section 3 of the main program "Input and assignment of values of variables". The variables VNAMEI and VNAMER are of type CHARACTER.

Identifiers of variables of type INTEGER are placed in VNAMEI and iIdentifiers of variables of type REAL are placed in VNAMER. See volume 1, chapter 7.1 "Free Format Input".

The record which assigns values to user variables has the following form:

VARI; identifiers; value/

VARI   name of the command for all records which assign
              values to variables

identifier   identifier of variable. This must already be entered
              in VNAMEI or VNAMER

value   the value of the variable which is to be read in
              free format

The subroutine XINPUT reads the record and places the value of the variable with the given identifier in IV if it is a variable of type INTEGER or in RV if it is a variable of type REAL.

The following statement assigns this value to the variable in the program whose identifier has just been read in.

Notes:

  * The user can follow the method for inputting previously defined varables. There is no difference between reading the 7 predefined variables and other user variables.

  * The user can also read formated variables. All the facilities of FORTRAN are available.

  * The order of the names of the variables in the section "Declaration of names" and the order of the assignments in the section "Assign values with free format input" must agree completely.

  * All variables which are to be read in free format must be assigned values in the section "Default values for free format input". These values are used if the variable does not appear in the VARI record.

The input variables must be identified to the subroutines in which they occur. The use of a block COMMON/ PRIV/ in which all input user variables occur is recommended. The block COMMON/PRIV/ should be declared in all user subprograms in which user variables can occur. This systematic method reduces the possibility of errors.

The main program and the following 6 user subprograms can contain user variables: EVENT, ACTIV, STATE, DETECT, TEST, and CHECK.

1.3.2 Problems

The problems demonstrate the input of free format variables.

* Problem 1

The variables a,b,c in the host parasite model are to be input.

Note:

   * The variable names a,b,c refer to variables of type REAL. The elements RV(4),RV(5) and RV(6) of the vector RV are assigned to them.

Note that the variable identifiers must be assigned in the same order as that in which the identifiers are declared.

The assignment of initial values and input is done as follows:

```
C       ASSIGN DEFAULT VALUES TO USER VARIABLES
C       =======================================
        A = 5. E-3
        B = 5. E-2
        C = 6. E-6
C
C
C       3. INPUT AND ASSIGNMENT OF VARIABLES
C       =====================================
C
C       DECLARATION OF NAMES OF INTEGER VARIABLES
C       =========================================
        VNAMEI(1) = 'IPRINT '
        VNAMEI(2) = 'ICONT  '
        VNAMEI(3) = 'SVIN   '
        VNAMEI(4) = 'SVOUT  '
C


C       DECLARATION OF NAMES OF REAL VARIABLES
C       ======================================
        VNAMER(1) = 'TEND   '
        VNAMER(2) = 'TXMAX  '
        VNAMER(3) = 'EPS    '
        VNAMER(4) = 'A      '
        VNAMER(5) = 'B      '
        VNAMER(6) = 'C      '
C
```

```
C          INITIAL VALUES FOR FREE FORMAT INPUT
C          =====================================
1000       IV(1) = IPRINT
           IV(2) = ICONT
           IV(3) = SVIN
           IV(4) = SVOUT
           RV(1) = TEND
           RV(2) = TXMAX
           RV(3) = EPS
           RV(4) = A
           RV(5) = B
           RV(6) = C
C
C          Input
C          =====
           CALL XINPUT(XEND,XNEW,XOUT,*9999)
C
C          ASSIGNMENT FOR FREE FORMAT INPUT
C          ================================
           IPRINT = IV(1)
           ICONT  = IV(2)
           SVIN   = IV(3)
           SVOUT  = IV(4)
           TEND   = RV(1)
           TXMAX  = RV(2)
           EPS    = RV(3)
           A      = RV(4)
           B      = RV(5)
           C      = RV(6)
```

The variables A, B, and C are made available to the main program and the following 6 user subprograms: EVENT, ACTIV, STATE, DETECT, TEST und CHECK in a block COMMON/PRIV/A,B,C.
The differential equations in STATE are now as follows:

```
1     DV(1,1) = A*SV(1,1) - C*SV(1,2)*SV(1,1)
      DV(1,2) = -B*SV(1,2) + C*SV(1,2)*SV(1,1)
```

The records to input the variables are now as follows:

```
VARI; TEND; 1000./
VARI; ICONT; 1/
VARI; EPS; 1.E-03/
VARI; A; 5.E-3/
VARI; B; 5.E-2/
VARI; C; 6.E-6/
```

* Problem 2

The initial conditions for the two differential equations are to be input.

Note:

   * The initial values of the numbers of hosts and parasites are to be input with the names X0 and Y0. Both variables must be present in the block COMMON/PRIV/:

```
COMMON/PRIV/A,B,C,X0,Y0
```

The event NE = 1, which sets the initial values is now as follows:

```
C
1      SV(1,1) = XO
       SV(1,2) = YO
       CALL BEGIN(1,*9999)
       RETURN
```

* Problem 3

The variables a, b and c should be altered interactively during the simulation run. Refer to Volume 1, chapter 7.4.2 "Interactive Mode".

1.4 Host Parasite Model III

The time at which conditional events will take place is not known in advance. These events occur when the system satisfies a particular condition: the condition is represented by a logical expression which contains the relevant state variables.

The conditions which occur in a model must be indexed by the user and placed in the logical function CHECK.

The user must ensure that the conditions are tested during the simulation run. The test flag TTEST = T which triggers the testing of the conditions must be set whenever a discrete variable which occurs in a condition is altered in the program. The test flag TTEST is set in the subroutine EQUAT for continuous variables. In the latter case the user does not have set the test flag.

1.4.1 Description of the Model

This example is also based on the host parasite model in chapter 1.1. It is extended as follows:

The hosts and parasites are part of an experiment in a laboratory. A lamp is switched on and off in the laboratory at intervals of 100 time units. The increased brightness causes a reduced mortality rate of the parasites.

$$dy/dt = c*x + y - b*y$$

	Light on	Light off
$b =$	0.02	0.05

The host population and the constant c are unaffected.

The experiment is continuously monitored. When the number of hosts becomes less than XMIN = 4000 or the number of parasites exceeds YMAX = 3500 then the number of parasites is halved.

At time T = 0 the light is switched on for the first time.

1.4.2 The Subroutine STATE

The initial setting of the private variables takes place in section 3 of the main program, "Input and assignment of variables of the main program".

```
C       Initialisation of the private variables
C
        A=0.005
        B=0.05
        C=6.E-6
Note:
```

* The quantities A,B,C are initialised here rather than input. The initial conditions for the number of hosts and parasites are given directly in the subroutine EVENT.
The differential equations in the subroutine STATE are as

follows:

```
      COMMON/PRIV/A,B,C
C
C     Equations for set 1
C
      DV(1,1) = A*SV(1,1)-C*SV(1,2)*SV(1,1)
      DV(1,2) = -B*SV(1,2)+C*SV(1,2)*SV(1,1)
```

1.4.3 Crossings and Conditions

Flags are also required to indicate whether the continuous variables $SV(1,1)$ and $SV(1,2)$ have crossed their boundaries:

IFLAG(1,1)   The number of hosts has reached the lower threshold XMIN.

IFLAG(1,2)   The number of parasites has reached the upper threshold YMAX.

An event occurs when a condition which is expressed in the logical function CHECK is satisfied. Thus the function is as follows:

```
C
C     Label selector
C     ==============
      GOTO(1),NCOND
C
C     Conditions
C     ==========
1     CHECK = IFLAG(1,1).EQ.1.OR.IFLAG(1,2).EQ.1
      GOTO 100
```

1.4.4 Events

Four events are required:

NE = 1   Initialisation of the state variables $SV(1,1)$ and $SV(1,2)$

NE = 2   Reduction of the number of parasites

NE = 3   Switching on the light

NE = 4   Switching off the light

Events 1 and 3 are first scheduled at time $T = 0$ in the main program.
Events 3 and 4 each schedule the other as its successor. Event 2 is a conditional event whose activation time cannot be previously determined.

The subroutine EVENT is as follows:

```
      COMMON/PRIV/A,B,C
C
C     Label selector
C     ==============
      GOTO(1,2,3,4), NE
C
C     Event processing
C     ================
1     SV(1,1) = 10000.
      SV(1,2) = 1000.
      CALL BEGIN(1,*9999)
      RETURN
C
2     CALL MONITR(1)
      SV(1,2) = SV(1,2)/2.
      CALL BEGIN(1,*9999)
      CALL MONITR(1)
      RETURN
C
3     CALL MONITR(1)
      B = 0.02
      CALL BEGIN(1,*9999)
      CALL MONITR(1)
      CALL ANNOUN(4,T+100.,*9999)
      RETURN
C
4     CALL MONITR(1)
      B = 0.05
      CALL BEGIN(1,*9999)
      CALL MONITR(1)
      CALL ANNOUN(3,T+100.,*9999)
      RETURN
```

Notes:

* The call of the subroutine BEGIN in the events NE=3 and NE=4
is necessary, because the differential equations of the subroutine STATE were modified by changing the value of the variable
B.

* An event in which the differential equations in the subroutine STATE are in any way modified should be preceded and
succeeded by calls of the subroutine MONITR.

1.4.5 Checking of Conditions

The user is responsible for checking the conditions. The logical
value of the relevant condition must be determined in the
subroutine TEST by calling the logical function CHECK(NCOND) and
then initiating the required activity.

There is only one condition in the host parasite model III.   The
event 2 is to be processed when this condition has the logical
value .TRUE.

The subroutine TEST is as follows:

```
C
C       Check the conditions
C       ====================
        IF(CHECK(1)) CALL EVENT(2,*9999)
        RETURN
```

The condition must be monitored by a call of the subroutine TEST, when a variable in the condition has changed its value. If this happens, the test indicator TTEST is set equal to T. This causes a call of the subroutine TEST by the subroutine FLOWC.

The test flag TTEST is set in the subroutine EQUAT when the variables IFLAG change their value from IFLAG=0 to IFLAG=1 due to the occurrance of crossings. In this case, GPSS-FORTRAN Version 3 initiates the monitoring of the conditions automatically.

Notes:

* Every condition in a model which contains several conditions must be monitored in TEST. The conditions are expressed in sequence in TEST. It follows that a call of TEST causes all conditions to be monitored and the appropriate activities to be scheduled if necessary.

* If a variable of the discrete part of the simulator occurs in a condition, the user must set the test flag TTEST = T when the value of this variable is altered.

The flags IFLAG(1,1) and IFLAG(1,2) are set in the subroutine CROSS, which must be called by the user in the subroutine DETECT as follows:

```
C       Call of subroutine CROSS for set 1
C       ==================================
1       CALL CROSS(1,1,1,0,0.,4000.,-1,1.,*977,*9999)
        CALL CROSS(1,2,2,0,0.,3500.,+1,1.,*977,*9999)
        RETURN
```

The parameter list of the subroutine CROSS is as follows:

CALL CROSS(NSET,NCR,NX,NY,CMULT,CADD,LDIR,TOL,EXIT1,EXIT2)

NSET = 1

There is only one set with the number NSET = 1.

NCR = 1 or NCR = 2

The crossings are indexed. The index of the crossing is equal to the index of the flag.

NX = 1 or NX = 2

The variable which effects the crossing is SV(1,1), the number of hosts, or SV(1,2), the number of parasites.

NY = 0

There are no crossed variables.

CMULT = 0

The multiplicative factor is not used.

CADD = 4000. or CADD = 3500.

The values of the threshold are 4000. or 3500.

LDIR = -1 or LDIR = +1

The variables reach the threshold value from above or below.

TOL = 1.

The size of the tolerance interval is 1.   The tolerance interval
is given as an absolute value and not in percent.

The addresses of the exits, *977 and *9999, are not to be altered
by the user. They point to fixed labels in the subroutine DETECT.

1.4.6   Summary of the Method Used

The following steps are necessary to implement the host parasite
model:

* Initialisation of private variables.   Declaration of the block
COMMON/PRIV/

* Definition of the differential equations in the subroutine
STATE

* Definition of the events in the subroutine EVENT

* Scheduling of the events 1 and 3 in the main program

* Definition of the condition for the conditional event NE = 2 in
the logical function CHECK

* Setting of the flags for the two crossings by two calls of the
subroutine CROSS in the subroutine DETECT

* Monitoring of the conditions which contain the two flags
IFLAG(1,1) and IFLAG(1,2) in the subroutine TEST

Note:

   * The method described above can be applied to all simulation
   models. All combined simulation models, independent of their
   size and complexity, can be dealt with in this way.

1.4.7 Results for Host Parasite Model III

The plot on the next page shows the dynamic behaviour of the
numbers of hosts and parasites. If the continuous variables
exceed or fall below the relevant threshold values, an event
causes the necessary changes. Events are shown by the symbol * in
the event column.

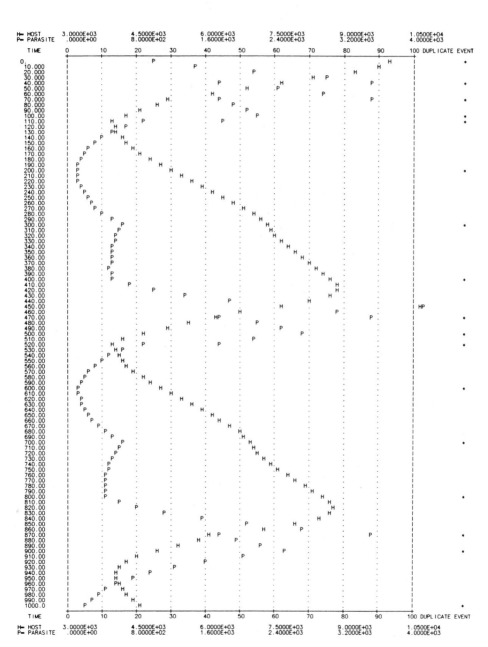

1.4.8 Problems

These examples demonstrate further applications of GPSS-FORTRAN Version 3.

* Problem 1

If the number of hosts becomes less than the value XMIN or the number of parasites becomes greater than YMAX, then the number of parasites is to be halved. This reduction of the number of parasites is to take place 20 time units later.

The number of parasites is not to be reduced again during this period, for example when the number of parasites exceeds the upper bound YMAX and shortly afterwards the number of hosts becomes less than the value XMIN.

Note:

    * The event which reduces the number of parasites must be sche-
duled for time T + 20., where T is the time at which the condition is satisfied. The flag variable IRED is given the value 1
after scheduling the event.   It indicates that the event which
reduces the number of parasites is already scheduled and a
further scheduling of the event NE = 2 should not occur.   The
value of IRED must be reset to 0 in the event NE = 2 after the
reduction has taken place. The subroutine TEST is as follows:

```
        IF(.NOT.CHECK(1)) GOTO 1
        CALL ANNOUN(2,T + 20.,*9999)
        IRED = 1
1       CONTINUE
        RETURN
```

The condition in the function CHECK is extended as follows:

```
1       CHECK = IRED.EQ.0.AND.(IFLAG(1,1).EQ.1.OR.IFLAG(1,2).EQ.1)
```

The variable IRED must be included in the block COMMON/PRIV/.

* Problem 2

Instead of reducing the number of parasites when the number of hosts becomes less than XMIN or the number of parasites exceeds YMAX, the light is to be switched off if it is on. The light is to be switched on again at the same time as it would have been switched on if this event had not occurred.

Note:

    * Instead of the previous conditional event NE = 2 there is a
new conditional event which switches off the light without
scheduling the switching on of the light at time T + 100.   The
new event is as follows:

```
C
2          CALL MONITR(1)
           B = 0.05
           CALL BEGIN(1,*9999)
           CALL MONITR(1)
           RETURN
```

If the light has been switched off by the event NE = 2, then the switching off is repeated by event NE = 4. This second switching off has no effect.

An alternative method is to schedule the next switching off and the next switching on in the event NE = 3. Then it is not necessary to schedule an event in the event NE = 4. Then problem 2 does not require the event NE = 2.

1.5 The Host Parasite Model IV

The structure of the model can be dynamically altered in GPSS-
FORTRAN Version 3. When a condition is satisfied, the simulation
proceeds with a new system of differential equations.

1.5.1 Description of the Model

The model is based on the simple host parasite model I which is
described in chapter 1.1. The differential equations of the host
parasite model I are based on the assumption of exponential
growth. This assumption is certainly wrong when the population
has grown beyond a certain size. The size of the population
approaches a limiting value in a more realistic model, i.e. the
population growth does not obey the differential equation of
expontial growth

dx/dt = a * x.

The logistic growth function is often used in such a situation.
It is defined by the following differential equation:

dx/dt = a * x * (k-x)/k

The variable k is the limiting value which the population
approaches. It is referred to as the capacitiy of the environment
for this population. The reader is recommended to consult a
textbook on population biology.

The host parasite system where both populations are determined by
the logistic growth function is described by the following system
of differential equations:

dx/dt = a*x*(k1 - x)/k1 - c*x*y*(k2 - y)/k2

dy/dt = c*x*y*(k2-y)/k2 - b*y

The host parasite model IV uses the simple system of equations
from chapter 1.1 for low population density. If the number of
hosts is greater than 9200., then this simple approximation is no
longer valid and the extended system of differential equations is
used.

The constants are:

          a = 0.005   k1 = 80000.
          b = 0.05   k2 = 8000.
          c = 6.E-6

Note:

   * The host parasite model IV contains a dynamic alteration of
   the structure of the model caused by a condition. When the
   number of hosts exceeds the value 9200., the system of
   differential equations which describe the structure of the
   model is replaced.

1.5.2 Implementation

Both systems of differential equations are defined in the subroutine STATE. A flag variable ISTATE determines which system describes the model at a particular time.

The flag variable ISTATE is assigned a value, dependent on the population, in an event.

The subroutine is as follows:

```
C
C       Label selector
C       ==============
        GOTO(1,2,3), NSET
C
C       Equations for NSET = 1
C       ======================
1       GOTO(11,12),ISTATE
11      DV(1,1) = 0.005*SV(1,1) - 0.000006*SV(1,2)*SV(1,1)
        DV(1,2) = -0.05*SV(1,2) + 0.000006*SV(1,2)*SV(1,1)
        RETURN
12      DV(1,1) = 0.005*SV(1,1)*(80000.-SV(1,1))/80000.
       *-0.000006*SV(1,2)*SV(1,1)*(8000.-SV(1,2))/8000.
        DV(1,2) = -0.05*SV(1,2)+0.000006*SV(1,2)*SV(1,1)
       **(8000.-SV(1,2))/8000.
        RETURN
```

Two crossings are defined in the subroutine DETECT to determine when the host population exceeds or falls below the boundary value 9200. :

```
C
C       Crossings for set 1
C       ===================
1       CALL CROSS(1,1,1,0,0.,9200.,+1,10.,*977,*9999)
        CALL CROSS(1,2,1,0,0.,9200.,-1,10.,*977,*9999)
        RETURN
```

The conditions in the logical function CHECK are:

```
1       IF(IFLAG(1,1).EQ.1) CHECK = .TRUE.
        GOTO 100
2       IF(IFLAG(1,2).EQ.1) CHECK = .TRUE.
        GOTO 100
```

The statements which test the conditions in the subroutine TEST are:

```
        IF(CHECK(1)) CALL EVENT(1,*9999)
        IF(CHECK(2)) CALL EVENT(2,*9999)
```

The events in subroutine EVENT are as follows:

```
C       Logistic growth curve
C       =====================
1       CALL MONITR(1)
        ISTATE = 2
        CALL BEGIN(1,*9999)
        CALL MONITR(1)
        RETURN
```

```
C
C         Exponential growth curve
C         ========================
2         CALL MONITR(1)
          ISTATE = 1
          CALL BEGIN(1,*9999)
          CALL MONITR(1)
          RETURN
C
C         Initial conditions
C         ==================
3         SV(1,1) = 10000.
          SV(1,2) = 1000.
          ISTATE = 2
          CALL BEGIN(1,*9999)
          RETURN
```

The event NE = 3 is to be scheduled in the main program in the normal way.

The events NE = 1 and NE = 2 are conditional events which set the flag variables. The event NE = 1 sets the flag variable ISTATE=2 when the boundary value 9200. for the host population is exceeded. This causes the selection of the extended system of differential equations in the subroutine STATE, which are based on the logistic growth curve.

Note:

   * The variable ISTATE must be included in the area COMMON/PRIV/.

1.5.3 Results of the Host Parasite Model IV

The plot on the next page shows the alteration in the form of the curve when the number of hosts exceeds or goes below 9200.

PLOT NR 1

VARIABLE	MINIMUM	MAXIMUM	MEAN	95%-CONFIDENCE INTERVAL	END OF SETTLING PHASE	DISPLACEMENT OF MEAN	DISPL. OF MEAN IN PER CENT
H = HOST	7.3948E+03	1.0000E+04	——	——	——	——	——
P = PARASITE	5.6131E+02	1.1823E+03	——	——	——	——	——

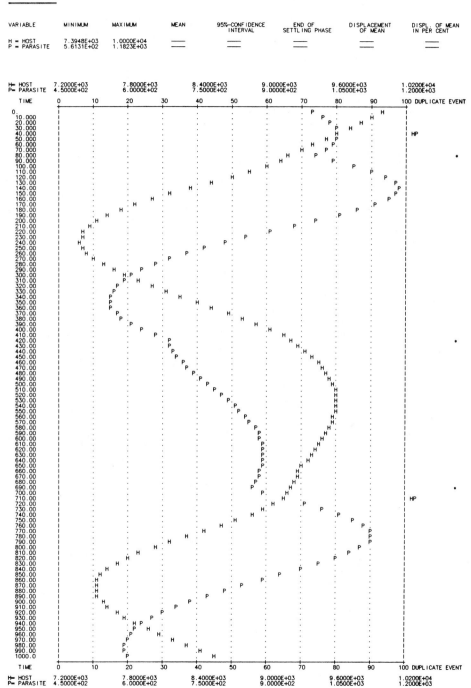

1.5.4 Problems

The problems deal with the behaviour of populations subject to a
logistic growth curve. Only the logistic growth curve is to be
used in the following problems.

* Problem 1

Investigate the host population when the model does not contain
any parasites. The results are to be compared with results
obtained for the exponential growth curve.

* Problem 2

Introduce a factor which prevents the number of parasites from
becoming less than a given threshold value. This is done by
modifying accordingly the equation for the parasites given in
Volume 2, chapter 1.5.1.

Investigate the number of parasites when there are no hosts.
Compare the results with those obtained from the exponential
growth curve on which the logistic growth curve is based.

* Problem 3

It is to be shown that a crossing discovered due to a discontinuity is also recognised by GPSS-FORTRAN Version 3. The number of
hosts is to be halved at time T = 100 in the original host
parasite model IV. The change of ISTATE becomes necessary because
the number of hosts sinks below 1000 is to be observed.

2. Queued Models

Queued models consist of stationary model components, called stations, and mobile model components, called transactions. The transactions move from one station to another; in particular they form queues at the stations. The most general station is the gate. This is characterised by a logical expression. The further processing of a transaction cannot take place as long as the value of this logical expression is equal to .FALSE. The transaction joins the queue at the gate and cannot leave it until the expression has the logical value .TRUE.

A model of a brewery is used to demonstrate the simulation of a queued model.

There are three versions of the model of the brewery. Each version demonstrates particular techniques.

Brewery model I   :   running of model

Brewery model II :   generation of random numbers and processing of statistical data

Brewery model III: combined model with continuous and transaction oriented components.

2.1 Brewery Model I

A very simple example is used to show the running of the model for the simulation of queued models. The interarrival times and service times are deterministic.

2.1.1 Description of Model

Beer barrels are delivered to a brewery and are filled up by a pump. The interarrival time for the barrels is always 10 time units.

The pump can deal with only one barrel at a time. Barrels which arrive when the pump is busy join a queue. The service time for a barrel is 11 time units.

The simulation is to be ended when 500 barrels have been dealt with.

The simulation should provide answers to the following questions:

What is the mean time spent in the queue by the barrels?

At what time does the last barrel leave the pump?

2.1.2 Implementation in Subroutine ACTIV

The function of the pump is implemented using a gate station; the barrels are represented by transactions.

The program which represents the model of the brewery is implemented in the subroutine ACTIV.

First the subroutine GENERA is used to generate transactions by the subroutine call:

        CALL GENERA(10.,1.,*9999)

The parameter list of the subroutine GENERA is as follows:

ET = 10.0

The time at which the next transaction is to be generated is the current value of the simulation clock T + 10.0 time units. This means that the next activation of a source is scheduled when a transaction is generated at time T. The parameter list provides the value of the interarrival time ET = 10.0.

PR = 1.

The priorities of the transactions are not used in the model of the brewery. Therefore all transactions are assigned the priority PR = 1.

*9999

The error exit returns control to the flow control and thence to the terminating section in the main program.

The time at which the transactions join the queue are entered in the element for user attributes, TX(LTX,9), after generation of the transaction.

The generated transactions then reach the call of the subroutine GATE. Here, they join a queue and remain blocked until the condition which allows them to proceed has the value .TRUE. This is done by the subroutine call:

        CALL GATE(1,1,1,0,2,*9000)

The condition expresses whether a barrel is at the pump or not. A variable IPUMP is used; it can take on of the following values:

IPUMP = 0   Pump free
IPUMP = 1   Pump occupied

The variable IPUMP is initialised to zero in section 3, "Input and initialisation of variables". IPUMP must be included in the block COMMON/PRIV/.

The parameter list of the subroutine GATE is as follows:

NG = 1
The index of the gate is NG = 1.

NCOND = 1
The condition which controls the gate has the index NCOND = 1 in
the function CHECK.

GLOBAL = 1
The logical expression selected by NCOND = 1 contains only global
parameters i.e. the logical expression does not contain any
variable which depends on the individual properties of the
blocked transaction.

IBLOCK = O
Every arriving transaction can test the condition.

ID = 2
The label of the subroutine call CALL GATE is 2.

*9000
This exit is used when the transaction is blocked. This transfers
control to a call of the flow control which selects a new
activation.

The condition of the gate is placed in the function CHECK with
the index NCOND = 1. It is:

1   CHECK = IPUMP.EQ.O

If the condition NCOND = 1 is satisfied and therefore further
processing is possible, the subroutine GATE is again called for
the selected transaction. Then the statement after the call of
GATE is executed.

The time required to fill the barrel is provided by the
subroutine ADVANC, which delays the transaction for AT = 11.0
time units. This is done by the subroutine call:

        CALL ADVANC(11.0,3,*9000)

The parameter list of the subroutine ADVANC is as follows:

AT = 11.0
The parameter AT is the service time.

IDN = 3
On completion of the service time the transaction proceeds to the
execution of the statement following the subroutine call CALL
ADVANC. This statement has the label 3.

*9000
Control is transferred to the flow control after the completion
of the service time has been scheduled.

The subroutine TERMIN which eliminates the transactions is called
on completion of the service time:

        CALL TERMIN(*9000)

The parameter of the subroutine TERMIN is:

*9000
Control is transferred to the flow control after the transaction
has been erased.

The variable IPUMP is set equal to 1 when a transaction has passed the gate and occupied the pump. The pump is freed by the statement following the subroutine call CALL ADVANC by the statement IPUMP = 0. Since IPUMP occurs in the condition NCOND = 1, this must be tested immediately. This is initiated by setting the test flag TTEST = T.

```
IPUMP = 0
TTEST = T
```

The test indicator causes the subroutine TEST to be called. This tests the condition NCOND = 1 and, if necessary, causes a transaction to be unblocked.

The subroutine TEST is as follows:

```
IF(CHECK(1))CALL DBLOCK(5,1,0,1)
```

Since it is known in this example that after the first transaction has been unblocked the logical condition NCOND = 1 has again the value .FALSE., it is not necessary to unblock all transactions at the gate.

Note:

   * In this very simple example it would be possible to test the condition in the subroutine ACTIV rather by calling the sub-routine TEST:

```
IPUMP = 0
IF(CHECK(1))CALL DBLOCK(5,1,0,1)
```

It is also possible to omit the test of the condition completely, since the condition is certainly satisfied when the test is performed. It would suffice to test when a transaction is deactivated:

```
IPUMP = 0
CALL DBLOCK(5,1,0,1)
```

These simplifications are possible because the model is short and simple. However the technique described above should always be used.

The subroutine DBLOCK unblocks a transaction by removing it from the queue of blocked transactions and scheduling its activation at the current time T. The flow control finds it in the scheduled transaction list, activates it, and passes it to the subroutine GATE.

The parameter list of DBLOCK is follows:

NT = 5
Every type of station is identified by an index. For gates NT=5.

NS = 1
The stations of a particular type are assigned consecutive indices. The index of the gate is NS = 1.

LFAM = 0
LFAM defines the family to which the transaction belongs. LFAM is
assigned the value zero because families are not used in the
model of the brewery.

MAX = 1
MAX is the number of transactions which are to be removed from
the queue at a time.

2.1.3 Main Program

The model is initialised by scheduling the generation of the
first transaction with a call of the subroutine START in section
5 "INITIALISATION" of the main program.

```
C       START SOURCE
C       ============
        CALL START(1,0.,1,*7000)
C
```

The parameter list of START is as follows:

NSC = 1
The source which generates the transaction has the index NSC = 1.

TSC = 0.
The time at which the first transaction is to be generated is TSC
= 0.

IDG = 1
The label of the subroutine call CALL GENERA in the subroutine
ACTIV is given by IDG = 1.

*7000
If an error occurs control is transferred to the terminating
section.

The statements discussed so far specify the running of the model.
They must be augmented by statements which collect statistical
data.

The following variables are used to accumulate statistical data:

WTG   Total time spent in the queue by all barrels
WTM   Average time spent in queue = total time spent in queue /
       number of barrels processed

These two private variables must be included in the block
COMMON/PRIV/:

```
        COMMON/PRIV/IPUMP,WTG,WTM
```

They are initialised with the value 0 in section 3 of the main
program "Input and initialisation of variables":

```
C       Initialise user variables
C       ==========================
        IPUMP = 0
        WTG = 0.
        WTM = 0.
```

The times spent by an individual transaction in the queue is given by:

time spent in queue = value of the simulation clock T when it leaves the queue - time of joining the queue

The time of joining the queue is stored in the element TX(LTX,9).

The total waiting time is obtained by adding the waiting time of the individual transactions.

WTG = WTG + (T - TX(LTX,9))

This is done whenever the transaction leaves the gate.

The mean waiting time is calculated in section 7 of the main program "Terminating section", according to the formula:

WTM = WTG/NTXC

NTXC is a variable representing the total number of transactions generated.

The simulation run is ended when all transactions have been processed and the flow control finds no further activities to be performed. The value of the simulation clock is the time at which processing is completed. Section 8 of the main program "Output of the results" is then as follows:

```
C        OUTPUT OF THE RESULTS
C        =====================
         WRITE(UNIT2,8010)
8010     FORMAT(////20X,43(1H*),2(/,20X,1H*,41X,1H*))
         WRITE(UNIT2,8020)WTM
8020     FORMAT
        +(20X,1H*,28H    MEAN TIME IN QUEUE: WTM  ,F10.3,4H    *)
         WRITE(UNIT2,8030)T
8030     FORMAT
        +(20X,1H*,28H    END OF PROCESSING:       ,F10.3,4H    *)
         WRITE(UNIT2,8040)
8040     FORMAT(2(20X,1H*,41X,1H*/),20X,43(1H*))
         WRITE(UNIT2,8050)
8050     FORMAT(1H1)
```

2.1.4 The Subroutine ACTIV

The subroutine ACTIV is as follows:

```
C
         COMMON/PRIV/IPUMP,WTG,WTM
C
C        Label selector
C        ==============
         GOTO(1,2,3), NADDR
C
```

```
C       Generate transactions
C       =====================
1       CALL GENERA(10.0,1.,*9999)
        TX(LTX,9)=T
C
C       Process transactions
C       =====================
2       CALL GATE(1,1,1,0,2,*9000)
        IPUMP=1
        WTG=WTG+(T-TX(LTX,9))
        CALL ADVANC(11.0,3,*9000)
3       IPUMP=0
        TTEST = T
C
C       Eliminate transactions
C       =====================
        CALL TERMIN(*9000)
C
C       Return to flow control
C       =====================
9000    RETURN
C
C       Exit to terminating section
C       ===========================
9999    RETURN1
        END
```

Notes:

*   The parameter IBLOCK in the parameter list of GATE   must
have   the value IBLOCK = 0 to ensure that the model   runs   correctly when a transaction reaches an empty station,   i.e.   when
IPUMP = 0. In this case there is no transaction which calls
the subroutine DLBOCK after leaving the station.   Thus the
transaction would always remain blocked.

Because IBLOCK = 0, the transaction can test the condition
NCOND=1 as soon as it reaches the station independently of
DBLOCK and if possible, be processed.

*   The model of the brewery would normally be implemented using
a facility and the subroutines SEIZE, WORK and CLEAR. Facilities are exactly suited for this type of model. If facilities are used,   the empty station would not create a problem.
Gates have been used in this model for didactic reasons.   We
will see below that gates are the most general type of stations, and all other station types, in particular facilities,
are special cases.

2.1.5 Input Data Records

The input data record for the model of the brewery is as follows:

VARI;TXMAX;500/
VARI;ICONT;0/
END/

The simulation run is to be ended when the number of transactions
reached 500. TEND is assigned a very high value so that the
simulation run is not ended by the simulation time reaching the

value of TEND. TEND is initialised to 1.E+10 in the subroutine PRESET and there is no need to change this value, therefore it is not necessary to input TEND.

Since this is a transaction oriented model without a continuous part, ICONT = 0. In this example, neither INTI- nor PLOT- data records are used.

The initial values of the other variables are left unaltered:

IPRINT = 0
SVIN = 0
SVOUT = 0

The simulation run has the following results:

Average time spent in queue WTM = 249.5

Time of completion of processing = 5500.0

2.1.6 Problem

The following problem contains a small extension of the model described in the previous section. It demonstrates the use of user attributes of transactions.

* Problem

The barrels are alternatively small and large.

Content of small barrels = 30 liters.
Content of large barrels = 50 liters.

The time required to fill a barrel is 0.275 units of time multiplied by the contents in litres.

Note:

    * The capacity of the barrel is a user attribute which is held in the second element reserved for this purpose in the TX array:

        CALL GENERA(10.0,1.,*9999)
        TX(LTX,10) = 30.
        IF(AMOD(TX(LTX,1),2.).LT.0.1) TX(LTX,10) = 50.

The last statement has the effect that all transactions with even transaction index are assigned the value 50. litres for the capacity of the barrel.

The service time assigned by the subroutine ADVANC is a function of the capacity:

        AT = 0.275*TX(LTX,10)
        CALL ADVANC(AT,3,*9000)

The subroutine ACTIV is otherwise unchanged.

2.2 Running of the Model

In event oriented simulation the events take place at an instant
of time and only one event is activated at a time. In transaction
oriented simulation several activities can be taking place at the
same time. A transaction is generated and is processed by
statements of the simulation program until it cannot be further
processed. This happens when a transaction commences an activity
which has a finite duration or when a condition necessary for
further processing is not fulfilled. The transaction is
deactivated in both cases, i.e., the transaction is placed in a
queue and the place in the simulation program at which the
processing of this tranaction is to continue when it is
reactivated, is recorded.

2.2.1 Example

A transaction is generated by calling the subroutine GENERA in
the brewery model. It then proceeds to the subsequent statements.

If IBLOCK = 0 the transaction tests the condition NCOND = 1 in
the subroutine GATE. If the station is free and thus the
condition is satisfied, the transaction can proceed to be
processed by subsequent statements. This continues until it
reaches the call of the subroutine ADVANC. Here it is deactivated
and its reactivation at time T+11.0 is scheduled. It is also
recorded that its processing at time T + 11.0 is to commmence at
the statement with label 3. Then control is transferred to the
flow control.

If the transaction reaches the subroutine call CALL GATE when
IPUMP = 1, then it cannot be processed further. The transaction
is placed in the queue at the gate and deactivated. Then control
is returned to the flow control.

Whenever a transaction is deactivated control must be returned to
the flow control which selects a new activation and lets it be
processed. For this reason subroutines in which transactions can
be deactivated have the exit *9000 which causes control to leave
the subroutine ACTIV by the normal RETURN exit. Control is
returned to the subroutine FLOWC which can later call ACTIV
again.

A transaction is active when the variable LTX contains the row
number of the transaction in the transaction array and the
transaction schedule.

* Example

TX(LTX,9) = 1

This statement assigns the value 1 to the first user attribute of
the active transaction.

The label selector of the subroutine ACTIV must contain the
labels of all statements at which the activation can begin.

Control is transferred to the call of the subroutine GENERA with
label 1 when a transaction is to be generated.

The next statement which requires a label is the call of the
subroutine GATE.

Control is transferred to this statement when an active
transaction reaches it from the subroutine GENERA. In this case
the label 2 is not required. However the subroutine GATE is also
called when a previously blocked transaction is to be activated
by calling the subroutine DBLOCK. In this case the processing of
the transaction starts with the statement CALL GATE.

The third and last label is required to indicate at which
statement the processing of transactions deactivated by the subroutine ADVANC is to continue.

The allocation of labels is made easier by the fact that all
labels in the label selector occur in the parameter lists of the
subroutines. Labels, which do not occur in the parameter lists of
the subroutines are not required for the flow control.

Label 1 occurs in the subroutine START which activates the
source in the main program.

Label 2 occurs in the parameter list of the subroutine GATE.

Label 3 occurs in the parameter list of the subroutine ADVANC as
the value of IDN.

The labels in the label selector start with the value 1 and are
consecutively numbered.

To show the order in which activities occur the trace is
activated between time 0 and 500.

Note:

   * The variable IPRINT is read in and assigned the value 1. An
   event NE = 1 is defined which sets the variable IPRINT = 0.
   This event is scheduled for T = 500.

In addition the transaction array, the arrays used by the flow
control, and the contents of the queue at the gate are to be
printed out.

Note:

   * System variables are printed using the report subroutines of
   GPSS-FORTRAN Version 3.

REPRT1(NT)   Print the queues at the stations with type index NT.
             For gates NT = 5.

REPRT2   Print the transaction array and the family array.
             (The family array is meaningless in this example).

REPRT3   Print the flow control arrays. REPRT2 and REPRT3
             have no parameters.

Thus the event is as following:

```
C
1       IPRINT = O
        CALL REPRT1(5)
        CALL REPRT2
        CALL REPRT3
        RETURN
```

Note:

* If several activities are scheduled to take place at the same time, then events are activated before other activities. This means IPRINT would be set equal to O and the printing of the arrays is stopped before transactions are generated or activated at time T = 500.

The queue at the gate is as follows:

        T = 500.000   RT = 500.000

        GATE   1
        ========

        QUEUE:

LTX	NUMBER OF TRANS.	DUPLICATE INDEX	LFAM	PRIORITY	LABEL FOR PREEMPTION	PROC.TIME REMAINING	RETURN INDICATOR	TIME OF BLOCKING
4	47.00	0.	0.	1.000	0.	0.	0.	460.0
1	48.00	0.	0.	1.000	0.	0.	0.	470.0
3	49.00	0.	0.	1.000	0.	0.	0.	480.0
5	50.00	0.	0.	1.000	0.	0.	0.	490.0

The lists of the flow control are as follows:

T =   500.0000   RT =   500.0000

TRANSACTION ARRAY
=================

LTX	CONTENT								TXI
1	48.00 / 470.0	0. / 0.	0. / 0.	1.000 / 0.	0. 0.	0. 0.	0. 0.	470.0 / 0.	0
2	46.00 / 450.0	0. / 0.	0. / 0.	1.000 / 0.	0. 0.	0. 0.	0. 0.	0. 0.	0
3	49.00 / 480.0	0. / 0.	0. / 0.	1.000 / 0.	0. 0.	0. 0.	0. 0.	480.0 / 0.	0
4	47.00 / 460.0	0. / 0.	0. / 0.	1.000 / 0.	0. 0.	0. 0.	0. 0.	460.0 / 0.	0
5	50.00 / 490.0	0. / 0.	0. / 0.	1.000 / 0.	0. 0.	0. 0.	0. 0.	490.0 / 0.	0

T =   500.0   RT =   500.0

ANKER THEAD - LHEAD
====================

	EVENTL	SOURCL	ACTIVL	CONFL	MONITL	EQUL
T	0.	500.0	506.0	0.	0.	0.
LINE	-1	1	2	-1	-1	-1

SOURCES
=======

LINE	T	ADDR	ANZ	CHAINS
1	500.0	1.000	.1000E+10	-1

TRANSACTION ACTIVATIONS
=========================

LINE	T/BLOCK	ADDR	CHAINT	CHAINB
1	-23.00	2.000	0	3
2	506.0	3.000	-1	0
3	-23.00	2.000	0	5
4	-23.00	2.000	0	1
5	-23.00	2.000	0	-1

TEST INDICATOR
==============

TTEST = -1.00000

2.2.2 Problems

The following problem demonstrates the structure and function of
the flow control. It is very important for understanding GPSS-
FORTRAN Version 3.

* Problem

The sequence of events for the first four transactions of the
brewery model is to be traced completely. The arrays of the flow
control are to be printed every time a transaction is to be
deactivated. The corresponding state transitions are to be
recorded.

Note:

   * The event NE = 1, which calls the subroutines REPRT1,
   REPRT2 and REPRT3 is scheduled after every deactivation of a
   transaction. The section "Return to flow control" in the subroutine ACTIV is as follows:

```
C       Return to flow control
C       ======================
9000    CALL ANNOUN(1,T,*9999)
        RETURN
```

It is recommended that the event NE = 1 is scheduled the first
time in the main program at time T = 0. By setting TXMAX = 4 in
the input data record VARI, the number of transactions generated
is limited to 4.

2.3 Brewery Model II

Random numbers are used to model stochastic systems. GPSS-FORTRAN Version 3 provides subroutines which generate random numbers with various distributions.

2.3.1 Description of the Model

The simple brewery model from chapter 2.1 is slightly extended to show the use of random numbers generators. The interarrival times and the sizes of the barrels are now random numbers.

Interarrival time ET:

The average interarrival time is 10.0. The distribution is exponential (Erlang distribution with K = 1), lower bound = 0.35, upper bound = 50.0.

Size of barrel:

The barrels can have the following sizes: 20, 30, 40, 50, 60 litres. All sizes occur with equal frequency. The time required to fill a barrel is 0.225 time units per litre.

The following questions are to be answered by simulation:

* What is the mean length of the queue?

* What is the mean time spent in the queue?

* What is the mean value of the sum of the time spent in the queue and the service time?

Altogether 5000 transactions are to be processed.

2.3.2 Calling the Random Number Generators

Every call of the subroutine ERLANG supplies a value for ET in the variable RANDOM. Taken together the values comprise an exponential distribution with mean 10.0.

The label 1 must be placed before the call of the subroutine ERLANG. The generation of the transaction is now as follows:

```
1       CALL ERLANG(10.,1,0.35,50.,1,RANDOM,*9999)
        CALL GENERA(RANDOM,1.,*9999)
```

To assign the capacity of the barrels uniformly distributed random numbers in the interval from 2.0 to 6.999 are generated by the subroutine UNIFRM. Integers from 2 to 6 are obtained by type conversion, and these are multiplied by 10.

The capacity of the barrels is calculated as follows:

```
        CALL UNIFRM(2.0,6.999,2,RANDOM)
        TX(LTX,9) = AINT(RANDOM)*10.
```

2.3.3 Collection and Processing of Statistical Data

The best method for obtaining the average length of the
queue, the time spent in the queue, and their sum is the use of
the method provided in GPSS-FORTRAN Version 3 to determine
average values with respect to time. See volume 1, chapter 5.1.

The transaction places a token in a bin by calling the subroutine
ARRIVE. The subroutine DEPART is used to remove a token.

The behaviour of the tokens in a bin is observed. The processing
of the information which has been collected about the behaviour
of the tokens in the bins during the running of a simulation is
performed by the subroutine ENDBIN which is called in section 7,
"Terminating section" of the main program.

The results are recorded in the BIN table and the BINSTA table.
The BIN table and the BINSTA table can be printed by calling the
subroutine REPRT4.

Section 7 "Terminating section" is as follows:

```
C       Final evaluation of the bins
C       =============================
        CALL  ENDBIN
        CALL  REPRT4
        CALL  REPRT5(1,2,0,0,0,0)
C
```

Examples:

* The following is the order of the subroutine calls when
averages connected with the behaviour of the queues are to be
determined:

```
        CALL ARRIVE
        CALL GATE
        CALL DEPART
        CALL ADVANC
        CALL TERMIN
```

In this case the transaction places a token in the bin when it
joins the queue. When the transaction has passed the subroutine
GATE, it occupies the station and therefore has left the queue. A
token is removed from the bin by calling the subroutine DEPART.
The number of tokens in the bin is the number of transactions in
the queue.

All properties of the bin are properties of the queue at the
gate. In this way the average length of the queue and the average
time spent in the queue can be determined.

The following is the sequence of the subroutine calls when
statistical data is to be collected about the behaviour of the
transactions in the station:

```
        CALL GATE
        CALL ARRIVE
        CALL ADVANC
        CALL DEPART
        CALL TERMIN
```

In this case the bin provides information about the mean processing time and mean number of transactions in the station.

* The time spent by a transaction in the queue and in the station is obtained by the subroutine calls:

```
CALL ARRIVE
CALL GATE
CALL ADVANC
CALL DEPART
CALL TERMIN
```

* It is of course possible to combine the methods described above without restrictions. For example two bins can be used to determine the time in the queue and the sum of the time in the queue and in the station. The sequence of subroutine calls is then as follows:

```
CALL ARRIVE(NBN = 1)
CALL ARRIVE(NBN = 2)
CALL GATE
CALL DEPART(NBN = 1)
CALL ADVANC
CALL DEPART(NBN = 2)
CALL TERMIN
```

The bin with NBN = 1 measures the time in the queue and the bin with NBN = 2 measures the time in the queue and in the station.

2.3.4 The Subroutine ACTIV

The subroutine ACTIV for the brewery model II is as follows:

```
C       Generate transactions
C       =====================
1       CALL ERLANG(10.,1,0.35,50.,1,RANDOM,*9999)
        CALL GENERA(RANDOM,1.,*9999)
        CALL UNIFRM(2.0,6.999,2,RANDOM)
        TX(LTX,9) = AINT(RANDOM)*10.
C
C       Process transactions
C       ====================
        CALL ARRIVE(1,1)
        CALL ARRIVE(2,1)
2       CALL GATE(1,1,1,0,2,*9000)
        CALL DEPART(1,1,0.,*9999)
        IPUMP = 1
        AT = 0.225*TX(LTX,9)
        CALL ADVANC(AT,3,*9000)
3       IPUMP = 0
        TTEST = T
        CALL DEPART(2,1,0.,*9999)
C
C       Eliminate transaction
C       =====================
        CALL TERMIN(*9000)
```

The subroutine ACTIV as described above specifies the model and the subroutines ARRIVE and DEPART measure the behaviour of the model.

The statistical data collected is processed by the subroutine
ENDBIN, which calculates the mean times in the station, and other
values. The results are printed by the subroutine REPRT4.

The subroutine REPRT5 must be called in the terminating section
in addition to REPRT4, in order to obtain information about the
behaviour of the bins as a function of time. See volume 1,
chapter 5.3.1, "The Report Subroutines".

Subroutine call

        CALL REPRT5(1,2,0,0,0,0)

2.3.5 The Results

The results for the brewery model II can be seen in the following
output of the BIN array and the BINSTA array.

The bin NBN = 1 contains information about the time in the queue
and the bin NBN = 2 about the the time in the queue and in the
station. The contents of the BIN array and BINSTA array are
described in volume 2, appendix A3, "Data Areas".

The plot of the mean number of tokens as a function of time
appears after the BIN table. It can be seen that it converges.
The following plot section covers the time from 2560. to 142080.

T = 497781.4765   RT = 497781.4765

BIN ARRAY
=========

NBN	QTY	MAX	SUMIN	SUMOUT	ARRIVE	DEPART	TOTALWT	LAST
1	0	38	50000	50000	50000	50000	.1839E+07	.4978E+06
2	0	39	50000	50000	50000	50000	.2288E+07	.4978E+06

BINSTA ARRAY
============

NBN	DURATION TIME	NUM. OF TOKEN	CONF.INT. PER CENT	DISPLACEM. PER CENT	END OF SETTLING PHASE
1	36.79	3.674	7.817	2.546	2560.
2	45.77	4.598	6.247	-.6182E-12	1920.

P L O T   NR 10

VARIABLE	MINIMUM	MAXIMUM	MEAN	95%-CONFIDENCE INTERVAL	END OF SETTLING PHASE	DISPLACEMENT OF MEAN	DISPL. OF MEAN IN PER CENT
1 = BIN 1	1.3200E+00	3.7403E+00	——	——	——	——	——
2 = BIN 2	.0000E+00	4.6424E+00	——	——	——	——	——

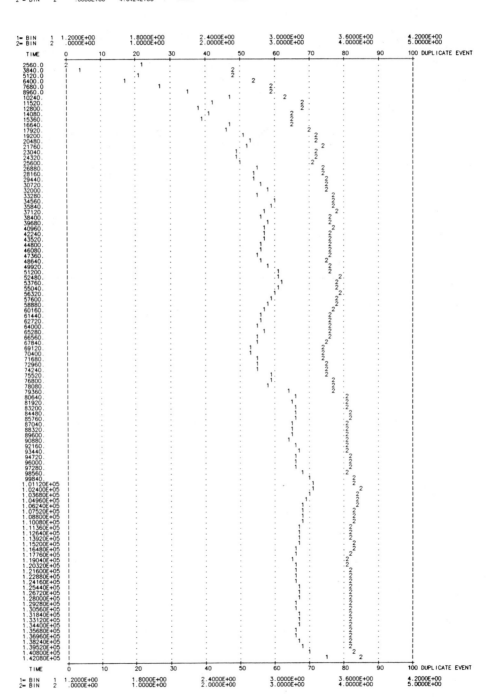

| 1= BIN   1 | 1.2000E+00 | 1.8000E+00 | 2.4000E+00 | 3.0000E+00 | 3.6000E+00 | 4.2000E+00 |
| 2= BIN   2 | .0000E+00 | 1.0000E+00 | 2.0000E+00 | 3.0000E+00 | 4.0000E+00 | 5.0000E+00 |

2.3.6 Problems

The problems show the use of the random number generators.

* Problem 1

The interarrival times have a normal distribution with average
10.0 and standard deviation 2.0.

Note:

   * The line

   1   CALL ERLANG(10.,1,0.35,50.,1,RANDOM,*9999)

   must be replaced by

   1   CALL GAUSS(10.,2.,2.,18.,1,RANDOM)

* Problem 2

The interarrival times are given by a normal distribution with
mean 10.0 and standard deviation 2.0. The lower limit is now MIN
= 5.0 and MAX = 15.0. The differences in the results of problem 1
and problem 2 are to be explained.

Note:

   * The random variations are reduced by the narrower boundaries
   of the interval containing the interarrival times in problem 2.
   Problem 2 is closer to a deterministic model. Thus the mean
   queue length is less in problem 2 and the confidence interval
   is smaller.

2.4 Brewery Model III

Queue oriented models can be extended by including event oriented and continuous components. The brewery model III is used to demonstrate the interaction of the queue oriented, event oriented, and continuous components in a combined model.

The brewery model III also shows how the structure of the model can be dynamically altered in GPSS-FORTRAN Version 3.

2.4.1 Description of the model

The brewery model III is an extension of the brewery model II. The rate at which the barrel is filled is more complicated. The rate at which the barrel is filled, RATE, depends on the contents of the barrel SV.

Initial rate: RATE = 1.0
Intermediate rate: RATE = 0.20*SV + 1.
Maximum rate: RATE = 6.0

The dimensions of RATE is litres/time units.

The rate at which the barrel is filled starts with 1.0 and then is increased proportionally to the contents of the barrel until the maximum rate is achieved. The filling process ends when the barrel is full.

As in brewery model II, the mean queue length, mean time spent in the queue, and mean time in the queue and in the station are to be determined. In addition, the contents of the barrel SV and the rate of filling the barrel RATE from T = 0 to T = 20 is to be plotted.

The interarrrival time in the brewery model III must be larger than the interarrival time in the brewery model II since more time is required to fill a barrel and the model must converge to a stationary state. The mean interarrrival time is 16.0 time units. The upper and lower limits are also changed accordingly.

2.4.2 The Subroutine ACTIV

The transaction oriented part of the model is described in the subroutine ACTIV. It deals with the generation of barrels, the entry to and departure from the filling station and the elimination of barrels from the system. The brewery model III differs from the brewery model II in that the process of filling the barrel no longer involves a constant amount of time and therefore it cannot be dealt with by the subroutine ADVANC.

In the brewery model II every barrel spends a predetermined time AT at the filling station. In the brewery model III the barrel remains in the filling station until the following condition is satisfied:

SV(1,1).EQ.CAP
SV(1,1) is the state variable which represents the contents of the barrel. CAP is the capacity of the barrel:

CAP = TX(LTX,9).

The condition is satisfied when the contents of the barrel are equal to its capacity. When this happens the next step in the process can begin.

The condition is represented in the logical function CHECK with NCOND = 2.

The transaction which occupies the filling station remains in the subroutine ACTIV at the gate NG = 2 until the condition is satisfied.

The subroutine call CALL ADVANC is replaced by

```
      CAP = TX(LTX,9)
      CALL ANNOUN(2,T,*9999)
3     CALL GATE(2,2,1,1,3,*9000)
      CALL ANNOUN(4,T,*9999)
```

The waiting for the scheduled activation of a transaction is replaced by waiting for a conditional activation. As soon as the barrel reaches the filling station, the capacity of the barrel is placed in the variable CAP. The variable IFILL is also set equal to 2.

IFILL indicates the state of the filling station:

IFILL = 1   The filling station is not empty.

IFILL = 2   The filling station is working. The filling rate has not yet reached its maximum value of 6.0.

IFILL = 3   The rate of filling has reached its maximum value.

Note:

   * The simulation is to be ended when the last transaction has been processed.

It is to be noted that the source is closed down when the number of transactions generated has reached the value TXMAX. The simulation itself is ended at time TEND.

After processing the last transaction the integration of the differential equation in the subroutine STATE with SV(1,1) = 0 and DV(1,1) = 0 will continue until time TEND unless special measures are taken to prevent this. The simulation is to be ended when the processing of the last transaction is complete. This is done by testing before the transaction is eliminated whether of the simulation can be ended. The section "Elimination of a transaction" is as follows:

```
C     Eliminate a transaction
C     =======================
      IF(TX(LTX,1).GT.TXMAX-1) TEND = T
      CALL TERMIN(*9000)
```

2.4.3 The Subroutine STATE

The filling of the barrel is a continuous process with respect to time. It is described in subroutine STATE.

The continuous variable SV(1,1) is the content of the barrel. The rate at which the content is increasing is represented by its derivative DV(1,1).

Thus the content of the barrel obeys the differential equation:

DV(1,1) = RATE

The rate at which the barrel is filled, RATE, depends on the state of the filling station:

IFILL = 1   station empty   RATE = 0.

IFILL = 2   station working   RATE = 0.20*SV(1,1)+1

IFILL = 3   maximum rate   RATE = 6.

Thus the differential equation is represented by the following statements in the subroutine STATE:

```
1       GOTO(10,20,30),IFILL

10      RATE = 0.
        GOTO 100

20      RATE = 0.20*SV(1,1) + 1.
        GOTO 100

30      RATE = 6.0
        GOTO 100

100     DV(1,1) = RATE
        RETURN
```

2.4.4 Crossings

The level of beer in the barrel is monitored using a crossing in the subroutine DETECT. The flag IFLAG(1,1) is set equal to 1 when the level of beer reaches its capacity. Similarly the time at which the rate of filling DV(1,1) reaches the maximum value must be recognised. This is indicated by the flag IFLAG(1,2).

The subroutine DETECT is as follows:

```
C       CALL SUBROUTINE CROSS FOR SET 1
C       ===============================
1       CALL CROSS(1,1,1,0,0.,CAP,1,0.1,*977,*9999)
        CALL CROSS(1,2,-1,0,0.,6.,1,0.01,*977,*9999)
        RETURN
```

The conditions in which the variables IFLAG(1,1) and IFLAG(1,2) appear are tested in the subroutine TEST.

The event NE = 1 is activated if the condition NCOND = 2 is satisfied and the contents of the barrel are equal to its capacity. The event NE = 1 includes all activities which occur when the barrel becomes full.

The event NE = 3 is activated if the condition NCOND = 3 is satisfied and the filling rate has reached its maximum value.

The subroutine TEST is as follows:

```
        IF(CHECK(1)) CALL DBLOCK(5,1,0,1)
        IF(CHECK(2)) CALL EVENT(1,*9999)
        IF(CHECK(3)) CALL EVENT(3,*9999)
        RETURN
```

2.4.5 Events

The event NE = 1 in subroutine EVENT is as follows:

```
C       Complete filling
C       ================
1       CALL MONITR(1)
        IFILL = 1
        CALL BEGIN(1,*9999)
        CALL MONITR(1)
        CALL DBLOCK(5,2,0,0)
        RETURN
```

IFILL = 1
This stops the filling process.

CALL DBLOCK(5,2,0,0)

The transaction which is waiting at the gate NG = 2 is activated by calling DBLOCK when the barrel is filled. It is then further processed in the subroutine ACTIV.

The event NE = 2 sets IFILL = 2. This begins the filling process. The event NE = 2 is activated in the subroutine ACTIV when a barrel enters the filling station. The event NE = 2 is as follows:

```
C       Begin filling process
C       =====================
2       CALL MONITR(1)
        IFILL = 2
        CALL BEGIN(1,*9999)
        CALL MONITR(1)
        RETURN
```

The event NE = 3 sets IFILL equal to 3. This indicates that the filling rate has reached its maximum value. The event NE = 3 is as follows:

```
C       Maximum rate of filling
C       =======================
3       CALL MONITR(1)
        IFILL = 3
        CALL BEGIN(1,*9999)
        CALL MONITR(1)
        RETURN
```

The event NE = 4 sets SV(1,1) equal to 0 after the barrel has left the filling station.

```
C       Clear the barrel
C       ================
4       CALL MONITR(1)
        SV(1,1) = 0.
        CALL BEGIN(1,*9999)
        CALL MONITR(1)
        RETURN
```

Note:

   * Remember that every change of a variable which occurs in the subroutine STATE requires a call of the subroutine BEGIN. The alteration is to be traced by two calls of MONITR.

2.4.6 Checking of Conditions

The logical function CHECK is as follows:

```
C
1       CHECK = IPUMP.EQ.0
        GOTO 100
C
2       CHECK = IFLAG(1,1).EQ.1
        GOTO 100
C
3       CHECK = IFLAG(1,2).EQ.1
        GOTO 100
```

The condition NCOND = 1 controls access to the filling station. The gate NG = 1 in the subroutine ACTIV blocks all arriving transactions when the condition NCOND = 1 has the value .FALSE.

The condition NCOND = 2 tests whether the barrel is full. If it is full the event NE = 1 is activated. Subroutine TEST checks the condition NCOND = 2 and processes the results.

The condition NCOND = 3 tests whether the maximum rate of filling has been reached. Subroutine TEST checks the condition and activates the event NE = 3.

Note:

   * The indicator variable IFLAG is to be used if an event is to be activated once only when the crossing line has been crossed. This means that IFLAG must appear in the logical condition. This is the case in the brewery model III.

The indicator variable JFLAG is to be used if, on the other hand, an event is to occur whenever the value of the continuous variable is above (or below) the value of a crossing. See volume 1, chapter 2.3, "Conditional State Transitions".

2.4.7 Main Program

The following variables are required in the block COMMON/PRIV/:

COMMON/PRIV/IPUMP,CAP,IFILL

It is recommended that the block COMMON/PRIV/ is included in all user subroutines, even if the variables do not occur in the particular subroutine. The block COMMON/PRIV/ should be included in the main program and the following six user' subroutines: EVENT, ACTIV, STATE, DETECT, TEST, CHECK.

The input file for the brewery model III is as follows:

```
TEXT; BREWERY MODEL III/
VARI; TXMAX; 100/
VARI; ICONT; 1 /
INTI; 1; 1; 0.01; 1; 1; 0.001; 10.; 0.001; 1.E04/
PLO1; 1; 0.; 20.; 0.5; 21;001001; -001001/
PLO3; 1;*X;CONTENT;*Y;&CONTENT/
END/
```

2.4.8 Summary of the Implementation

The following steps are necessary to implement the brewery model III:

* Initialise the user variables. Declare the block COMMON/PRIV/.

* Describe the transaction oriented part of the model in the subroutine ACTIV.

* Define the differential equation for the filling process in the subroutine STATE.

* Define the events NE = 1, NE = 2, NE = 3 in the subroutine EVENT.

* Define the conditions for the occurrence of events in the logical function CHECK.

* Define the crossings in the subroutine DETECT.

* Test the conditions in the subroutine TEST.

The brewery model III shows that GPSS-FORTRAN Version 3 can also deal with complex models with event oriented, transaction oriented, and continuous components. The modular structure of the simulator can be seen. The various model components are described independently of each other in the subroutines EVENT, ACTIV and STATE. The connections between the components of the model are created by conditions which are defined in the logical function CHECK.

In addition, the subroutines DETECT and TEST are required to locate the crossings and test the conditions.

Even very complex models can be represented in a clear and well structured form in this way.

2.4.9 The Results

The results of the brewery model III are shown below.

The data for the time spent by the barrels in the queue and the
time spent in the queue together with being filled are obtained
from the bins NBN = 1 and NBN = 2.

The next page shows the plot of the filling process for one
barrel.

PLOT NR 1

VARIABLE	MINIMUM	MAXIMUM	MEAN	95%-CONFIDENCE INTERVAL	END OF SETTLING PHASE	DISPLACEMENT OF MEAN	DISPL. OF MEAN IN PER CENT
X = CONTENT	.0000E+00	3.0028E+01	⎯	⎯	⎯	⎯	⎯
Y = CONTENT'	.0000E+00	6.0026E+00	⎯	⎯	⎯	⎯	⎯

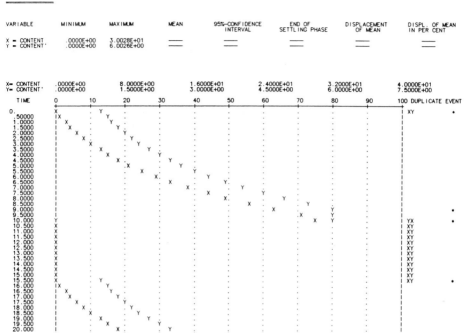

X= CONTENT	.0000E+00	8.0000E+00	1.6000E+01	2.4000E+01	3.2000E+01	4.0000E+01
Y= CONTENT'	.0000E+00	1.5000E+00	3.0000E+00	4.5000E+00	6.0000E+00	7.5000E+00

X= CONTENT	.0000E+00	8.0000E+00	1.6000E+01	2.4000E+01	3.2000E+01	4.0000E+01
Y= CONTENT'	.0000E+00	1.5000E+00	3.0000E+00	4.5000E+00	6.0000E+00	7.5000E+00

2.4.10 Problems

The problems show how complex systems can be dealt with using
GPSS-FORTRAN Version 3. The problems are not simple but the
reader is strongly recommended to work through them because they
provide valuable training.

* Problem 1

Disturbances in the filling process caused by a momentary
blockage of the valve are to be included. The barrel is not
filled during the stoppage. The times at which the stoppages
occur are normally distributed with mean 30.0 and standard
deviation 10.0; the length of a stoppage is always exactly 4.0.
The first stoppage occurs at time 5.0.

Note:

  * Two additional events are required which deal with the
  beginning and end of the stoppage.

Event NE = 5 stops the barrel from being filled by setting
IFILL=1. It also schedules the next occurrence of the event at a
later time. The delay until the next occurrence of this event is
normally distributed. In addition, the event NE = 6 is scheduled
for time T + 4. at which the stoppage ends.

The following events must be included in the subroutine EVENT:

```
C
5       CALL MONITR(1)
        IFILL = 1
        CALL BEGIN(1,*9999)
        CALL MONITR(1)
        CALL GAUSS(30.0,10.0,10.,50.,3,RANDOM)
        CALL ANNOUN(5,T+RANDOM,*9999)
        CALL ANNOUN(6,T+4.,*9999)
        RETURN

6       CALL MONITR(1)
        IFILL = 2
        CALL BEGIN(1,*9999)
        CALL MONITR(1)
        RETURN
```

The label selector in the subroutine EVENT must be extended to
include the labels 5 and 6.

The event NE = 5 is to be scheduled in the main program at time
T = 5.

* Problem 2

The filling procedure is modified. The rate of filling is
continuously reduced, starting when a barrel is 3/4 full. The
rate of filling may not become less than the initial rate of 1.0.

The following applies when the barrel is not yet 3/4 filled:

RATE = 0.20*SV(1,1) + 1
RAMAX = AMIN1(RATE,6.)

If the barrel is 3/4 full, the rate is given by:

RATE = RAMAX*(0.75*CAP/SV(1,1))**8.

Note:

* The variable IFILL is extended to represent the following two states:

IFILL = 4   The barrel is 3/4 full
IFILL = 5   The rate of filling has been reduced to 1.0

The subroutine DETECT checks whether the level has reached 3/4 of the capacity using the flag IFLAG(1,3) and whether the rate of filling has been reduced to 1.0 using the flag IFLAG(1,4).

The two new conditions are defined in NCOND = 4 and NCOND = 5 in the logical function CHECK. The subroutine TEST performs the necessary checking.

Two events NE = 5 and NE = 6 are used to set the flag variable IFILL. They are activated in the subroutine TEST if the conditions NCOND = 4 or NCOND = 5 are satisfied.

The subroutine STATE is extended to include the two new statements which compute RATE.

Note:

* If the value of the state variable is exactly on the crossing line and then moves back from this line, this is not treated as a crossing. A crossing only occurs when a crossing line is actually crossed.

* Problem 3

User attributes of a transaction can occur in the condition of a gate. The brewery model III is slightly modified to show this:

If a barrel of size 20 litres arrives at the filling station, it leaves it immediately without being filled.

This change affects the gate NG = 2. The gate can be passed when a barrel is full or when a barrel with 20 litres contents reaches it.

The call of the subroutine GATE is as follows:

        CALL GATE(2,2,0,0,3,*9000)

The values of the parameters IGLOBL and IBLOCK are to be particularly noted.

The condition NCOND = 2 in the logical function CHECK is as
follows:

2   IF(LTX.NE.0) CHECK = FLAG(1,1).EQ.1 OR TX(LTX,9).EQ.20

It is particularly important that CHECK is only set in the
condition NCOND = 2 when LTX.NE.0. This rule must be obeyed in
combined models which contain user attributes of transactions in
the conditions of the gates. It is possible in combined models
that the logical function CHECK is called to test the conditions
from a point in the program which does not refer to the
transaction. In this case, LTX.EQ.0. This would lead to an error.

3. The Facilities

The most general type of station in queued models is the gate.
Arriving transactions are blocked and placed in a queue when the
logical condition of the gate has the value .FALSE. The logical
condition is provided by the user. GPSS-FORTRAN Version 3
supports other frequently occurring types of stations as well as
gates. They represent special cases with a fixed logical
condition. Here, it is not necessary for the user to formulate
the logical condition and arrange for its testing. Both are done
by the simulator.

The facility is a very simple type of station. It is used to
represent simple servers in a model. The following examples will
be used to show how facilities can be included in a model.

Model of a squirrel   Use of simple facility

Model of a repair workshop   Facility with preemption

Model of job administration   Dynamic assignment of priorities

Model of a group practice   Use of multifacility

3.1 Model of a Squirrel

The model of a squirrel shows the use of a simple facility, and
how the execution of a simulation run can be repeated.

3.1.1 Structure of the Model

Ten nuts lie on the ground under a walnut tree. A squirrel begins
to crack them at time T = 0. It requires on average four minutes
per nut. A new nut falls from the tree on average every five
minutes, with the first nut falling at time T = 6. As soon as
there are no nuts left on the ground, the squirrel goes
elsewhere.

The random events have an exponential distribution.

The simulation is to provide answers to the following two
questions:

* How many nuts does the squirrel crack?

* How long is the squirrel on average engaged in cracking nuts?

The simulation is to be repeated a hundred times to compute the
averages.

Confidence intervals are to be computed for the averages.

3.1.2 Implementation

The squirrel and its nuts can be represented by a single server
with a queue. The squirrel is represented by a facility which is
occupied when a nut is being cracked. All the nuts which fall
from the tree form a queue.

The subroutine ACTIV contains the series of subroutine calls
which are typical of a server.

```
3          CALL SEIZE(1,3,*9000)
           CALL ERLANG(4.,1,0.14,20.,2,RAND2,*9999)
           CALL WORK(1,RAND2,0,4,*9000,*9999)
4          CALL CLEAR(1,*9000,*9999)
```

The generation of the first 10 transactions is done by the source
NSC = 1. It is started by the following call in the main program:

```
           CALL START(1,0.,1,*9999)
```

The corresponding call of the subroutine GENERA in ACTIV is as
follows:

```
1          CALL GENERA(0.,1.,*9999)
```


3.1.3 Main Program

The user must assign the value of the maximum number of transactions which can be generated by a source in section 4 of the
main program "Assign values of constants and initialise model."

```
C
C          Initialise Source Array
C          =======================
           SOURCL(I,3) = 10.
```

The third column of the source array contains the number of
transactions to be generated by a particular source. This
statement assigns the value 10. for the source NSC = 1, which
occupies the first row of the source array.

No data need be provided for the source NSC = 2. The default
value is used which was assigned in the subroutine PRESET:

```
           SOURCL(1,3) = 1.E+10
```

All further transactions which enter the model during the
simulation run are generated by the source NSC = 2. This source
is also started in the main program.

```
           CALL START(2,6.,2,*7000)
```

The corresponding call of the subroutine GENERA in ACTIV is as follows:

```
2         CALL ERLANG(5.,1,0.17,25.,1,RAND1,*9999)
          CALL GENERA(RAND1,1.,*9999)
```

The simulation is to be ended when there are no nuts left on the ground. This means that the queue for the facility must be empty.

The generation of further nuts is then stopped by closing down the source NSC = 2 by a call of the subroutine START. The flow control finds no further activations and transfers control to section 7 of the main program "Terminating section".

3.1.4 The Subroutine ACTIV

The subroutine ACTIV is as follows:

```
C
C         Generation of the first ten transactions
C         ========================================
1         CALL GENERA(0.,1.,*9999)
          GOTO 21
C
C         Generation of the subsequent transactions
C         =========================================
2         CALL ERLANG(5.,1,0.17,25.,1,RAND1,*9999)
          CALL GENERA(RAND1,1.,*9999)
C
C         Enter and leave the facilities
C         ==============================
21        CALL ARRIVE(1,1)
3         CALL SEIZE(1,3,*9000)
          CALL DEPART(1,1,0.,*9999)
          CALL ERLANG(4.,1,0.14,20.,2,RAND2,*9999)
          CALL WORK(1,RAND2,0,4,*9000,*9999)
4         CALL CLEAR(1,*9000,*9999)
C
C         Test if the simulation is completed
C         ===================================
          IF(BIN(1,1).LE.0.01) CALL START(2,-1.,2,*9999)
C
C         Eliminate the transaction
C         =========================
          CALL TERMIN(*9000)
```

The first thing a transaction does after it has been generated is to place a token in the bin NBN = 1. Then it calls the subroutine SEIZE.

All transactions generated by GENERA reach the subroutine SEIZE. A test is made to determine whether the facility is free or occupied. If it is free, the transaction occupies it, otherwise the transaction is blocked. However control can be transferred directly to the subroutine SEIZE when the facility has become free and there are transactions queued for it. In this case a transaction has left the facility and called the subroutine CLEAR.

If the queue for the facility is not empty, then the first transaction is removed from the queue and scheduled for activation by the state transition "Unblock". The section "Unblock the next transaction" unblocks the next transaction from the queue in the subroutine CLEAR. This transaction is found by the subroutine FLOWC in the flow control and activated at the statement with label 3.

When control has left the subroutine SEIZE via the normal RETURN exit, then the transaction has found a free facility which it can now occupy.
The subroutine DEPART is called next. The bin with NBN = 1 collects statistical data about the behaviour of transactions in the queue.

Then the service time is computed. The subroutine WORK is called to deactivate the transaction and place it in the scheduled state. The token is reactivated at the end of the service time at the successor statement whose label is supplied as a parameter of the subroutine WORK. It is the subroutine call CALL CLEAR with label 4.

The transaction reaches the test of the criterion for ending the simulation after the subroutine CLEAR. Then it is eliminated from the model by calling the subroutine TERMIN.

Notes:

* Control must be returned to the flow control when a transaction has been deactivated. This means that all subroutines in which a transaction can be blocked must have an exit *9000 which returns control to the flow control. In the squirrel model this applies to the subroutines SEIZE, WORK, and TERMIN.

* The condition which must be satisfied for a transaction to pass the subroutine call CALL SEIZE and not be placed in the queue is:

"The facility is free".

This test can be found in the subroutine SEIZE:

        IF(FAC(NFA,1).NE.0) GOTO 200

* The condition is tested in the subroutine CLEAR. Since a transaction frees the facility in the subroutine CLEAR the next transaction can immediately be scheduled for activation at the facility. This means that the testing of the condition and the call of the subroutine DBLOCK takes place in the subroutine CLEAR and need not be done by the user. The statement in subroutine CLEAR which does this is:

        IF(BHEAD(NFA).GT.0) CALL DBLOCK(1,NFA,0,1)

It is necessary for the correct execution of the simulation that a transaction which has been blocked and is scheduled for activation is immediately processed. No other activation may precede this. This is achieved by placing the transaction at the head of the list of scheduled transactions. It is found here by the subroutine FLOWC in the flow control before all other transactions and is immediately activated.

3.1.5 Repetition of the Simulation

The previous description refers to a single simulation run. The
problem requires that this is repeated a hundred times.

This is achieved by placing the three sections of the main
program

5. Start model
6. Model
7. Terminating section

in a DO-loop with I = 1,100.

The following five points are to be considered in constructing
the DO-loop:

All data areas must be reinitialised for each new simulation run.
Thus the subroutines RESET and PRESET must also be called inside
the DO-loop.

* Since PRESET and RESET are also called inside the DO-loop and
thus are after the call INPUT, all values read in are overwritten
by the initialisation.

The call of PRESET initialises in the source table the number of
transactions to be generated by each source. Therefore the
assignment

        SOURCL(1,3) = 10.

must be executed for the source NSC = 1 in every simulation run.

The random number generators must not be reinitialised. Otherwise
each simulation run would have an identical series of random
numbers and therefore identical results. The subroutine INIT1 may
not be called from inside the DO-loop.

The number of nuts which were cracked in each run and the time
which was necessary for this are recorded in the vectors SUM and
TIM. Both data areas are declared in section 1 of the main
program "General FORTRAN definitions" as follows:

        DIMENSION SUM(100), TIM(100)

The mean of the values in SUM and TIM and the corresponding
confidence intervals are computed using the subroutine ANAR.

The two means SUMM and TIMM and the widths of the confidence
intervals HALFS and HALFT are output.

Thus sections 5 - 8 of the main program are as follows:

```
        DO 7500 I = 1,100
C
        CALL RESET
        CALL PRESET
        SOURCL(1,3) = 10.
C
```

```
C         5. Start model
C         ==============
C         Start sources
C         =============
          CALL START(1,0.,1,*7000)
          CALL START(2,6.,2,*7000)
C
C         6. Model
C         ========
6000      CALL FLOWC(*7000)
C
C         Terminating section
C         ===================
7000      CONTINUE
C


C         Final computation of the bins and determination
C         ===============================================
C         of the confidence intervals
C         ===========================
          CALL ENDBIN
C
C         Final computation of user quantities
C         ====================================
          SUM(I) = BIN(1,3)
          TIM(I) = BIN(1,8)
7500      CONTINUE
C
C         Determination of the averages and the confidence intervals
C         ==========================================================
          CALL ANAR(SUM,100,1,0.95,SUMM,HALFS,JMIN,KMIN,IP,0,*8001)
8001      CALL ANAR(TIM,100,2,0.95,TIMM,HALFT,JMIN,KMIN,IP,0,*8005)
C
C         8. Output of the results
C         ========================
          IF (ICONT.NE.0) CALL ENDPLO(0)
C
C         Output of user quantities
C         =========================
8005      CONTINUE
          WRITE(UNIT2,8010)
8010      FORMAT(/////16X,45(1H*),2(/16X,1H*,43X,1H*))
          WRITE(UNIT2,8020) SUMM,TIMM
8020      FORMAT(16X,1H*,2X,20H THE SQUIRREL CRACKS,
         +10HON AVERAGE,11X,1H*,/16X,1H*,2X,F5.2,
         +9H NUTS IN ,F6.2,12H TIME UNITS.,9X,1H*,/16X,1H*,
         +43X,1H*)
          WRITE(UNIT2,8030) HALFS,HALFT
8030      FORMAT(16X,1H*,2X,20HCONFIDENCE INTERVAL ,
         +14HFOR NUTS:(+/- ,F4.1,2H ),1X,1H*,/16X,
         +1H*,2X,34HCONFIDENCE INTERVAL FOR TIME:(+/- ,
         +F4.1,2H ),1X,1H*)
          WRITE(UNIT2,8040)
8040      FORMAT(2(16X,1H*,43X,1H*/),16X,45(1H*))
          WRITE(UNIT2,8050)
8050      FORMAT(1H1)
C
```

3.1.6 Results

```
************************************************
*                                              *
*                                              *
*    THE SQUIRREL CRACKS ON AVERAGE            *
*    48.87 NUTS IN 194.88 TIME UNITS.          *
*                                              *
*    CONFIDENCE INTERVAL FOR NUTS:(+/-   .9 )  *
*    CONFIDENCE INTERVAL FOR TIME:(+/- 24.0 )  *
*                                              *
*                                              *
************************************************
```

3.1.7 Problems

The problems show three possible modifications of the model of
the squirrel.

* Problem 1

At the beginning of the simulation there are 15 walnuts on the
ground.

Note:

    * The statement in the main program which determines how many
nuts are to be generated by the source SCR = 1 must be altered:

        SOURCL(1,3) = 15

Further changes are not necessary.

* Problem 2

The squirrel loses interest in cracking nuts after 250 time
units. It does not start a new nut if the time is greater than
250.

Comment:

The criterion for ending the simulation is to be modified to:

```
        IF(T.GE.250) GOTO 9999
        IF(BIN(1,1).LE.EPS) CALL START(2,-1.,2,*9999)
```

When interpreting the results it should be borne in mind that
HALFW is set less than 0 when ANAR cannot determine a confidence
interval. See volume 1 chapter 5.1.6 "The Calculation of the
Confidence Interval and the Determination of the Settling Time".

* Problem 3

In problem 2, the squirrel always finishes a nut which it has
started. The criterion for ending the simulation is only tested
when it has finished a nut.

In problem 3 the squirrel stops at time T = 250., i.e. a nut
which it has started is left unfinished.

Note:

    * A scheduled event is required which interferes in the flow
control at time T = 250. and sets the end of the processing
time equal to the value of the simulation clock T:

```
1       LTX1 = FAC(1,1)
        CALL NCHAIN(3,LTX1,*9999)
        ACTIVL(LTX1,1) = T
        CALL TCHAIN(3,LTX1,*9999)
        RETURN
        END
```

3.2 The Model of a Repair Workshop

Each queue can be processed in GPSS-FORTRAN Version 3 according to an individual policy suited to the queue. This example deals with a station whose queue is processed using the policy PFIFO. The setting up time required for the preemption should be taken into account.

3.2.1 Description of the Model

A repair workshop deals with its current jobs in the order of their priority. If a job arrives whose priority is higher than that of the job being processed, then the latter is interrupted and replaced by the new job.

The jobs arrive with exponentially distributed interarrival times with MEAN = 3.0. 20 % of the jobs have a high priority equal to 2; the other jobs have priority equal to 1.

The processing time of the jobs is normally distributed with mean 1.8 and standard deviation 0.6. The following questions are to be answered by simulation:

* What is the mean time spent in the queue and the mean length of the queue at the workshop? The averages are to be determined separately for jobs of higher and lower priorities.

* What percentage of the total time is spend on setting the job up? This is equal to the total setting up time * 100 / total processing time.

10000 jobs are to be processed.

3.2.2 Implementation

First transactions are generated. The subroutine TRANSF makes a random selection of 20 % of the transactions and transfers them to the statement with label 10. There they are assigned the higher priority 2.

The processing time is determined for all transactions and stored in the private parameter TX(LTX,9).

```
C       Generate the transactions
C       ==========================
1       CALL ERLANG(3.0,1,0.1,15.,1,RAND1,*9999)
        CALL GENERA(RAND1,1.,*9999)
        CALL TRANSF(0.2,3,*10)
        TX(LTX,4) = 1.
        GOTO 11
10      TX(LTX,4) = 2.
11      CALL GAUSS(1.8,0.6,0.2,3.4,2,RAND2)
        TX(LTX,9) = RAND2
```

The processing of the transactions starts after the generation. First, statistical information about the behaviour of the transactions in the queues is collected. This is done by calling the subroutines ARRIVE and DEPART.

Notes:

* The behaviour of the transactions is monitored using two bins NBN = 1 and NBN = 2. The index of the bin is the same as the priority of the transaction.

Although the transactions are arranged in order in the queue, they are registered separately in two different bins according to their priorities.

* Because the index of the appropriate bin is a parameter of the subroutines ARRIVE and DEPART it is sufficient to write the statements:

        CALL ARRIVE(NINT(TX(LTX,4)),1)   or
        CALL DEPART(NINT(TX(LTX,4)),1,0,*9999) respectively,

only once.

See chapter 8.2 "Combination of Model Components to Struc-tures".

* A preempted transaction is returned to the queue. On leaving the facility, it must place another token in the bin for the statistical data to be correctly collected.   This is done by the call

        CALL ARRIVE(NINT(TX(LTX,4)),1)

in the section "Counting the preemptions".

The occupation of the station is programmed as follows:

```
C       Processing the transactions
C       ===========================
        CALL ARRIVE(NINT(TX(LTX,4)),1)
2       CALL PREEMP(1,2,*9000)
        CALL DEPART(NINT(TX(LTX,4)),1,0,*9999)
        CALL SETUP(1,0.4,3,*9000,*9999)
3       CALL WORK(1,TX(LTX,9),0,4,*9000,*9999)
4       CALL KNOCKD(1,0.4,5,*9000,*9999)
5       CALL CLEAR(1,*50,*9999)
        GOTO 100

C       Counting the preemptions
C       ========================
50      ICOUNT = ICOUNT + 1
        CALL ARRIVE(NINT(TX(LTX,4)),1)
        GOTO 9000

C       Eliminating the transactions
C       ============================
100     CALL TERMIN(*9000)
```

When a transaction has left the facility, it leaves the subroutine CLEAR via the normal RETURN exit to the statement following the calling statement.   In this case control is transferred to a call of the subroutine TERMIN, which eliminates the transaction.

If the transaction has been preempted it is blocked in the subroutine CLEAR. In this case control leaves the subroutine via the label which is supplied as a parameter. Control must be returned to the flow control either directly or indirectly, so that the next transaction can be activated. In the repair workshop model, control is transferred to the statement with the label 50 after a preemption. This records in ICOUNT the number of preemptions. Then control is returned to the flow control.

The variable ICOUNT is initialised in section 2 of the main program "Assign default values to user variables" with ICOUNT = 0. It is accessed in the subroutine ACTIV in the block COMMON/PRIV/.

The results are processed in section 7 of the main program "Terminating section".
The subroutine ENDBIN evaluates the two bins NBIN=1 and NBIN=2. This determines the mean queue length and the mean waiting time for jobs with lower and higher priority.

The percentage of time devoted to setting up new jobs is given by

OVERH = FLOAT(ICOUNT)*0.8*100./T

3.2.3 Results

The results of the repair workshop model are given in the following.

The results for the behaviour of the queue are contained in the values for the bin NBN = 1.

The time lost in setting up is 3.3 %.

T = 29748.9978   RT = 29748.9978

BIN ARRAY
=========

NBN	QTY	MAX	SUMIN	SUMOUT	ARRIVE	DEPART	TOTALWT	LAST
1	0	18	8007	8007	9216	9216	.1014E+06	.2975E+05
2	0	3	1993	1993	1993	1993	1259.	.2975E+05

BINSTA ARRAY
============

NBN	DURATION TIME	NUM. OF TOKEN	CONF.INT. PER CENT	DISPLACEM. PER CENT	END OF SET-TLING PHASE
1	12.67	3.413	12.12	.2147	400.0
2	.6315	.4236E-01	7.817	.5242E-12	80.00


```
***************************************
*                                     *
*                                     *
*   TIME LOST IN SETTING UP:  3.3 %   *
*                                     *
*                                     *
***************************************
```

3.2.4 Problems

The problems show how preemption occurs.

* Problem 1

The number of times a preemption does not occur, because the transaction to be preempted is already in the closing down phase, is to be determined.

Note:

  * If preemption cannot occur the arriving transaction is blocked. Exit from the subroutine PREEMP transfers control to the statement with label 9000.

Those transactions which have a high priority PR = 2 but could not preempt because the transaction to be preempted was in the closing down phase are selected from the blocked transactions. This is done by the following statements:

```
9000   LTX1 = FAC(1,1)
       IF(FAC(1,3).EQ.3.AND
       + TX(LTX,4).GT.TX(LTX1,4))  IKNOCK = IKNOCK + 1
       RETURN
```

* Problem 2

The number of times an immediate preemption does not occur because the transaction to be preempted is in the setting up phase is to be counted.

3.3 Job Administration Model

GPSS-FORTRAN Version 3 allows priorities to be assigned
dynamically. The priorities of the transactions can be
recalculated by the subroutine DYNVAL.

3.3.1 Description of the Model

The orders which a firm receives are assigned one of six possible
priorities.
The interarrival times are exponentially distributed with mean
MEAN1 = 50. The processing time of the orders is also
exponentially distributed with mean MEAN2 = 40. units of time.

The probability that a job is assigned a particular priority is
1/6, i.e. all priorities have the same probability.

Dynamic priority assignment according to WTL (Waiting Time Limit)
is used to decrease the mean waiting times of the orders with
lower priorities. The new priority is given by

$$P = P(0) + WZ/100.$$

The variables have the following meaning:

P   Reassigned prioritiy
P(0)   Initial priority when the job enters the model
WZ   Waiting time, ie. time since the job entered the model

This means that an order is transferred to the next higher
priority class after a waiting time of 100. The initial priority,
P(0), is taken into account.

The priorities are recalculated when the server is free and a new
order is to be selected. The reassignment of the priorities does
itself not use any time in the model.

The following two questions are to be investigated by simulation:

* What is the average waiting time of the orders as a function of
their initial priority P(0) if the priorities are fixed?

* What is the average waiting time of the orders as a function of
their initial priority P(0)?

The average time in the queue as a function of the initial
priority P(0) is to be plotted.

The simulation is to be ended when the last 20 values of the mean
waiting time of the orders with initial priority P(0) = 1 are in
the interval (average - 10 %, average + 10 %). The number of
transactions between successive tests is NE = 100.

3.3.2 Implementation

First the transactions are generated and assigned their initial
priorities. The initial priority P(0) is placed in TX(LTX,9).
TX(LTX,4) contains the current priority which is recalculated by

the subroutine DYNVAL. TX(LTX,9) = TX(LTX,4) if the priorities are not changed.

The transaction occupies the facility and later leaves the facility at the end of the service time. If IPRIOR.EQ.1 the priorities are to be reassigned dynamically between a transaction leaving the facility and the next transaction entering it.

Seven bins are used to store statistical information. The bins with index NBN = 1,...,6 refer to transactions with initial priority P(0) = 1,...,6. It follows that: NBN = TX(LTX,9).
All transactions are registered in the bin with NBN = 7, independent of their priorities.
The position of the calls of ARRIVE and DEPART show that the transactions are monitored while they are in the queue.

A histogram table TAB1 is used to represent graphically the dependence of the mean waiting time on the initial priority. X is the initial priority and Y is the time spent in the queue of the transaction.
The subroutine SIMEND is used to decide when the simulation is to be ended. NBN = 1 for the queue of transactions with initial priority P(0) = 1.

The results first of all show the seven queues.
The immediate processing and output of the frequency table TAB1 would show the number of observed transactions as a function of the initial priority P(0). According to the definition of the model the result must be a uniform distribution.
The mean waiting times as a function of the priority are monitored and stored in the elements TAB2(I,2) of a second frequency table. The histogram is computed by the subroutine ENDTAB and plotted by the subroutine GRAPH.

The time the transaction joins the queue is recorded in the user attribute TX(LTX,10). Thus the waiting time of a transaction is given by:

$$Y = T - TX(LTX,10)$$

The subroutine ACTIV is as follows:

```
C        Generate transactions
C        ======================
1        CALL ERLANG(50.,1,1.7,250.,1,RAND1,*9999)
         CALL GENERA(RAND1,1.,*9999)
C
C        Determine initial priority
C        ==========================
         CALL UNIFRM(1.0,6.999,2,RAND2)
         TX(LTX,4) = AINT(RAND2)
         TX(LTX,9) = TX(LTX,4)
         TX(LTX,10) = T
C
C        Enter and leave the facility
C        ============================
         CALL ARRIVE(NINT(TX(LTX,9)),1)
         CALL ARRIVE(7,1)
2        CALL SEIZE(1,2,*9000)
         CALL DEPART(7,1,0.,*9999)
         CALL DEPART(NINT(TX(LTX,9)),1,0.,*9999)
```

```
          X = TX(LTX,9)
          Y = T - TX(LTX,10)
          CALL TABULA(1,6,X,Y,1.,1.)
          CALL ERLANG(40.,1,1.4,200.,3,RAND3,*9999)
          CALL WORK(1,RAND3,0,3,*9000,*9999)
3         CALL CLEAR(1,*9000,*9999)
C
C         Dynamic priority assignment
C         ===========================
          IF(IPRIOR.EQ.1) CALL DYNVAL(1,1,0,ICOUNT)
C
C         Eliminate transactions
C         ======================
          CALL SIMEND(1,100,10.)
          CALL TERMIN(*9000)
```

3.3.3 Main Program

The variable IPRIOR is input by the main program and is available
to the subroutine ACTIV in the block COMMON/PRIV/.

IPRIOR = 0 no dynamic priority assignment
IPRIOR = 1 dynamic priority assignment

The processing of the results takes place in section 7 of the
main program "Terminating section". The histogram tables are
also processed in this section:

```
          CALL ENDTAB(1,2,0.,0.)
          DO 8100 I=1,6
          VFUNC(1,I) = FLOAT(I)
          IF(TAB(I+1,2,1).LT.EPS) GOTO 8100
          VFUNC(2,I) = TAB(I+1,4,1,)/TAB(I+1,2,1)
8100      CONTNUE
          CALL GRAPH(VFUNC,6,0.,0.,TEXT)
```

The totals of the times spent in the queues by the transactions,
arranged according to priorities, are found in the sixth column
of table 1 with the title CUMY. These values are in the fourth
column of the table TAB.

Note:

    *   The upper bounds of the intervals are found in table   1
    under the heading X. A transaction with priority 1 is placed
    in the interval with upper bound   1.   See   volume   1,
    chapter 5.2 "Construction of Histograms".

The mean waiting time is computed from the total waiting time of
all transactions with the same priority. This is done by dividing
the total waiting time by the number of transactions which occur
in this interval.
The mean values are printed in the seventh column with the
heading E(Y).
The priorities and the mean waiting times are placed in the table
VFUNC in order to plot the mean values.

Notes:

   *   The table VFUNC and the array TEXT required for the   names
   of the tables must be dimensioned as follows:

   CHARACTER * 4 TEXT
   DIMENSION VFUNC(2,6), TEXT(8)

   * The headings of the tables must be placed in the array   TEXT.
   See volume 1, chapter 7.3 "Output of Plots by GRAPH":

        TEXT(1) = 'WAIT'
        TEXT(2) = 'ING '
        TEXT(3) = 'TIME'

   * It is recommended that the table VFUNC is initialised with
   zeros   in the main program in the section "Assign default
   values to user variables".

The subroutine GRAPH prints VFUNC as a histogram. VFUNC(1,I)
contains the values of x, and VFUNC(2,I) the corresponding values
of y.

Note:

   *   The   subroutine SIMEND tests whether the simulation can be
   ended. It is called before a transaction is eliminated. If the
   criterion for ending the simulation is satisfied, control is
   transferred   from SIMEND to the label *9999, which begins
   the terminating section of the program.

3.3.4 The Subroutine DYNVAL

DYNVAL performs the dynamic assignment of the priorities. It is
called when a transaction has left the facility and before it is
reoccupied.
The priority of a transaction is computed by the function DYNPR.
The user must provide in DYNPR the function which computes the
priority.

The function DYNPR is as follows:

```
C       Determine the priority
C       ========================
        IF(TX(LTX1,4).GT.6.-EPS) GOTO 10
        PR = TX(LTX1,9) + (T - TX(LTX1,10))/100.
        IF(PR.LT.6.) GOTO 20
10      PR = 6.
20      DYNPR = PR
        RETURN
        END
```

The priority is computed as follows:

$$P = P(0) + WZ/100.$$

The time spent in the queue by a transaction is given by the
difference between the time at which it was generated and the
current value of time. Both times are entered in the transaction
table by the subroutine ACTIV:

TX(LTX,9) initial priority
TX(LTX,10) time of generation

Notes:

*   The subroutine DYNVAL works through the queue recomputing
the priority of each transaction. The row index of the transaction for which the priority is recomputed is determined in
DYNVAL and passed to the function DYNPR in its parameter list.

* The function DYNPR is one of the GPSS-FORTRAN Version 3 subroutines to be written by the user. See volume 2, appendix A6.

3.3.5 Results

The results of the order processing model are shown below:

The following two histograms show the mean time spent in the
queue as a function of the initial priority P(O) for policies
with and without dynamic priority assignment.

One sees that the orders with low initial priority are less
discriminated against with dynamic priority assignment than with
static priority assignment. On the other hand orders with high
initial priority fare worse with dynamic priority assignment.

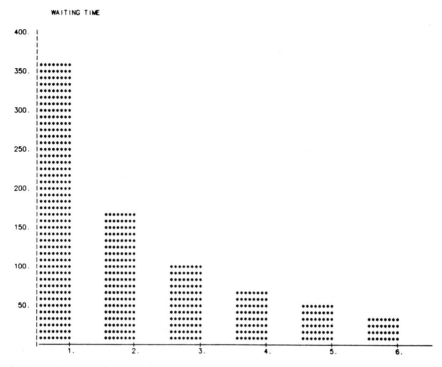

WAITING TIME

SCALE OF X — AXIS: .10E+01
SCALE OF Y — AXIS: .10E+01

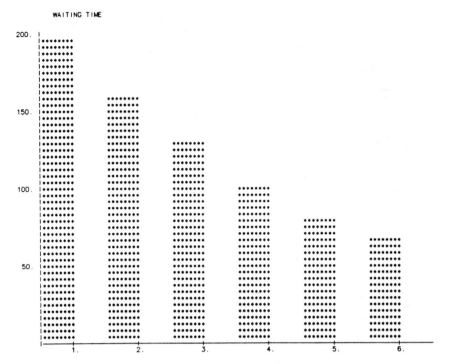

WAITING TIME

SCALE OF X - AXIS: .10E+01
SCALE OF Y - AXIS: .10E+01

3.3.6 Problems

The problems contain modifications of the order processing model.

* Problem 1

The number of possible priority classes is increased to eight.

Note:

   * The following alterations are required:

   Determination of the priority:

```
CALL UNIFRM(1.0,8.999,2,RAND2)
```

   Record the waiting time:

```
CALL TABULA(1,8,X,Y,1.,1.)
```

   Process the histogram:

```
DO 8100 I = 1,8
```

* Problem 2:

The criterion for ending the simulation run is to be modified. The simulation is to be ended when the last twenty values for orders with initial priority $P(0) = 1$ are within an interval containing values within 20% of the mean.

3.4 Group Practice Model

A multifacility consists of several simple servers which are
arranged in parallel and service a common queue. GPSS-FORTRAN
Version 3 provides subroutines which enable transactions to enter
and leave the service elements of a multifacility.

3.4.1 Description of Model

Four doctors have a group practice. The practice consists of 4
separate consulting rooms and 3 separate waiting rooms for normal
patients, urgent patients, and emergencies.

The interarrival time of the patients is exponentially
distributed with MEAN = 30. The percentage of urgent patients is
30 %. They are treated before the normal patients.

The patients in a particular waiting room are selected according
to the policy FIFO. The patients cannot choose a doctor. When a
consulting room is free, the waiting room for urgent patients is
checked first. If this is empty, the patient who has been waiting
in the waiting room for normal patients is selected. The time of
treatment is normally distributed with MEAN2 = 100. and SIGMA=5.
In addition, 3 minutes are needed for setting up at the beginning
of each treatment and an additional 3 minutes for closing down.

If several consulting rooms are free, the plan LFIRST is used to
assign a newly arrived patient. A special rule applies to
emergency patients, who comprise 1 % of the total. They are dealt
with immediately: if all consulting rooms are occupied, then the
treatment of one of the patients is interrupted. If there is a
choice, a normal patient is interrupted rather than an urgent
patient. If the treatment of a patient has been interrupted,
then it can be continued by another doctor.

The model is shown in figure 1. The following question is to be
answered by simulation.

* What is the average waiting time for normal patients, urgent
patients and emergencies?

The simulation is ended when the last 20 values of the mean
waiting time of emergency patients is in the interval (mean -
10%, mean + 10%). The number of transactions between successive
tests is NE = 5.

3.4.2 Implementation

The consulting rooms can be represented by the elements of a
multifacility. The 3 waiting rooms are represented by 3 queues.
The priorities are allocated as follows:

Normal patient   priority TX(LTX,4) = 1.
Urgent patient   priority TX(LTX,4) = 2.
Emergency patient   priority TX(LTX,4) = 3.

First the transactions are generated. Emergency cases and urgent
cases are generated with the given probabilities. The processing
time is stored in the user attribute TX(LTX,9). The normal

patients and urgent patients reach the subroutine call CALL MSEIZE. The setting up and closing down times are administered by the subroutines MSETUP and MKNOCK. The subroutine call CALL MCLEAR with label 6 frees the consulting room.

The emergency cases are treated in a separate branch of the program which starts at label 2 and performs the preemption.

The waiting times are monitored by the following bins:

Waiting time of normal patient   NBN = 1
Waiting time of urgent patient   NBN = 2
Waiting time of emergency patient   NBN = 3

3.4.3 Main Program

The plan array PLAMA must be initialised by the user in section 4 of the main program.

The plan for occupying an element LFIRST has the value 1. The statement

        PLAMA(1,1) = 1

assigns LFIRST to the multifacility MFA = 1.In the same way the statement

        PLAMA(1,2) = 1

assigns the plan for clearing an element PRIOR to the multifacility MFA = 1.

The number of elements in the multifacility must also be initialised in section 4 of the main program. This is done by the statement

        MFAC(1,2) = 4

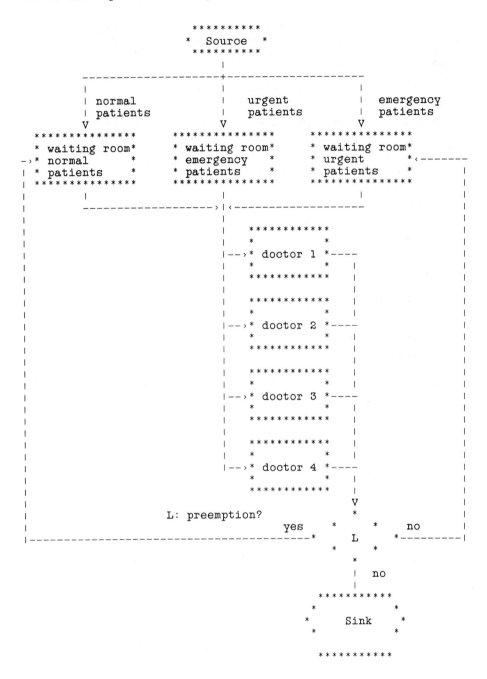

Figure 1 Structure of the group practice model

```
C
C        4. INITIALISATION OF CONSTANTS AND VARIABLES
C        ================================================
4000     CONTINUE
C
C        INITIALISE POLICY, STRATEGY, AND PLAN TABLE
C        ===============================================
         PLAMA(1,1) = 1
         PLAMA(1,2) = 1
C
C        END OF INITIALISATION OF POLICY, STRATEGY AND PLAN TABLE
C        ==========================================================
C        SET CAPACITY OF MULTIFACILITIES
C        ===============================
         MFAC(1,2) = 4
```

3.4.4 The Subroutine ACTIV

The subroutine ACTIV is as follows:

```
C        Generate transactions
C        =====================
1        CALL ERLANG(30.,1,1.,150.,1,RAND1,*9999)
         CALL GENERA(RAND1,1.,*9999)
         CALL GAUSS(100.,5.,50.,150.,2,RAND2)
         TX(LTX,9) = RAND2
C
C        Assign priorities
C        =================
         CALL TRANSF(0.01,3,*21)
         CALL TRANSF(0.2,4,*11)
C
C        Enter without preemption
C        ========================
         CALL ARRIVE(1,1)
         GOTO 2
11       TX(LTX,4) = 2.
         CALL ARRIVE(2,1)
2        CALL MSEIZE(1,2,*9000)
         GOTO 31
C
C        Enter with preemption
C        =====================
21       CALL ARRIVE(3,1)
         TX(LTX,4) = 3.
3        CALL MPREEM(1,3,*9000)
C
C        Processing time
C        ===============
31       CALL DEPART(NINT(TX(LTX,4)),1,0.,*9999)
         CALL MSETUP(1,3.,4,*9000,*9999)
4        CALL MWORK(1,TX(LTX,9),0,5,*9000,*9999)
5        CALL MKNOCK(1,3.,6,*9000,*9999)
C
C        Leave
C        =====
6        CALL MCLEAR(1,*100,*9999)
C
```

```
C       Eliminate transactions
C       =======================
        CALL SIMEND(3,5,10.)
        CALL TERMIN(*9000)
C
C       Reentry of preempted transactions in a bin
C       ==========================================
100     CALL ARRIVE(NINT(TX(LTX,4)),1)
        GOTO 9000
```

3.4.5 Results

The following are the results of the simulation of the group practice.

T = 541092.4526   RT = 541092.4526

BIN ARRAY

NBN	QTY	MAX	SUMIN	SUMOUT	ARRIVE	DEPART	TOTALWT	LAST
1	1	19	14332	14331	14449	14448	.1120E+07	.5411E+06
2	0	4	3672	3672	3672	3672	.5810E+05	.5411E+06
3	0	1	175	175	175	175	346.4	.5411E+06

BINSTA ARRAY

NBN	DURATION TIME	NUM. OF TOKEN	CONF.INT. PER CENT	DISPLACEM. PER CENT	END OF SET- TLING PHASE
1	78.14	2.071	10.55	3.682	3200.
2	15.82	.1073	6.507	2.606	.1536E+06
3	1.980	.6399E-03	14.81	.1084E-11	7000.

3.4.6 Problems

The problems deal with modifications of the group practice model.
The user of GPSS-FORTRAN Version 3 should be able to construct
the models without further assistance.

* Problem 1

The number of emergency patients is increased from 1 % to 4 %.

* Problem 2

The number of times normal patients and urgent patients are
preempted is to be calculated.

4. Pools and Storages

GPSS-FORTRAN Version 3 provides pools of resources and storages as model elements. First the station type pool is described. Storages are an extension of pools in which input and output strategies can be specified: further information about their occupation is provided.

The computer model shows the use of pools and storages:

Computer model I   The model uses pools with the appropriate subroutines.

Computer model II   The problem is extended causing the use of storages to be necessary.

4.1 Computer Model I

Computer model I shows the use of pools. It is not necessary to keep records of the occupation of individual elements. Therefore, a pool of resources can be used for the construction of the model.

4.1.1 Description of Model

A computer consists of a processor, a main memory with a capacity of 32 K and a secondary memory with a capacity of 128 K.

The interarrival time and the processing time of jobs are exponentially distributed. The memory requirements are uniformly distributed. The means, minima, and maxima are shown in table 1.

A job entering the computer first tries to obtain main memory. If the main memory is occupied it enters secondary memory.

The administration of the memory does not involve the use of a processor and does not consume any time in the model.

The processor selects the next job in main memory according to a round robin strategy. The processor is assigned to this job for one time unit.

The job returns the main memory allocated to it when it is completed. At the same time a test is made to determine whether availability of this free memory allows further jobs to be loaded from secondary memory. The selection is according to FIFO.

Table 1   Parameter for the computer model

Parameter	Average	Minimum	Maximum
Interarrival time	5.0	0.17	25.0
Processing time	4.8	0.17	24.0
Memory requirement	5 K	2 K	8 K

Simulation is to be used to answer the following two questions:

* What is the average occupation of the two memories?

* What is the mean waiting time of the jobs as a function of their memory requirement (Waiting time = time from entry of the job into the computer to the beginning of processing)? The relationship is to be plotted.

The simulation is to be ended when the last 20 values for the total time spent in the model of all jobs in the system are in the interval average - 10 %, and average + 10 %. The number of transactions generated between two tests is NE = 100.

4.1.2 Implementation

First, jobs with the required characteristics must be generated. In this example their processing time and memory requirements must be specified.

On entering the model a test is made to determine whether the job can immediately enter main memory or whether it is to be stored in secondary memory. This decision is made by the following test:

        CONTEN = POOL(1,2) - POOL(1,1)
        IF(TX(LTX,10).LE.CONTEN) GOTO 4

If the memory requirement is less than the available main memory, main memory can be occupied by a the call of the subroutine ENTER with label 4. At the same time the job joins the queue for the processor. It waits to be processed with the other jobs which currently occupy main memory.

If there is no room in main memory for the job which has just entered the system, it is placed in secondary memory. This is done by the subroutine ENTER with label 3.

* When a job enters the main memory, there are two cases to be distinguished:

a) The job entered main memory directly; it was not previously in secondary memory. In this case it can immediately join the queue for the processor.

b) The job was in secondary memory and is transferred to main memory. In this case the space which it occupied in secondary memory must be freed. At the same time a test must be made to determine whether the requirements for secondary memory of jobs which are queued for it can be satisfied. This means that the subroutine LEAVE which frees secondary memory must be called after the job has occupied main memory. Then the subroutine call CALL DBLOCK allows the memory requirements of jobs queued for secondary memory to be tested.

The processor is regarded as a server which is occupied by the subroutine SEIZE and freed by the subroutine CLEAR. The service time is the length of a time slice. If the remaining processing time of a job is less than the time slice, then the service time is equal to the remaining processing time.

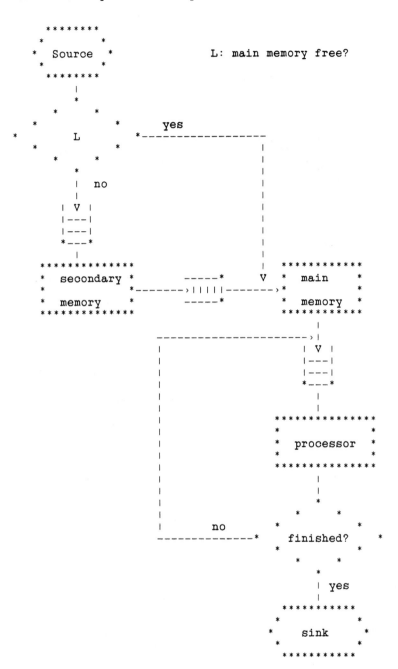

Figure 2 Structure of the Computer Model

When the job has been completed it frees its section of main memory. It also allows jobs in secondary memory, waiting for main memory, to test their memory requirement for main memory. Finally the job leaves the model by calling the subroutine TERMIN.

Note:

> * The capacity of the two pools is determined by an entry in the pool array. This is done in section 4 of the main program.

4.1.3 Settling Phase

The settling phase is avoided by starting the model in a state which is approximately the same as the state after settling.

Queueing theory shows that the computer model will reach a steady state because the mean processing time is less than the mean interarrival time.

An estimate of the average number of jobs in the system is given by:

$$MEAN = ALPHA/(1 - ALPHA)$$

where
> ALPHA = average processing time / average interarrival time

It follows for the present example that MEAN = 24.

These 24 jobs are on average half way through their processing. This is equivalent to 12 newly arrived and not yet started jobs. For this reason 12 jobs are generated at time T = 0. and distributed between the two memories.
The occupation of the two memories is recorded by registering arrivals and departures using the subroutines ARRIVE and DEPART. The number of units for each arrival and departure corresponds to the number of memory locations. The mean memory occupation can be calculated from the results obtained in this way.

The subroutines TABULA and ENDTAB are used to determine how the average waiting time of the job depends on its memory requirement. The number of times a job with a particular memory requirement obtains the processor is recorded. This is done by entering the memory requirements of the jobs in a frequency table. The mean waiting time is regarded as the dependent variable. The average waiting time as a function of the memory requirement can be determined in this way.

4.1.4 The Subroutine ACTIV

The subroutine ACTIV for the computer model I is as follows:

```
C
C       Generate the first 12 jobs
C       ==========================
1       CALL GENERA(0.,1.,*9999)
        CALL ARRIVE(1,1)
        GOTO 201
```

```
C
C      Generate the remaining jobs
C      ============================
2      CALL ERLANG(5.,1,0.17,25.,1,RAND1,*9999)
       CALL GENERA(RAND1,1.,*9999)
       CALL ARRIVE(1,1)
201    CALL ERLANG(4.8,1,0.17,24.,2,RAND2,*9999)
       TX(LTX,9) = RAND2
       CALL UNIFRM(2.,8.999,3,RAND3)
       TX(LTX,10) = AINT(RAND3)
       TX(LTX,11) = T
C
C      Test main memory
C      ================
       CONTEN = POOL(1,2) - POOL(1,1)
       IF(TX(LTX,10).LE.CONTEN) GOTO 4
C
C
C      Occupy secondary memory
C      =======================
3      CALL ENTER(2,NINT(TX(LTX,10)),0,3,*9000)
       CALL ARRIVE(2,NINT(TX(LTX,10)))
       TX(LTX,12) = 1.
C
C
C      Occupy main memory
C      ==================
4      CALL ENTER(1,NINT(TX(LTX,10)),0,4,*9000)
       CALL ARRIVE(3,NINT(TX(LTX,10)))
       IF(TX(LTX,12).LT.1.) GOTO 5
C
C      Free secondary memory
C      =====================
       CALL LEAVE(2,NINT(TX(LTX,10)),*9999)
       CALL DEPART(2,NINT(TX(LTX,10)),0.,*9999)
       CALL DBLOCK(3,2,0,0)
C
C      Ocuppy and free the processor
C      =============================
5      CALL SEIZE(1,5,*9000)
       IF(NINT(TX(LTX,13)).EQ.1) GOTO 501
       X = TX(LTX,10)
       Y = T-TX(LTX,11)
       CALL TABULA(1,8,X,Y,2.,1.)
       TX(LTX,13) = 1.
501    WT = RTZ
       IF(TX(LTX,9).LT.RTZ) WT = TX(LTX,9)
       CALL WORK(1,WT,1,6,*9000,*9999)
6      CALL CLEAR(1,*9000,*9999)
       TX(LTX,9) = TX(LTX,9) - WT
       IF(TX(LTX,9).GT.EPS) GOTO 5
C
C      Free main memory
C      ================
       CALL LEAVE(1,NINT(TX(LTX,10)),*9999)
       CALL DEPART(3,NINT(TX(LTX,10)),0.,*9999)
       CALL DBLOCK(3,1,0,0)
```

```
C
C      Eliminate transactions
C      ======================
       CALL DEPART(1,1,0.,*9999)
       CALL TERMIN(*9000)
C
C      Exit to flow control
C      ====================
9000   CALL SIMEND(1,100,10.)
       RETURN
```

4.1.5 Main Program

It is to be noted that the first activation of the sources NSC=1
and NSC=2 are scheduled in the main program at time T = 0. This
is done by the statement:

```
       CALL START(1,0.,1,*7000)
       CALL START(2,0.,2,*7000)
```

The number of transactions to be generated by the source NSC=1
must be assigned by the statement:

```
       SOURCL(1,3) = 12.
```

The capacity of the pools NPL = 1 and NPL = 2 must be assigned in
section 3 of the main program "Initialisation of constants".

```
       POOL(1,2)= 32
       POOL(2,2)= 128
```

The criterion for ending the simulation run is tested after every
deactivation.
The histograms are computed and output in section 7 of the main
program "Terminating section".

```
C      Final calculation for user variables
C      ====================================
       CALL ENDTAB(1,1,0.,0.)
       DO 8100 I=2,8
       VFUNC(1,I-1) = FLOAT(I)
       IF(TAB(I,2,1).LT.EPS) GOTO 8100
       VFUNC(2,I-1)=TAB(I,4,1)/TAB(I,2,1)
8100   CONTINUE
       CALL GRAPH(VFUNC,7,0.,120.,TEXT)
```

The size of the arrays VFUNC and TEXT must be specified. The text
for the table headings is placed in TEXT.

```
       DIMENSION VFUNC(2,7)
       CHARACTER * 4 TEXT
       DIMENSION TEXT(8)
       TEXT(1) = 'WAIT'
       TEXT(2) = 'ING '
       TEXT(3) = 'TIME'
```

The size of the time slice used by the processor is assigned in
the main program by the statement RZT=1. RZT is available to the
subroutine ACTIV in COMMON/PRIV.

Furthermore, the contents of the array VFUNC must be initialized to zero:

```
      DO 90 I = 1,2
      DO 80 J = 1,7
        VFUNC(I,J) = 0.
80    CONTINUE
90    CONTINUE
```

4.1.6 The Results

The simulation run produces the following results for the model Computer I:

The mean number of occupied locations in main memory and secondary memory are contained in the bins NBN = 3 and NBN = 2.

The waiting time of a job as a function of the memory requirement is shown in the diagram below.

T = 25269.2086   RT = 25269.2086

BIN ARRAY
=========

NBN	QTY	MAX	SUMIN	SUMOUT	ARRIVE	DEPART	TOTALWT	LAST
1	27	61	5127	5100	5127	5100	.3976E+06	.2527E+05
2	128	128	19609	19481	3757	3738	.1367E+07	.2527E+05
3	29	32	25565	25536	5105	5100	.6873E+06	.2527E+05

BINSTA ARRAY
============

NBN	DURATION TIME	NUM. OF TOKEN	CONF.INT. PER CENT	DISPLACEM. PER CENT	END OF SET-TLING PHASE
1	77.75	15.71	31.68	1.776	1280.
2	69.94	53.94	41.38	-7.325	2048.
3	26.90	27.19	6.165	-.1412	320.0

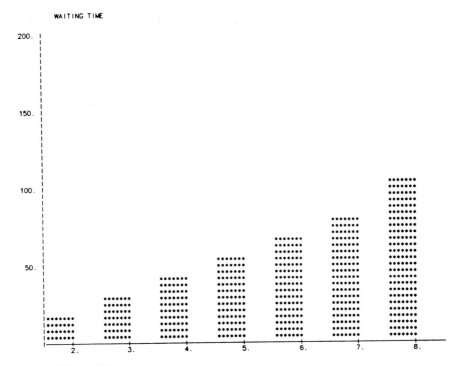

SCALE OF X — AXIS: .10E+01
SCALE OF Y — AXIS: .10E+01

T =   25269.2086   RT =   25269.2086

BIN ARRAY
==========

NBN	QTY	MAX	SUMIN	SUMOUT	ARRIVE	DEPART	TOTALWT	LAST
1	27	61	5127	5100	5127	5100	.3976E+06	.2527E+05
2	128	128	19609	19481	3757	3738	.1367E+07	.2527E+05
3	29	32	25565	25536	5105	5100	.6873E+06	.2527E+05

BINSTA ARRAY
=============

NBN	DURATION TIME	NUM. OF TOKEN	CONF.INT. PER CENT	DISPLACEM. PER CENT	END OF SET-TLING PHASE
1	77.75	15.71	31.68	1.776	1280.
2	69.94	53.94	41.38	-7.325	2048.
3	26.90	27.19	6.165	-.1412	320.0

4.1.7 Problems

The problems deal with modifications of the model Computer I.

* Problem 1

The memory assigned to a job is freed when the processing of the job is finished. Jobs which are waiting in peripheral memory then test whether their memory requirements can now be satisfied. The order in which the jobs perform this test is FIFO.

The effect of a policy in which priority is given to jobs with the greatest memory requirements on the memory usage and the waiting times of the jobs is to be investigated.

Hint:

The priority of the jobs is set equal to the memory requirement in the section "Generate the remaining jobs":

$$TX(LTX,4) = TX(LTX,10)$$

Further alterations are not required.

* Problem 2

The effect of a policy in which jobs with the smallest memory requirements have the highest priority on the memory utilisation as well as the waiting times of the jobs is to be investigated.

* Problem 3

The simulation run is to be repeated without the model initially containing 12 jobs. The effect on the end of the settling phase is to be investigated.

The end of the settling phase is found in the matrix BINSTA, which can be printed using the subroutine REPRT4.

4.2 Computer Model II

Computer model II differs from the computer model I in that the
occupancy of the memory is directly represented in the model.
This makes it possible to take into account gaps in the allocated
memory or to investigate the effect of different strategies.

4.2.1 Alterations to Computer Model I

The occupation of the two memories in computer model II uses the
first fit strategy. Otherwise the model is the same as computer
model I. The subroutine calls of ENTER and LEAVE in the
subroutine ACTIV are replaced by calls of ALLOC and FREE. For
example the section "Allocation of main memory" changes to:

```
4        CALL ALLOC(1,NINT(TX(LTX,10)),1,0,LINE,4,*9000)
         TX(LTX,14) = FLOAT(LINE)
         CALL ARRIVE((3,NINT(TX(LTX,10)))
         IF(TX(LTX,12).LT.1.) GOTO 5
```

The parameter LINE returns the starting address of the block of
memory assigned. It is used subsequently to free the block.

The parameter MARK can be used to characterise the memory
locations occupied. This is not used in the computer model II.
MARK is set equal to 1 for all transactions.

The section "Freeing main memory" is as follows:

```
         CALL FREE (1,NINT(TX(LTX,10)),
        +NINT(TX(LTX,14)),LINE,*9999)
         CALL DEPART(3,NINT(TX(LTX,10)),0.,*9999)
         CALL DBLOCK(4,1,0,0)
```

The parameter KEY contains the starting address of the area of
memory to be freed. This was placed in the private parameter
TX(LTX,14) when the block was occupied.

The parameter LINE returns the start address of the remaining
area if part of the block is freed. It is not used in computer
model II. Since the occupied area is returned as a whole, LINE is
set equal to 0 for every transaction in the model Computer II.

Secondary memory is treated similarly to main memory.

The section "Test main memory" must also be modified for computer
model II. It is no longer sufficient to examine whether there is
sufficient free memory for the job. It is now necessary to find a
sufficiently large unoccupied block in memory. The subroutine
STRATA is used to determine whether such a block is available.
It identifies a sufficiently large block and returns its starting
address in the parameter LSM. LSM returns the value 0 if there is
no such block available. In this case the main memory cannot be
occupied.

Note:

   * The variable LSM belongs to the block COMMON/STO/. It does
not belong to the parameter list of the subroutine STRATA.

The section "Test main memory" is now as follows:

```
        CALL STRATA(1,NINT(TX(LTX,10)))
        IF(LSM.NE.0) GOTO 4
```

In addition, the strategy to be used to occupy the two memories must be provided in section 4 "INITIALISATION". There are no default values for the strategies. Therefore the matrix STRAMA must be assigned values. It can be seen from the subroutine STRATA that for first fit:

```
C
C       INITIALISE POLICY, STRATEGY, AND PLAN ARRAY
C       ===========================================
        STRAMA(1,1) = 1
        STRAMA(2,1) = 1
```

It is to be noted that the model computer II uses storages of station type NT = 4. It follows that the station type NT must be set equal to 4 in both calls of the subroutine DBLOCK. In addition, the capacity of the storages must be assigned in the main program by the following statements:

```
        SBM(1,2) = 32
        SBM(2,2) = 128
```


4.2.2 Results

The results of the simulation of the computer model II are shown below.

The average number of memory locations occupied is given in the bins NBN = 3 and NBN = 2.

The bar chart below shows the relation between waiting time and memory requirement.

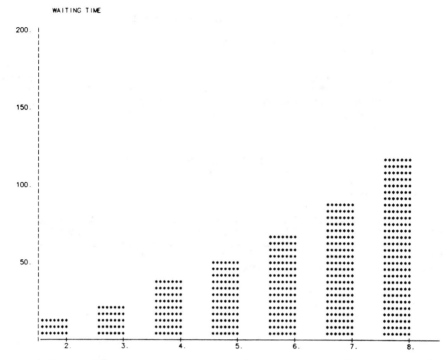

T = 25274.4913   RT = 25274.4913

BIN ARRAY
=========

NBN	QTY	MAX	SUMIN	SUMOUT	ARRIVE	DEPART	TOTALWT	LAST
1	28	63	5128	5100	5128	5100	.3953E+06	.2527E+05
2	120	128	19309	19189	3548	3529	.1404E+07	.2527E+05
3	32	32	25572	25540	5106	5100	.6497E+06	.2527E+05

BINSTA ARRAY
============

NBN	DURATION TIME	NUM. OF TOKEN	CONF.INT. PER CENT	DISPLACEM. PER CENT	END OF SET- TLING PHASE
1	77.29	15.61	30.89	.6771	960.0
2	72.94	55.43	29.66	3.389	3040.
3	25.42	25.69	6.180	-.1961E-01	160.0

4.2.3 Problems

The problems show the structure of the storages.

* Problem 1

The strategy best fit is to be used instead of the strategy first fit.

Note:

   * The initialisation of the strategy matrix STRAMA in the main program is to be changed.

* Problem 2

The distribution of the length of the unused gaps is to be recorded and plotted.

Note:

   * An event NE = 1 is included which examines the segment matrix SM for the storages NST = 1 and NST = 2 and identifies the free areas every ten time units. The length of the free areas is entered into a histogram and output at the end of the simulation run.

The subroutine EVENT is as follows:

```
1         CONTINUE
C
C         Identification of free gaps in main memory
C         ==============================================
          NST = 1
          I = SBM(NST,1)
          IE = I+SBM(NST,2)-1
10        IF(SM(I,2).NE.-1) GOTO 20
          XSM = FLOAT(SM(I,1))
          CALL TABULA(3,100,XSM,0.,0.,1.)
20        I = I + SM(I,1)
          IF(I.LE.IE)  GOTO 10
C
C         Identification of free gaps in peripheral memory
C         ====================================================
          NST = 2
          I = SBM(NST,1)
          IE = I+SBM(NST,2)-1
30        IF(SM(I,2).NE.-1) GOTO 40
          XSM = FLOAT(SM(I,1))
          CALL TABULA(4,100,XSM,0.,0.,1.)
40        I = I+SM(I,1)
          IF(I.LE.IE) GOTO 30
C
C         Schedule the next event
C         =========================
          CALL ANNOUN(1,T+10.,*9999)
```

The first call of the event must be scheduled in the main program. This must be done at time T = 1., since the first twelve jobs already occupy both memories at this time.

The two frequency tables NTAB = 3 and NTAB = 4 must be processed
by two calls of the subroutine NTAB.

Notes:

* To understand the event NE = 1, the reader should look at the
description of the subroutine FFIT. In addition, the structure
of the   segment matrix SM and the storage basis matrix SBM
should be understood.

* An understanding of the storages is essential for problem 2.

5. The Coordination of Transactions

GPSS-FORTRAN Version 3 provides subroutines for the most frequently occuring situations involving the coordination of transactions. The following examples show how these subroutines can be used:

Model: transport of parcels Coordination of transactions in a single branch

Model: scenic mountain Coordination of transactions in parallel branches

Model: car telephones Coordination of simultanious transactions

5.1 Model of Parcel Transport

This model shows the coordination of transactions in a single branch.

5.1.1 Description of Model

Parcels must be loaded on to a wagon. The interarrival time of the parcels is exponentially distributed with mean 10.0 units of time. The capacity of the wagon is 12 parcels; it leaves when it is full.

The length of time required to load the wagon is to be investigated. The mean and the distribution of the loading time are to be determined. The simulation run should include 2000 loadings of the wagon.

5.1.2 Implementation

First transactions are generated in the usual way. The upper limit of the transactions TXMAX is set equal to 2.4E04. This represents 2000 wagons. The subroutine GATHR1 collects the transactions and then allows them to proceed. The user clock RT is used to determine the time to load the wagon. RT must be reset to 0. when the wagon leaves.

The packets proceed when twelve have been collected. The blocked transactions can then be eliminated. The first transaction to enter the wagon has an additional function. It causes the time spent waiting in the wagon to be registered and resets the user clock RT to 0.

Note:

 * The user may not alter the simulation clock T because this could lead to errors in the flow control. The user should use the user clock RT to measure the passage of time. It can be modified without restriction. The user clock runs synchronous-

ly with the simulation clock T.

The subroutine ACTIV is as follows:

```
C
C       Address calculation
C       ===================
        GOTO(1,2),NADDR
C
C
C       Generation of transactions
C       ==========================
1       CALL ERLANG(10.0,1,0.32,50.,1,RANDOM,*9999)
        CALL GENERA(RANDOM,1.,*9999)
C
C       Addition to and dissolution of the queue
C       ========================================
2       CALL GATHR1(1,12,2,*9000)
        IF(RT.LT.EPS) GOTO 20
        CALL TABULA(1,24,RT,0.,48.,8.)
        RT=0.
C
C       Ellimination of the transactions
C       ================================
20      CALL TERMIN(*9000)
```

The frequency table must be processed in the main program using
the subroutine ENDTAB.

5.1.3. The Results

The model of parcel transport has the following results:

The histogram of the frequency distribution of the lapse of time
between departures is seen to have the shape of an Erlang
distribution with K = 12 and mean 120.0.

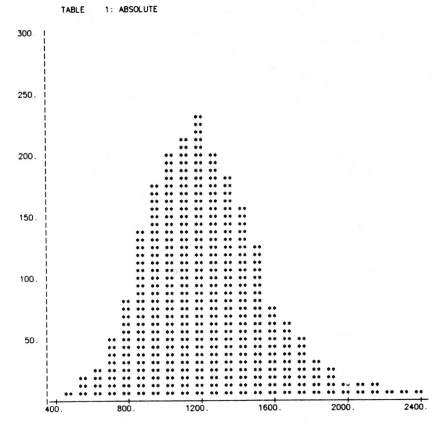

TABLE   1: ABSOLUTE

SCALE OF X — AXIS: .10E+00
SCALE OF Y — AXIS: .10E+01

5.1.4. Problems

As has been pointed out before, the gate is the most general type
of station. All other types of stations, e.g. facilities,
storages, gather stations, are special cases which contain a
specific condition. Any type of station can be represented using
gates. In this case, the user must himself define the required
state variables, formulate the condition, and arrange for the
testing of the condition.

* Problem 1

The model of parcel transport is to be programmed using gates. A
trace is to be generated for the first 500 time units.

Note:

    * The relevant state variable is the number of packets which
    are already in the wagon. IPAKET is incremented whenever a
    parcel arrives. This is done by transferring control to the
    statement with label 21 after the transaction is blocked.
    Control is returned to the flow control after this has been
    done in the usual way. The condition which allows an activity
    is defined in the logical function CHECK:

        CHECK = IPAKET.EQ.12

The condition is tested in the subroutine TEST whenever a
transaction is blocked. This is caused by setting the test
indicator TTEST. The testing of the condition in the subroutine
TEST is as follows:

        IF(CHECK(1)) CALL DBLOCK(5,1,0,0)

The subroutine ACTIV is as follows:

```
C
C       Generation of transactions
C       ================================
1       CALL ERLANG(10.0,1,0.32,50.,1,RANDOM,*9999)
        CALL GENERA(RANDOM,1.,*9999)
C
C       Addition to and dissolution of the queue
C       =========================================
2       CALL GATE(1,1,1,1,2,*21)
        IF(RT.LT.EPS) GOTO 20
        CALL TABULA(1,24,RT,0.,48.,8.)
        RT=0.
C
C       Elimination of the transactions
C       ================================
20      CALL TERMIN(*9000)
C
C       Return to the flow control
C       ==========================
21      IPAKET = IPAKET + 1
        TTEST = T
9000    RETURN
```

The variable IPAKET must be initialised and included in the block COMMON/PRIV/.

IPRINT is set equal to one to cause a trace. At time T = 500., the scheduled event NE = 1 sets IPRINT to zero.

* Problem 2

The capacity of the wagon varies. It is uniformly distributed between MIN=5. and MAX=15.

Note:

  * The parameter ICAP of the subroutine GATHER1 is a uniformly distributed random variable.

The variable ICAP is recalculated after each departure of the wagon. ICAP is initialised to ten in the main program. This specifies the capacity of the first wagon. The statement with label 2 must be altered. In addition, the capacity of the next wagon must be determined after every departure. The section "Addition to and dissolution of the queue" is now as follows:

```
C
C       Addition to and dissolution of the queue
C       =========================================
2       CALL GATHR(1,ICAP,2,*9000)
        IF(RT.LT.EPS) GOTO 20
        CALL TABULA(1,24,RT,0.,48.,8.)
        RT = 0.
        CALL UNIFRM(5.,15.999,1,RANDOM)
        ICAP = AINT(RANDOM)
```

5.2 Model of a Scenic Mountain

The model of a scenic mountain shows the coordination of tokens
in two parallel processing branches.   Initially the user chains
and trigger stations are used.

Problem 2 shows how the model of a scenic mountain can be
constructed using gates as a general station type.

5.2.1. Description of the Model

The visitor of a scenic mountain must use a bus. The interarrival
time of the visitors is exponentially distributed with mean
MEAN1 = 6.

The bus can hold 8 people.   It does not leave unless it contains
at least 3 people.   The travel time including getting in and out
of the bus is 15 minutes.   The time spent by the visitors at the
top of the mountain is normally distributed with MEAN2 = 40. and
SIGMA = 10.   The following two questions are to be answered using
simulation:

* What is the mean time visitors have to wait for the bus in
order to go up or go down?

* What is the frequency distribution of the number of people in
the bus?

The simulation is to be ended when the last twenty values of the
mean time waiting to go up are all in the interval MEAN +/- 10%.
The number of transactions between sucessive tests is 100.

5.2.2. Implementation

The bus is represented by a transaction which is generated at
the beginning of the simulation run and continues to move in the
model.

The entry of visitors into the bus is initiated by calling the
subroutine UNLIN1. Separate user chains are required for visitors
waiting to go up and for visitors waiting to go down.

Visitors join the queues at the trigger stations and wait until
they can enter the bus.

The number of visitors taking part in each upward or downward
journey is counted in the variable ICOUNT and included in the
histogram by calling the subroutine TABULA.

The model of the scenic mountain is as follows:

```
C
C       Generate the bus
C       ================
1       CALL GENERA(0.,0.,*9999)
        CALL START(1,-1.,1,*9999)
```

```
C
C        Journey upwards
C        ===============
2        CALL UNLIN1(1,3,8,2,*9000)
         CALL ADVANC(15.,3,*9000)
C
C        Journey downwards
C        =================
3        CALL UNLIN1(2,3,8,3,*9000)
         CALL ADVANC(15.,2,*9000)
C
C        Generation of the visitors
C        ==========================
4        CALL ERLANG(6.,1,0.21,30.,1,RAND1,*9999)
         CALL GENERA(RAND1,1.,*9999)
C
C        Waiting for the bus at the bottom of the mountain
C        =================================================
         CALL ARRIVE(1,1)
5        CALL LINK1(1,5,*9000)
C
C        Upward journey of the visitors
C        ==============================
         CALL DEPART(1,1,0.,*9999)
         ICOUNT=ICOUNT+1
         CALL ADVANC(15.,6,*9000)
C
C        Leaving the bus at the top of the mountain
C        ==========================================
6        IF(ICOUNT.EQ.0) GOTO 65
         COUNT=FLOAT(ICOUNT)
         CALL TABULA(1,6,COUNT,0.,3.,1.)
         ICOUNT=0
C
C        Time spent at the top of the mountain
C        =====================================
65       CALL GAUSS(40.,10.,0.,80.,2,RAND2)
         CALL ADVANC(RAND2,7,*9000)
C
C        Waiting for the bus at the top of the mountain
C        ==============================================
7        CALL ARRIVE(2,1)
8        CALL LINK1(2,8,*9000)
C
C        Downward journey of the visitors
C        ================================
         CALL DEPART(2,1,0.,*9999)
         ICOUNT=ICOUNT+1
         CALL ADVANC(15.,9,*9000)
C
C        Leaving the bus at the bottom of the mountain
C        =============================================
9        IF(ICOUNT.EQ.0) GOTO 95
         COUNT=FLOAT(ICOUNT)
         CALL TABULA(1,6,COUNT,0.,3.,1.)
         ICOUNT=0
C
C        Eliminating the transaction
C        ===========================
95       CALL SIMEND(1,100,10.)
         CALL TERMIN(*9000)
```

Notes:

* Both sources must be started in the main program. This is done by the following two statements:

        CALL START(1,0.,1,*7000)
        CALL START(2,0.,4,*7000)

* The histogram must be computed and printed by calling ENDTAB in section 7 "Terminating section" in the main program.

The model of the scenic mountain has the following results:

The mean time waiting for the bus going up is found in the values of the BINSTA matrix for NBN = 1 and for the bus going down in NBN = 2.

The next page shows the histogram of the number of people in the bus.

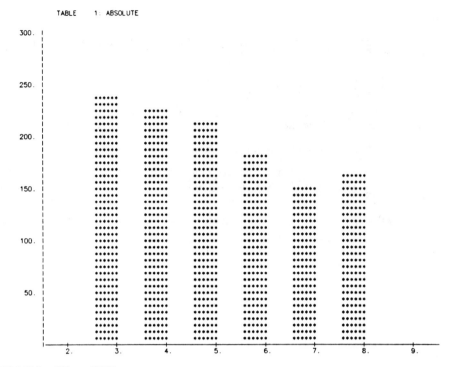

TABLE   1: ABSOLUTE

SCALE OF X – AXIS: .10E+01
SCALE OF Y – AXIS: .10E+01

5.2.3. Problems

The problems demonstrate further ways to coordinate transactions
in parallel branches.

* Problem 1
20% of the visitors decide to leave the mountain by walking down.
The new problem shows a situation in which a complete blockage of
the system can occur. Suppose the bus arrives at the top of the
mountain with three people in it. If one visitor decides to leave
by walking down, there are only two visitors left to travel down
in the bus. Since the bus will not leave without three people,
it will always remain at the top of the mountain.

A counter, IVISIT, must be included which counts the number of
visitors at the top of the mountain who intend to use the bus. If
there are not sufficient visitors the parameter MIN in the
subroutine UNLIN1 is reduced to the number of visitors who are
actually waiting to go down in the bus.

If the bus is at the top of the mountain, and all the visitors
at the top of the tower intend to leave on foot, one of them must
use the bus to take it down.

Note:

    * The decision to leave by bus or on foot is taken in the
    section "Leave the bus at the top of the mountain".

```
C
C       Leave the bus at the top of the mountain
C       ========================================
6       CALL TRANSF(0.2,2,*61)
        TX(LTX,9) = 1.
        IVISIT = IVISIT + 1
61      IF(ICOUNT.EQ.0) GOTO 65
        COUNT = FLOAT(ICOUNT)
        CALL TABULA(1,6,COUNT,0.,3.,1.)
        ICOUNT = 0
```

The visitors who leave on foot are selected after the section
"Time spent at the top of the mountain". Then the section
"Waiting for bus at the top of the mountain" is as follows:

```
C
C       Waiting for the bus at the top of the mountain
C       ==============================================
7       IF(TX(LTX,9).GT.EPS.OR.IVISIT.GT.0) GOTO 71
        TX(LTX,9) = 1.
        IVISIT = IVISIT + 1
71      IF(TX(LTX,9).LT.EPS) GOTO 95
        IF(IVISIT.LT.3) MIN = IVISIT
        CALL ARRIVE (2,1)
8       CALL LINK1(2,8,*9000)
        IVISIT = IVISIT - 1
```

The number of visitors wanting to go down in the bus is placed
in MIN if this is less than three. The section "Downward journey
of the visitors" is as follows:

```
C
C        Downward journey of the visitors
C        ==================================
3        CALL UNLIN1(2,MIN,8,3,*9000)
         MIN = 3
         CALL ADVANC(15.,2,*9000)
```

* Problem 2
The model of the scenic mountain is to be constructed using gates.

Note:

   * The state variable BUS is to be used with the following meaning:

```
BUS = 0   The bus is at the bottom of the mountain
    = 1   The bus is in motion
    = 2   The bus is at the top of the mountain
```

The variable BUS is altered by the last transaction which enters or leaves the bus. It is not necessary to represent the bus by a transaction.

The user must define the conditions and arrange for their testing.

Example:

The section "Waiting for the bus at the top of the tower" is now as follows:

```
C
C        Waiting for the bus at the top of the mountain
C        ==================================================
         CALL ARRIVE(1,1)
5        CALL GATE(1,1,1,1,5,*9000)
```

The condition NCOND = 1 in the logical function CHECK is as follows:

```
         CHECK = IBUS.EQ.0.AND.BIN(1.1).GE.3.
```

In this case, up to eight transactions can leave the gate and begin the upward journey. The last transaction to leave the gate set IBUS = 1.

5.3 The Coordination of Simultaneous Activities

GPSS-FORTRAN Version 3 is specially concerned with simultaneous
activities. The sequence in which simultaneous activities occur
is as follows:

1) Processing of events
2) Starting sources
3) Activating transactions
4) Collecting of information for bins
5) Collecting of information for plots
6) Integration of sets

Example:

* When the processing of an event and the generation of a
transaction are scheduled for the same time, the event is
processed first.

The   order   in which transactions are activated   when   the
activations are scheduled for the same time is determined by the
type number:

1) Facilities
2) Multifacilities
3) Pools
4) Storages
5) Gates
6) Gather stations
7) Gather stations for families
8) User chains for transactions
9) Trigger stations for transactions
10) User chains for families
11) Trigger stations for families
12) Match stations

The index of the station determines the order of activation
within a particular station type.

Example:

* If the activation of a transaction which is to enter a facility
is to occur at the same time as a transaction which is to enter a
storage, then the transaction at the facility will be activated
first.

If there are transactions queued for various facilities which can
be activated, then the transaction queued at the facility with
the smallest station index is activated first.

If this is not adequate for dealing with transactions which can
be activated at the same time, then a MATCH station should be
used. A match station collects all transactions which are active
at the same time T and allows them to proceed in a predetermined
order.

5.3.1. Model of Car Telephones

The model is assumed to contain ten cars. Telephones in the cars
send signals to a receiver. Signals which are received within a
single time interval are regarded as simultaneous. Only the
signal with the highest intensity in a group of simultaneous
signals is processed. All other signals are disregarded.

The times between the transmission of successive signals by a
particular car are exponentially distributed with mean 42. The
intensity of the signals is normally distibuted with:

mean = 120.0
sigma = 20.0
min = 10.0
max = 1000.0

The simulation should determine what percentage of the signals
cannot be processed, because they occur simultaneously with other
signals, as a function of the size of the time interval.

The size of the time interval is varied from 5.0 to 10.0 in steps
of 1.0.   10000 signals are to be used in the simulation run for
each interval of time.

5.3.2. Structure of the Car Telephone Model

The fact that all signals within an interval of time are to be
regarded as simultaneous is represented in the model by arranging
that all signals to occur within a single time interval are
generated by the sources at the same time. The transactions which
represent the signals then proceed to a match station. The first
transaction to leave the match station is further processed. The
remaining transactions are registered and eliminated.   The
intensity of a received signal is its priority. The transaction
with the highest priority has thus the highest intensity and so
leaves the match station first. This means that the queue which
contains all transactions to be simultaneously activated is to be
processed using the policy PFIFO.

The subroutine ACTIV is as follows:

```
C
C       Generating the signals
C       ======================
1       CALL ERLANG(42.,1,1.3,210.,1,RAND1,*9999)
        RAND2 = FLOAT(IFIX(RAND1/SLOTX))* SLOTX
        IF (RAND2.LE.0.01) GOTO 1
        CALL GAUSS(120.,20.,10.,1000.,2,RAND3)
        CALL GENERA(RAND2,RAND3,*9999)
C
C       Register simultanious signals
C       =============================
2       CALL MATCH(1,2,*9000)
        IF(TMATCH.NE.T) GOTO 20
        ICOUNT = ICOUNT + 1
        CALL TERMIN(*9000)
C
C       Identification of the signal with the highest intensity
C       =======================================================
20      TMATCH = T
```

        CALL TERMIN(*9000)
The variable SLOTX contains the width of the time interval. The
variable ICOUNT contains the number of signals which could not be
processed. This is converted to a percentage in the section
"Terminating section" and placed in the array RESULT. When the
results are available for all interval widths the values of the
array RESULT are output by the subroutine GRAPH.

Notes:

   * The simulation run must be repeated for each value of the
   width of the time interval. This is done in a DO loop which is
   executed six times and increments the values of SLOTX from 5.0
   to 10.0 in steps of 1.0.

   * It is to be noted that the subroutines RESET and PRESET are
   called again within the DO loop. See Volume 2, chapter 3.1
   "Model of a Squirrel".

   * Each car is represented by a seperate source. It follows that
   each individual source must be started in the main program:

        DO 7200 J=1,10
        CALL START(J,0.,1,*7000)
   7200   CONTINUE

   * The subroutine GENERA generates transactions for each source.
   It is not necessary that each source in the subroutine ACTIV
   has an individual call of GENERA. The subroutine call of GENERA
   has the label 1 for all sources.

   * The results of a simulation run for a particular width of
   the time interval are placed in the array RESULT. Section
   seven "Terminating section" of the main program is as follows:

```
C
C       Final calculation of private quantities
C       =========================================
        RESULT(1,I) = SLOTX
        RESULT(2,I) = FLOAT(ICOUNT)*100. / TXMAX
        SLOTX = SLOTX + 1.
7500    CONTINUE
```

The results are output as a graph after the six simulation runs
have taken place:

        CALL GRAPH(RESULT,6,0.,0.,TEXT)

5.3.3. Results

The following bar chart shows the dependance of the number of signals not processed on the width of the time interval.

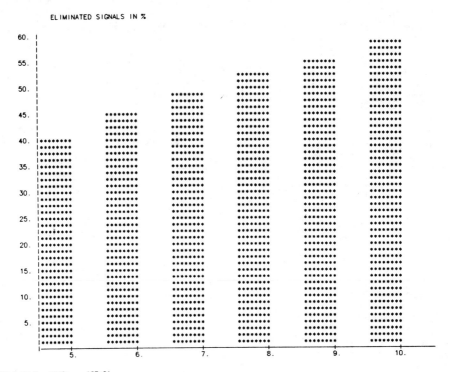

ELIMINATED SIGNALS IN %

SCALE OF X − AXIS: .10E+01
SCALE OF Y − AXIS: .10E+01

5.3.4. Problems

The problems show further possibilities for using match stations.

* Problem 1
The number of cars is to be reduced by eight. Otherwise, the problem remains unchanged.

* Problem 2
The signals which are not processed because their intensity is too low are transmitted again in the following time interval. If they cannot be processed in the second attempt they are eliminated as before.

Note:

   * The transactions are not eliminated in the section "Register simultaneous signals". Instead they are delayed by a time SLOTX using the subroutine ADVANC and then returned to the match station. The transactions which were not processed and the newly generated transactions both arrive at the beginning of the time interval at the match station.

Transactions which failed to be processed once are marked accordingly. This mark leads to their elimination if they fail to be processed a second time.

6. Tanker Fleet Model

There are certain standard examples from the area of combined simulation which appear repeatedly in the literature. The tanker fleet model is one of these. It appeared first in "The GASP IV Simulation Language" /1/.

The tanker model is sufficiently simple to be easily understood. It is however sufficiently complex to demonstrate and test the capability of a simulator.

In its structure, the tanker fleet model resembles the brewery model III. It consists of a queued system with a continuous part.

Notes:

* The transaction oriented part is implemented in GASP IV using events, since GASP IV does not directly support queued systems. This results in a slight increase in the effort required in comparison to GPSS-FORTRAN Version 3. Otherwise the implementations are very similar.

* The use of sets in GPSS-FORTRAN Version 3 makes it significantly more advanced than GASP IV in the area of continuous models. The set concept is explained using the example of the host parasite model V in chapter 7.

6.1 Description of the Tanker Fleet Model

A fleet of fifteen tankers transports oil from Valdez, Alaska to Seattle, Washington. The capacity of a tanker is 150 tb (thousand barrels). It is assumed that any number of tankers can be loaded simultaneously in Valdez. In Seattle there is only one dock and the tankers must be unloaded successively.

The oil from the tanker is pumped into a storage tank with a capacity of 2000 tb at a constant rate of RIN = 300 tb per day. A tanker is regarded as unloaded and can leave Seattle when it contains less than 7.5 tb oil.

The storage tank is connected to a refinery, which removes oil at a constant rate of ROUT = 150 tb per day.

The dock in Seattle is open from 6:00 till 24:00. Tankers are not unloaded when the dock is closed. The unloading is interrupted and continues on the next day.

The unloading is also interrupted when the tank has reached its capacity of 2000 tb. The unloading of the tanker in the dock is continued when the level of the tank has fallen to 1600 tb.

The removal of oil from the tank by the refinery must stop when the tank is empty. It can start again when the contents of the tank reaches 50 tb.

The times of the voyage are as follows:

Voyage from Valdez to Seattle loaded:
Normal distribution
MEAN = 5.0 days
SIGMA = 1.5

Voyage from Seattle to Valdez unloaded:
Normal distribution
MEAN = 4.0 days
SIGMA = 1.0

Loading time in Valdez:
Uniform distribution
min A = 2.9 days
max B = 3.1 days

Initial conditions are as follows:

* The contents of the tank at time T = 0. is 1000 tb.

* The first tanker arrives at Valdez at time T = 0. The other tankers follow it at intervals of half a day.

The following are to be determined by simulation:

* The mean length of the queue at the dock in Seattle.

* The mean time waiting to enter the dock at Seattle.

* The mean level of the tank.

* The level of the tank as a function of the time over 365 days.

The unloading of a ship from T = 9.25 to T = 10.307 is to be presented graphically.

The behaviour of the model is to be observed for 365 days.

6.2 The Structure of the Model

The state variables, the definition of the conditions and events and the description of the tanker and its respective behaviour must be specified for the model construction.

6.2.1 State Variables

The model of the tanker fleet consists of a queued system with an event oriented part and a continuous part which are connected via conditions.

The following state variables are needed to describe the system:

SV(1,1)   Level of the tank

SV(1,2)   Contents of the tanker in the dock

DV(1,1)   Rate of change of the level of the tank

DV(1,2)   Rate of change of the contents of the tanker

RIN   Rate of unloading the tanker
           This is the rate at which oil is pumped from the ship
           to the tank.
           RIN = 300.0 tb when unloading takes place
           RIN = 0. tb when unloading does not take place

ROUT   Rate of discharge of the tank
           This is the rate at which oil is pumped from the tank
           to the refinery.
           ROUT = 150.0 tb when discharging
           ROUT = 0.0 tb when not discharging

It follows:

DV(1,1) = RIN - ROUT
DV(1,2) = -RIN

In addition, the following variables are required to describe the model:

IOPEN   State of the dock

           IOPEN = 0 The dock is closed from 24:00 to 6:00.
           IOPEN = 1 The dock is open from 6:00 to 24:00.

ISHIP   Occupation of the dock

           ISHIP = 0 There is no ship in the dock.
           ISHIP = 1 There is a ship in the dock.

IFULL   No unloading

> There is an unusual case which must be taken into
> account. A tanker becomes empty when the tank reaches
> its capacity of 2000 tb. In this case a new tanker
> cannot start unloading but must wait in the dock until
> the level of the tank has gone down to 1600 tb.
>
> IFULL = 0 Unloading possible
> IFULL = 1 Unloading not possible

6.2.2. The Events

The events which occur in the model of the tanker fleet are
collected in the subroutine EVENT.

Event 1   Interrupt unloading because tank is full.

Event 2   Tank level becomes less than 1600 tb.
            Normally the unloading of the tanker can now start.
            There is a special case where unloading is interrupted
            because the tank was full and at the same time the ship
            became empty and could leave the dock. This case is
            characterised by IFULL = 1.

Event 3   Connect refinery
            The refinery begins to pump from the tank when the
            level of the tank has risen to 50 tb.

Event 4   Disconnect refinery
            The refinery ceases to pump from the tank because the
            tank is empty.

Event 5   Conclude unloading
            The unloading is concluded because the tanker is empty.
            The tanker which is waiting before the gate in
            subroutine ACTIV must be unblocked.

Event 6   Start unloading
            Unloading starts when there is a ship in the dock, the
            harbour is open, and IFULL = 0.

Event 7   Interrupt unloading the tanker because the harbour
            closes at 24.00

Event 8   Tanker enters dock
            The amount of oil which must be unloaded is stored in
            the state variable SV(1,2), the contents of the tanker.

Event 9   Open the harbour at 6:00 (IOPEN = 1)

Event 10   Close the harbour at 24:00 (IOPEN = 0)

Event 11   Set initial conditions

Events NE = 1 to 8 are conditional events which occur when the
corresponding conditions become true. These conditions are all
placed in the logical function CHECK. The conditions are indexed
according to the indices of the events.

Events 9 to 11 are scheduled events. All three events are initially scheduled in section 5 of the main program "Set initial conditions". The events NE = 9 and NE = 10 always schedule themselves for the following day.

```
C       Label selector
C       ==============
100     CONTINUE
        GOTO(1,2,3,4,5,6,7,8,9,10,11), NE
C
C       Process events
C       ==============
C
C       Interrupt the unloading because the tank is full
C       ===============================================
1       RIN = 0.
        IFULL = 1
        CALL BEGIN(1,*9999)
        CALL MONITR(1)
        CALL MONITR(2)
        RETURN
C
C       Tank level becomes less than 1600 tb
C       ====================================
2       IFULL = 0
        TTEST = T
        CALL BEGIN(1,*9999)
        CALL MONITR(1)
        CALL MONITR(2)
        RETURN
C
C       Connect refinery
C       ================
3       ROUT = 150.
        CALL BEGIN(1,*9999)
        CALL MONITR(1)
        CALL MONITR(2)
        RETURN
C
C       Disconnect refinery
C       ===================
4       ROUT = 0.
        CALL BEGIN(1,*9999)
        CALL MONITR(1)
        CALL MONITR(2)
        RETURN
C
C       Conclude unloading
C       ==================
5       CALL MONITR(1)
        CALL MONITR(2)
        ISHIP = 0
        RIN = 0.
        SV(1,2) = 0.
        CALL DBLOCK(5,1,0,1)
        CALL BEGIN(1,*9999)
        CALL MONITR(1)
        CALL MONITR(2)
        RETURN
C
```

```
C         Start unloading
C         ================
6         RIN = 300.
          CALL BEGIN(1,*9999)
          CALL MONITR(1)
          CALL MONITR(2)
          RETURN
C
C         Interrupt unloading because harbour closes at 24.00
C         ===================================================
7         RIN = 0.
          CALL BEGIN(1,*9999)
          CALL MONITR(1)
          CALL MONITR(2)
          RETURN
C
C         Tanker enters dock
C         ==================
8         SV(1,2) = TX(FAC(1,1),10)
          CALL BEGIN(1,*9999)
          CALL MONITR(1)
          CALL MONITR(2)
          RETURN
C
C         Harbour opens
C         =============
9         IOPEN = 1
          TTEST = T
          CALL ANNOUN(9,T+1.,*9999)
          CALL MONITR(1)
          CALL MONITR(2)
          RETURN
C
C         Harbour closes
C         ==============
10        IOPEN = 0
          TTEST = T
          CALL ANNOUN(10,T+1.,*9999)
          CALL MONITR(1)
          RETURN
C
C         Set initial conditions
C         ======================
11        SV(1,1) = 1000.
          SV(1,2) = 0.
          RIN = 0.
          ROUT = 150.
          IFULL = 0
          IOPEN = 0
          CALL BEGIN(1,*9999)
          RETURN
```

6.2.3. Setting the Flags

Flags are set when a continuous variable SV or DV has reached the
given threshold in order to formulate the conditions for
executing the conditional events.

IFLAG(1,1) Tank level SV(1,1) reaches maximum of 2000 tb.

IFLAG(1,2)   Tank level SV(1,1) has fallen to 1600 tb.

IFLAG(1,3)   Tank level SV(1,1) has risen to 50 tb.

IFLAG(1,4)   Tank is empty, i.e. SV(1,1) = 0

IFLAG(1,5)   Tanker is empty, i.e. SV(1,2).LE.7.5 tb

The flags are set in the subroutine DETECT by calling the subroutine CROSS. Thus the subroutine DETECT is as follows:

```
C
C       FLAG1: tank full
C       ===============
1       CALL CROSS(1,1,1,0,0.,2000.,+1,1.,*977,*988)
C
C       FLAG2: tank level 1600 TB
C       =========================
        CALL CROSS(1,2,1,0,0.,1600.,-1,1.,*977,*988)
C
C       FLAG3: tank level.GE.50 TB
C       ==========================
        CALL CROSS(1,3,1,0,0.,50.,+1,0.5,*977,*988)
C
C       FLAG4: tank empty
C       =================
        CALL CROSS(1,4,1,0,0.,5.,-1,0.1,*977,*988)
C
C       FLAG5: tanker empty
C       ===================
        CALL CROSS(1,5,2,0,0.,7.5,-1,0.1,*977,*988)
C
C       Return to Flow Control
C       ======================
        RETURN
C
C       Return to EQUAT
C       ===============
977     RETURN1
C
C       Error exit
C       ==========
988     RETURN2
        END
```

6.2.4 The Conditions

The conditional events NE = 1 to 7 in the subroutine EVENT occur when the corresponding conditions in the logical function CHECK have become true.

The logical function CHECK contains the following conditions:

NCOND 1   Tank full
           Consequence: Event NE = 1
                        Unloading interrupted because tank full

NCOND 2   Tank level has fallen to 1600 tb.
           Consequence: Event NE = 2
                        Restart unloading

NCOND 3   Tank level has risen to 50 tb.
           Consequence: Event NE = 3
                        Connect refinery

NCOND 4   Tank empty
           Consequence: Event NE = 4
                        Disconnect refinery
NCOND 5   Tanker empty
           Consequence: Event NE = 5
                        Conclude unloading

NCOND 6   Unloading possible
           Consequence: Event NE = 6
                        Start unloading

NCOND 7   Harbour closed
           Consequence: Event NE = 7
                        Interrupt unloading

The logical function CHECK is as follows:

```
C
      CHECK = .FALSE.
C
C     Label selector
C     ==============
      GOTO(1,2,3,4,5,6,7), NCOND
C
C     Conditions
C     ==========
C     Tank full
C     =========
1     IF(IFLAG(1,1).EQ.1) CHECK=.TRUE.
      GOTO 100
C
C     TANK.LE.1600 TB
C     ===============
2     IF(IFLAG(1,2).EQ.1.) CHECK=.TRUE.
      GOTO 100
C
C     TANK.GE.50 TB
C     =============
3     IF(IFLAG(1,3).EQ.1.AND.ROUT.LT.0.01)
     +CHECK=.TRUE.
      GOTO 100

C
C     Tank empty
C     ==========
4     IF(IFLAG(1,4).EQ.1.) CHECK=.TRUE.
      GOTO 100
C
C     Tanker empty
C     ============
5     IF(IFLAG(1,5).EQ.1.) CHECK=.TRUE.
      GOTO 100
C
C     Unloading possible
C     ==================
6     IF(IOPEN.EQ.1.AND.ISHIP.EQ.1.AND.IFULL.EQ.0) CHECK=.TRUE.
      GOTO 100
```

```
C
C       Harbour closes with ship in dock
C       =================================
7       IF(IOPEN.EQ.0.AND.ISHIP.EQ.1.AND.JFLAG(1,5).EQ.1)
       +CHECK=.TRUE.
        GOTO 100
```

Notes:

* The condition NCOND = 6 must be true if a ship which has just arrived in the harbour can begin to unload. In addition, the truth of this condition allows unloading to be continued if it had been interrupted because the tank had reached its capacity of 2000 tb.

* The condition NCOND = 7 is necessary to interrupt the unloading of the ship when the harbour closes at night.

6.2.5 Testing the Conditions

It is the responsibility of the user to test conditions in which discrete variables occur. The testing of such conditions must be initiated by the user by setting the test indicator TTEST = T when such a discrete variable has changed.

When a crossing of a continuous variable is localised, the test indicator is set automatically in the subroutine EQUAT. It is not necessary for the user to do anything in this case.

Discrete variables occur in the conditions NCOND=6 and NCOND=7.

Condition NCOND = 6

The condition NCOND = 6 contains the variables IOPEN, ISHIP and IFULL. When one of these variables is assigned a value a test must be initiated by the statement TTEST = T.

IOPEN is set equal to one in the event NE = 9 (open the dock). ISHIP is set equal to one in subroutine ACTIV after the ship enters the dock.

IFULL is set equal to zero in event NE = 2 (tank level under 1600 tb).

If the condition is satisfied event NE = 6 must be activated by the subroutine TEST:

IF(CHECK(6)) CALL EVENT(6,*9999)

Condition NCOND = 7

The condition NCOND = 7 checks if the following are satisfied:
IOPEN = 0, ISHIP = 1, and JFLAG(1,5)=1.
If one of these variables is assigned a value the condition must be tested. This is done by setting the test indicator TTEST = T.
If the condition is satisfied the event NE = 7 (interrupt unloading, dock closes) must be activated by the subroutine TEST.
This is done by the statement:

        IF(CHECK(7)) CALL EVENT(7,*9999)

The value of IOPEN is set to zero in event NE = 10 (close the dock).
ISHIP is set to one in the subroutine ACTIV when a ship has entered the dock. It is not necessary to test the condition NCOND = 7 here because the unloading process was in any case interrupted before the ship entered the dock.
IFLAG(1,5) is set equal to one in the subroutine DETECT as long as the tank level is over 7.5 tb.

The conditions 1 to 5 contain only flags. In this case the test indicator is set in EQUAT.

The subroutine TEST is as follows:

```
C
C       Tank full
C       =========
        IF(CHECK(1)) CALL EVENT(1,*9999)
C
C       Tank.LE.1600 tb
C       ===============
        IF(CHECK(2)) CALL EVENT(2,*9999)
C
C
C       Tank.GE.50 tb
C       =============
        IF(CHECK(3)) CALL EVENT(3,*9999)
C
C       Tank empty
C       ==========
        IF(CHECK(4)) CALL EVENT(4,*9999)
C
C       Tanker empty
C       ============
        IF(CHECK(5)) CALL EVENT(5,*9999)
C
C
C       Unloading possible
C       ==================
        IF(CHECK(6)) CALL EVENT(6,*9999)

C       Harbour closes with ship in dock
C       ================================
        IF(CHECK(7)) CALL EVENT(7,*9999)
C
C       Return to flow control
C       ======================
        RETURN
C
C       Exit to terminating section
C       ===========================
9999    RETURN 1
        END
```

6.2.6 The Subroutine ACTIV

The generation and movement of the tankers is described in the subroutine ACTIV.
The capacity of the tankers is entered in the private parameter TX(LTX,10) = 150. This value is placed in the state variable

SV(1,2) in event NE = 8 (tanker enters dock).

The dock is represented by a facility. A ship which has entered the dock is queued at a gate NG = 1. It is blocked there until the condition NCOND = 5 (tanker empty) is satisfied. In this case, the event NE = 5 is activated. This ends the unloading, unblocks blocked transaction, and so allows its further processing in the subroutine ACTIV.

The subroutine ACTIV is as follows:

```
C          Label selector
C          ===============
           GOTO(1,2,3,4,5,6), NADDR
C
C          Model
C          =====
C
C          Generate tanker
C          ===================
1          CALL GENERA(0.5,1.,*9999)
           TX(LTX,10)=150.
C
C          Loading in Valdez
C          =================
2          CALL UNIFRM(2.9,3.1,1,TLOAD)
           CALL ADVANC(TLOAD,3,*9000)
C
C          Voyage to Seattle
C          =================
3          CALL GAUSS(5.,1.5,3.,7.,2,TTOS)
           CALL ADVANC(TTOS,4,*9000)
C
C          Unloading in Seattle
C          ====================
4          CALL ARRIVE(1,1)
5          CALL SEIZE(1,5,*9000)
           CALL DEPART(1,1,0.,*9999)
           CALL EVENT(8,*9999)
           ISHIP=1
           TTEST = T
6          CALL GATE(1,5,1,1,6,*9000)
           CALL CLEAR(1,*9999,*9999)
           ISHIP=0
C
C          Voyage to Valdez
C          ================
           CALL GAUSS(4.,1.,2.5,5.5,3,TTOV)
           CALL ADVANC(TTOV,2,*9000)
C
C          Exit to flow control
C          ====================
9000       RETURN
C
C          Exit to terminating section
C          ===========================
9999       RETURN 1
           END
```

6.2.7 Subroutine STATE

Subroutine STATE contains the differential equations which describe the behaviour of the state variables $SV(1,1)$ and $SV(1,2)$. Both equations are extremely simple. The subroutine STATE is as follows:

```
C
C       Differential equations for the tanker model
C       ============================================
1       DV(1,1) = RIN - ROUT
        DV(1,2) = -RIN
        RETURN
C
9999    RETURN1
        END
```

6.2.8 Main Program

As usual the input data is read in the main program. It is as follows:

```
TEXT;TANKER-MODEL/
VARI;IPRINT;0/
VARI;ICONT;1/
VARI;SVIN;0/
VARI;TEND;365./
VARI;TXMAX;15/
INTI;1;1;0.01;2;2;1.E-4;1.;1.E-4;100000/
PLO1;1;0.;100.;1.;21;001001/
PLO2;1;0;2;1;0.;0./
PLO3;1;*A;TANK/
PLO1;2;9.25;10.307;0.01;21;001001;001002/
PLO3;2;*A;TANK;*B;SHIP/
END/
```

The user variables are declared in the block:

COMMON/PRIV/IOPEN,IFULL,ISHIP,RIN,ROUT

The block COMMON/PRIV must be declared in all seven user routines.

The first events are scheduled in section 5 of the framework:

```
C
C       Schedule the first events
C       =========================
        CALL ANNOUN(11,0.,*9999)
        CALL ANNOUN(9,0.25,*9999)
        CALL ANNOUN(10,1.,*9999)
```

In addition, the source which generates the first tanker must be started:

```
C
C       START SOURCE
C       ============
        CALL START(1,0.,1,*9999)
```

The REPORT routines are used to output the results:

```
C       Output of results
C       =================
C
C       Output of plots
C       ===============
        IF(ICONT.NE.0) CALL ENDPLO(1)
C
C       Output of user quantities
C       =========================
        CALL REPRT1(1)
        CALL REPRT1(5)
        CALL REPRT2
        CALL REPRT3
        CALL REPRT4
        CALL REPRT5(1,0,0,0,0,0)
        CALL REPRT6
```

Note:

  * The complexity of the model allows many variations in its implementation. In particular, simplifications which speed up the testing of the conditions are possible.

6.2.9 Results of the Model of the Tanker Fleet

The plots of the level of the tank and the unloading of the tanker are output first. It can be seen from plot 1 that the mean contents of the tank is 1589.0 tb.
The following graph contains a section from PLOT1 for the first hundred days. PLOT2 shows the unloading of the ship. The interruption of the unloading during the night can be seen.
The output from subroutine REPRT4 show the values of the mean queue length and the mean waiting time with confidence intervals:

Mean waiting time: 1.06 days +/- 14.8%
Mean queue length: 1.16 +/- 14.8%

PLOT NR 1

VARIABLE	MINIMUM	MAXIMUM	MEAN	95%-CONFIDENCE INTERVAL	END OF SETTLING PHASE	DISPLACEMENT OF MEAN	DISPL. OF MEAN IN PER CENT
A = TANK	4.9349E+00	1.7700E+03	973.5		– SETTLING PHASE CANNOT BE DETERMINED –		

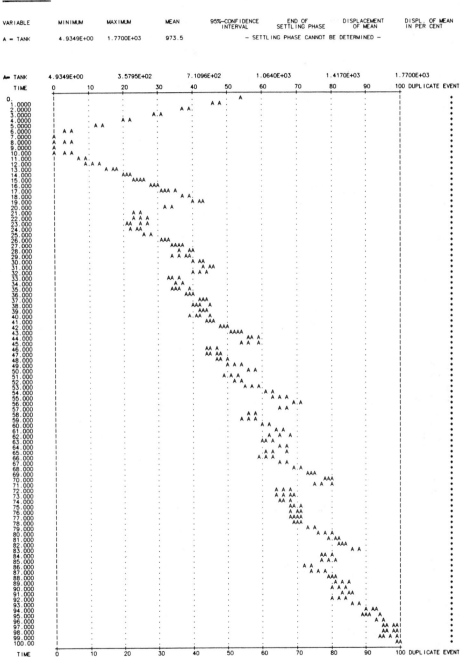

PLOT NR 2

VARIABLE	MINIMUM	MAXIMUM	MEAN	95%-CONFIDENCE INTERVAL	END OF SETTLING PHASE	DISPLACEMENT OF MEAN	DISPL. OF MEAN IN PER CENT
A = TANK	4.9349E+00	9.0291E+01	43.70		– SETTLING PHASE CANNOT BE DETERMINED –		
B = SHIP	.0000E+00	1.5000E+02	41.92	39.86	.2500	11.70	27.91

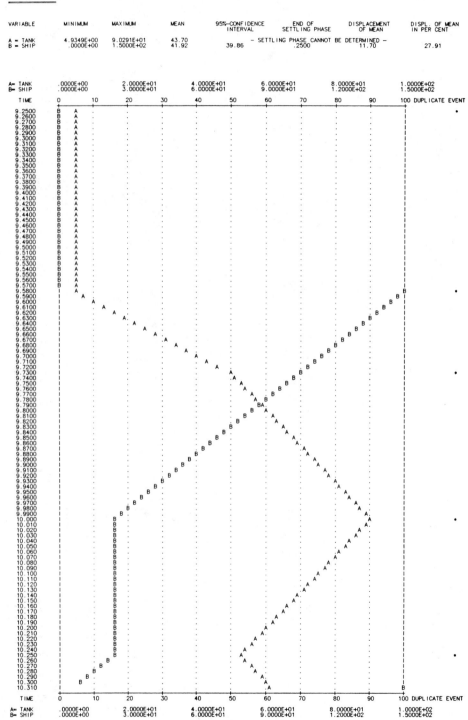

6.2.10 Problems on the Tanker Fleet Model

The model of the tanker fleet shows how behaviour of the model is influenced by complex conditions. The problems are intended to show the affect of changes made in the assumptions.

* Problem 1

PLOT1 shows that the model does not settle down until time T = 100. has been reached. The assumptions are to be altered so that the model begins in a state as close as possible to its state after settling.

Note:

    * There are many ways to make the model settle as quickly as possible. The simplest is to start the refinery at time T = 10. and initialise the tank level with 1800 tb.

* Problem 2

If a tanker contains less than 15 tb., then the unloading is completed even though it is midnight and the dock should close.

Note:

    * An additional flag IFLAG(1,6) must be introduced which indi-cates when the tanker level is less than 15 tb.
The unloading in event NE = 7 is only interrupted if IFLAG(1,6) = 0. The condition NCOND = 7 is as follows:

        IF(IOPEN.EQ.0.AND.ISHIP.EQ.1.AND.IFLAG(1,5).EQ.1.AND.
        IFLAG(1,6).EQ.1) CHECK = .TRUE.

The correct behaviour of the model is to be verified.

7. The Set Concept in GPSS-FORTRAN Version 3

The set concept in GPSS-FORTRAN Version 3 simplifies the specification and investigation of continuous models which consist of loosely coupled submodels.
The submodels are specified by separate sets of differential equations. The coupling is performed by events which are triggered by conditions specified by the user.

The set concept has the following advantages:

* Loosely coupled models have a clear and modular structure.

* A significant saving of computer time is possible, because the flow control of GPSS-FORTRAN Version 3 treats the sets separately. This means that crossings need only be sought inside a set and that each set is integrated separately. The independent integration of sets is particularly important when the time scale of the dynamic behaviour of the sets is very different and thus the integration step sizes vary highly.

The use of the set concept is demonstrated using a very simple example, the host parasite model. The full advantages of the set concept are however only apparent with more complex examples.

7.1 Host Parasite Model V

The host parasite model V is an extension of the host parasite model I.
The host parasite model V contains two separate populations of hosts and parasites. Both populations are described by the following two differential equations:

$$dx/dt = a*x - c*x*y$$
$$dy/dt = c*x*y - b*y$$

$a = 0.005$
$b = 0.05$
$c = 6.E-06$

x = Number of hosts
y = Number of parasites

The initial conditions for both populations are the same:

$x(0) = 10000.$
$y(0) = 1000.$

If the number of hosts in population 1 becomes less than XMIN =
7500.0, the number of parasites in population 1 is reduced by
10%. The parasites removed are added to population 2.
The simulation is to be concluded when the number of hosts in
population 2 becomes less than 6200.0

Problem:

The dynamic behaviour of both populations from T = 0. till the
end of the experiment is to be graphically shown in two separate
plots.

7.2 Structure of the Model

The complete model consists of the two populations which can be considered as loosely coupled submodels. The two submodels are loosely connected by an event, which decreases the number of parasites in the one population and increases it in the other. The event is activated by a condition.

7.2.1 The Subroutine STATE

Both sets are specified in the subroutine STATE:

```
C
C        Label selector
C        ==============
         GOTO(1,2,3),NSET
C
C        Equations for NSET=1
C        ====================
1        DV(1,1)=0.005*SV(1,1)-0.000006*SV(1,2)*SV(1,1)
         DV(1,2)=-0.05*SV(1,2)+0.000006*SV(1,2)*SV(1,1)
         RETURN
C
C        Equations for NSET=2
C        ====================
2        DV(2,1)=0.005*SV(2,1)-0.000006*SV(2,2)*SV(2,1)
         DV(2,2)=-0.05*SV(2,2)+0.000006*SV(2,2)*SV(2,1)
         RETURN
C
C        Equations for NSET=3
C        ====================
3        RETURN
C
```

Note:

  * The differential equations for both sets are identical in this example. This is normally not so.

7.2.2 The Events in Subroutine EVENT

The following three events are necessary:

```
C
C        Alter the number of parasites
C        =============================
1        CALL MONITR(1)
         CALL MONITR(2)
         DIFF = SV(1,2)/10.
         SV(1,2) = SV(1,2)-DIFF
         SV(2,2) = SV(2,2)+DIFF
         CALL BEGIN(1,*9999)
         CALL BEGIN(2,*9999)
         CALL MONITR(1)
         CALL MONITR(2)
         RETURN
C
```

```
C          Completion of run
C          =================
2          TEND = T
           RETURN
C
C          Set initial conditions
C          ======================
3          SV(1,1) = 10000.
           SV(1,2) = 1000.
           CALL BEGIN(1,*9999)
           SV(2,1) = 10000.
           SV(2,2) = 1000.
           CALL BEGIN(2,*9999)
           RETURN
```

The events $NE = 1$ and $NE = 2$ are conditional events which are processed in the subroutine TEST. The event $NE = 3$ initialises the model. It must be scheduled in section 5 of the framework "schedule the first events" by

```
           CALL ANNOUN(3,0.,*9999)
```

7.2.3 Setting of Flags

The following flags are required:

IFLAG(1,1) = 1 The number of hosts in population 1 has become
                less than 7500.0
IFLAG(2,1) = 1 The number of hosts in population 2 has become
                less than 6200.0

The flags are set in subroutine DETECT using CROSS. Subroutine DETECT is as follows:

```
C
C          Label selector
C          ==============
           GOTO(1,2,3), NSET
C
C          Call of subroutine CROSS for set 1
C          ==================================
1          CALL CROSS(1,1,1,0,0.,7500.,-1,10.,*977,*9999)
           RETURN
C
C          Call of subroutine CROSS for set 2
C          ==================================
2          CALL CROSS(2,1,1,0,0.,6200.,-1,10.,*977,*9999)
           RETURN
C
C          Call of subroutine CROSS for set 3
C          ==================================
3          RETURN
C
C          Return to EQUAT
C          ===============
977        RETURN1
9999       RETURN2
           END
```

7.2.4 The Conditions and Their Testing

The conditions are expressed in the logical function CHECK:

```
C
C       Label selector
C       ==============
        GOTO(1,2), NCOND
C
C       Alter the number of hosts
C       =========================
1       IF(IFLAG(1,1).EQ.1)CHECK=.TRUE.
        GOTO 100
C
C       Completion of run
C       =================
2       IF(IFLAG(2,1).EQ.1) CHECK=.TRUE.
        GOTO 100
```

The subroutine TEST:

```
C
C       Test the conditions
C       ===================
        IF(CHECK(1)) CALL EVENT(1,*9999)
        IF(CHECK(2)) CALL EVENT(2,*9999)
        RETURN
        END
```

7.2.5 The Input Data

The input data for the host parasite model is as follows:

```
TEXT; HOST-PARASITE MODELL V /
VARI; ICONT; 1/
INTI; 1;1;0.1;2;2;0.01;;5.;1.E-04;10000/
INTI; 2;1;1.;2;2;0.01;10.;1.E-03;10000/
PLO1; 1;0.;1000.;10.,21;001001;001002/
PLO3; 1;*H;HOST1;*P;PARASIT1/
PLO1; 2;0.;1000.;10.;22;002001;002002/
PLO3; 2;*W;HOST2;*P;PARASIT2/
END/
```

Since there are two sets to be integrated, two INTI records are necessary. It is assumed in the host parasite model that the set NSET=2 can be integrated with a lower accuracy.

Plot 1 shows the state variables $SV(1,1)$ and $SV(1,2)$ in graphical form. These two variables from set 1 are referred to in the plot record PLO1 as 001001 and 001002.
Similarly the variables $SV(2,1)$ and $SV(2,2)$ from set NSET = 2 are referred to as 002001 and 002002.

Notes:

* The data for the two plots are written to two files with numbers 21 and 22. Therefore two extra files must be opened in addition to the scratch file.

> *   Since the simulation is terminated by the event NE = 2, it
> is not necessary to input a value for TEND. The default
> TEND=1.E+10.

7.3 The Results

The graphical representation of the state variables shows the
following behaviour:

Plot 1 shows the number of hosts and parasites in set 1. As soon
as the number of hosts has gone below the crossing line 7500, an
event reduces the number of parasites. The occurrence of an event
is indicated by a star in the event column.
The number of parasites in set 2 as shown in plot 2 is increased
at the same time by the same amount.

The integration statistics which are printed above the plots show
that about twice as many integration steps are necessary for set
1 as for set 2. This is caused by the difference in the required
accuracy. See chapter 7.2.5, "The Input Data". The integration
statistics also show the number of crossings and the average
number of additional steps necessary to localize a crossing.

P L O T   NR 1

VARIABLE	MINIMUM	MAXIMUM	MEAN	95%-CONFIDENCE INTERVAL	END OF SETTLING PHASE	DISPLACEMENT OF MEAN	DISPL. OF MEAN IN PER CENT
H = HOST1	7.0281E+03	1.0000E+04	—	—	—	—	—
P = PARASIT1	4.6969E+02	1.4645E+03	—	—	—	—	—

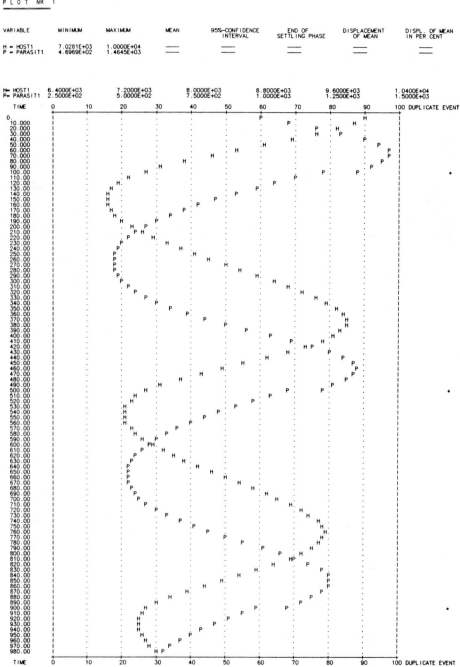

H⊢ HOST1   6.4000E+03   7.2000E+03   8.0000E+03   8.8000E+03   9.6000E+03   1.0400E+04
P⊢ PARASIT1 2.5000E+02   5.0000E+02   7.5000E+02   1.0000E+03   1.2500E+03   1.5000E+03

TIME   0   10   20   30   40   50   60   70   80   90   100 DUPLICATE EVENT

PLOT NR 2

VARIABLE	MINIMUM	MAXIMUM	MEAN	95%-CONFIDENCE INTERVAL	END OF SETTLING PHASE	DISPLACEMENT OF MEAN	DISPL. OF MEAN IN PER CENT
H = HOST2	6.1937E+03	1.0665E+04	——	——	——	——	——
P = PARASIT2	3.2554E+02	1.8008E+03	——	——	——	——	——

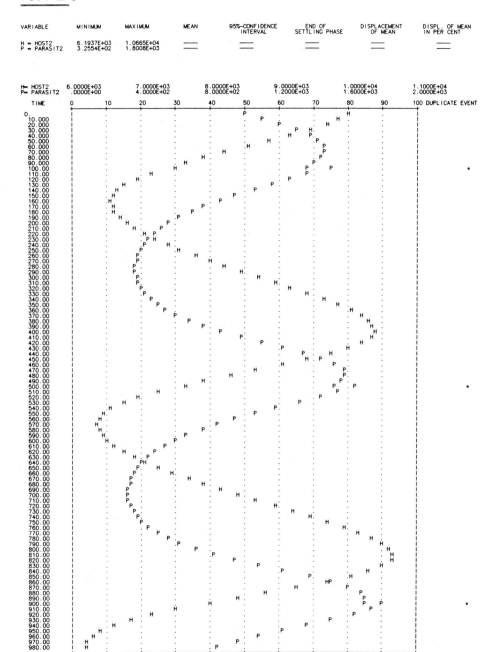

7.4 Problems

The problems on the host parasite model V should demonstrate how
the set concept in GPSS-FORTAN Version 3 is to be used.

* Problem 1

Since parasites are repeatedly added to population 2, there is a
danger that the number of hosts in population 2 will be reduced
too far. This is counteracted by testing every 100 time units
whether the number of parasites in population two has exceeded
the value of 1000.0. In this case, the number of parasites in
population 2 is reduced to 1000.0. The parasites removed are
added to population 3.
Population 3 contains only parasites. Therefore their number will
decrease according to the equation:

$$DV(3,1) = -0.05 * SV(3,1)$$

$SV(3,1)$ is to be graphically represented in a third plot. The
simulation run is to end at TEND = 1000.0.

Notes:

* A scheduled event NE = 4 must be included which tests the
number of parasites in population 2 and reduces it if appropriate. The differential equation for the set NSET = 3 must be
added to the subroutine STATE.

* The standard setting of the array bounds of GPSS-FORTRAN
Version 3 allows for three sets. If more sets are required the
dimensions must be redefined. See Appendix A4 "Array bounds".

* Problem 2

The number of parasites in population 1 is to be reduced by 30%
when the following relation between the number of hosts and
parasites in population 2 holds:

    $SV(2,1)/SV(2,2).GE.6$

i.e. the transfer of parasites from population 1 to population 2
should only occur when the number of hosts in population 2 is
sufficiently large.

A new continuous variable SV(2,3) is included in set 2 for this
purpose, which represents the ratio of hosts to the number of
parasites:

    $SV(2,3) = SV(2,1) / SV(2,2)$

The simulation is to end at T=1000.

It is to be noted that the transfer of parasites from population
1 to population 2 can only occur when at the same time the number
of hosts in population 1 is less than XMIN = 7500. and in
population two the ratio of the number of hosts to the number of
parasites is greater than six.

It is possible that in population 1 the number of hosts is already less than XMIN = 7500. and continues to fall, while the ratio of the number of hosts to the number of parasites in population 2 becomes less than 6.0 at a later time.

It is similarly possible that the ratio of the number of hosts to the number of parasites in population two is already less than six, but the transfer of parasites must wait until the number of hosts in population 1 has fallen below 7500.0.
The condition which leads to a transfer of parasites can therefore not be formulated using IFLAG since IFLAG is only set at the moment when the value crosses the crossing line.

Since no transfer should take place as long as the number of hosts in population 1 is less than the crossing value and the ratio of the number of hosts to the number of parasites in population 2 is larger than the crossing value, the flag variable JFLAG appears in the logical condition:

```
JFLAG(1,1) = + 1    Number of hosts greater than 7500.0
JFLAG(1,1) = - 1    Number of hosts less than 7500.0

JFLAG(2,1) = + 1    Ratio of hosts to parasites greater than 6.0
JFLAG(2,1) = - 1    Ratio of hosts to parasites less than 6.0
```

The condition for the transfer of parasites from population one to population two is expressed in the logical function CHECK:

```
1       IF(JFLAG(1,1).EQ.-1.AND.JFLAG(2,1).EQ.+1) CHECK=.TRUE.
        GOTO 100
```

The relevant crossings must be defined in the subroutine DETECT for each set. In the current example it is as follows:

```
C
C       Call of subroutine CROSS for set 1
C       ==================================
1       CALL CROSS(1,1,1,0,0.,7500.,0,10.,*977,*9999)
        RETURN
C
C       Call of subroutine CROSS for set 2
C       ==================================
2       CALL CROSS(2,1,3,0,0.,6.,0,0.1,*977,*9999)
        RETURN
```

Notes:

   * It is of course possible that flags from different sets occur in a condition.

   * The definition of the crossing is also necessary if JFLAG is used. The flag variable JFLAG changes sign when a crossing occurs.

   * If the condition is still true after a single transfer of parasites to population two, then a further reduction of the parasites in the population 1 occurs after the next integration step.

The testing of the condition in subroutine TEST is as follows:

```
C
C     Test the conditions
C     ====================
      IF(CHECK(1)) CALL EVENT(1,*9999)
```

The events in subroutine EVENT are as follows:

```
C
C     Alter the number of parasites
C     =============================
1     CALL MONITR(1)
      CALL MONITR(2)
      DIFF = SV(1,2)*0.3
      SV(1,2) = SV(1,2)-DIFF
      SV(2,2) = SV(2,2)+DIFF
      CALL BEGIN(1,*9999)
      CALL BEGIN(2,*9999)
      CALL MONITR(1)
      CALL MONITR(2)
      RETURN


C
C     Initialise
C     ==========
2     SV(1,1) = 10000.
      SV(1,2) = 1000.
      SV(2,1) = 10000.
      SV(2,2) = 1000.
      CALL BEGIN(1,*9999)
      CALL BEGIN(2,*9999)
      RETURN
```

Notes:

  * The new variable for the ratio hosts to parasites must be included in the subroutine STATE in the section "Equations for set 2".

$$SV(2,3) = SV(2,1)/SV(2,2)$$

  * The new variable $SV(2,3)$ is not defined by a differential equation. It is only introduced to define the crossing conveniently.

  * It is sensible to output as a plot the ratio of hosts to parasites in set NSET=2 in order to check the correct performance of the simulation model.

  * The new variable must be included in the input data for the INTI, PLO1 and PLO3 records:

```
INTI;2;1;1.;3;2;0.01;10.;1.E-03;10000/
PLO1;2;0.;1000.;20.;22;002001;002002;002003/
PLO3;2;*H;HOST2;*P;PARASIT2;*R;RATIO/
```

8. Specializations

GPSS-FORTRAN Version 3 supports many techniques for constructing and running a model and for presenting the results.

Six examples are given which show how a model can be simply and effectively constructed.

Cedar Bog Lake model   Variables and their graphical representation.

Supermarket model   Combination of model components to structure

Snowtire supply model   Representation of System Dynamics models in GPSS-FORTRAN Version 3

Wheel suspension model I   The treatment of higher order differential equations

Wheel suspension model II Continuous stochastic systems

Host parasite model VI   The use of delay variables

8.1 Variables and their Graphical Representation

Models of continuous systems often contain variables which are not defined by differential equations. The Cedar Bog Lake model shows how these variables must be treated in GPSS-FORTRAN Version 3.

8.1.1 Cedar Bog Lake Model

The Cedar Bog Lake model shows the gradual conversion of a lake into dry land. It was first described in "Computer Simulation of Energy Flow in Cedar Bog Lake" by R.B. Williams, in /2/.

The model starts with three state variables:

SV(1,1)   Plants
SV(1,2)   Herbivorous animals
SV(1,3)   Carnivorous animals

The variables are given in units of energy. This unit was chosen, to simplify the description, absorption of energy, loss of energy and exchange of energy. The amount of energy is proportional to the amount of plants or animals.
The organic material which collects at the bottom of the lake must also be declared:

SV(1,4)   Dead organic material

The absorption of energy from solar radiation and the loss of energy to the enviroment are represented by the following variables:

SV(1,5)   Loss of energy to the environment
SV(1,6)   Energy absorption from solar radiation

The absorption of energy, loss of energy and exchange of energy are described by the following differential equations:

DV(1,1) = SV(1,6) - 4.03*SV(1,1)
DV(1,2) = 0.48*SV(1,1) - 17.87*SV(1,2)
DV(1,3) = 4.85*SV(1,2) - 4.65*SV(1,3)
DV(1,4) = 2.55*SV(1,1) + 6.12*SV(1,2) + 1.95*SV(1,3)
DV(1,5) = 1.0*SV(1,1) + 6.90*SV(1,2) + 2.7*SV(1,3)
SV(1,6) = 95.9*(1. + 0.635*SIN(2.*3.14*T))

The first equation, for example, shows that the energy contained in the plants is initially subject to exponential decay. The absorption is due to solar radiation which supports plant growth.

The second equation similarly describes the rate of change of the energy content of the herbivorous animals. The loss of energy is counteracted by energy obtained from the plants eaten.

The energy contained in the dead organic material as well as the amount of dead organic material is described by the fourth differential equation. It states that the rate of change of the energy which is contained in the dead organic material is proportional to the quantities of plants, herbivorous and carni-vorous animals. The behaviour of the variables is to be represented graphically over two years.

8.1.2 Construction of the Model

The Cedar Bog Lake model describes a continuous system. The differential equations are defined in the subroutine STATE.

The variable SV(1,6) is a special case, because it is not defined by a differential equation. It would be possible to introduce this variable without using a state variable SV, e.g.:

        SUN = 95.9*(1. + 0.635*SIN(2.+3.14*T))
        DV(1,1) = SUN - 4.03*SV(1,1)

In this example, we want to plot the value of energy obtained from solar energy, to compare it with the values of the other state variables.

Only state variables can be plotted in GPSS-FORTRAN Version 3. Therefore this variable must be represented by the state variable SV(1,6), not by the private variable SUN.

Notes:

    * When assigning indices to the continuous variables, those which are defined by differential equations must be given lower indices than those which are only defined as continuous varia-bles in order to plot them. In the Cedar Bog Lake example, the variable which represents the energy obtained from the sun is

thus given the index 6.

* The number of continuous variables SV must be distinguished
in the INTI data record from the number of differential
quotients DV. The difference SV-DV is the number of continuous
variables which are not defined by differential equations, and
are included only because they are to be plotted.
The   order of the equations in subroutine STATE must be chosen
so that every variable which occurs on the right hand side
of an equation has been previously computed.

All continuous variables SV, which are defined by differential
equations, have already been assigned the correct values when
STATE is called. STATE is called in order to compute the values
of the   differential quotients DV from the values of   the
continuous variables SV at time T.

For the Cedar Bog Lake model this means that the order of the
differential equations has no significance.   It is however
necessary that the variable SV(1,6) is computed in the subroutine
STATE before the equation

        DV(1,1) = SV(1,6) - 4.03*SV(1,1)

The following is a possible order of the equations in the
subroutine STATE:

```
SV(1,6) = 95.9*(1. + 0.635*SIN(2.*3.14*T))
DV(1,1) = SV(1,6) - 4.03*SV(1,1)
DV(1,2) = 0.48*SV(1,1) - 17.87*SV(1,2)
DV(1,3) = 4.85*SV(1,2) - 4.65*SV(1,3)
DV(1,4) = 2.55*SV(1,1) + 6.12*SV(1,2) + 1.95*SV(1,3)
DV(1,5) = 1.0*SV(1,1) + 6.90*SV(1,2) + 2.7*SV(1,3)
```

The initial values must be specified in an event as usual.   The
subprogram then has the following form:

```
C
C       Label selector
C       ==============
        GOTO(1),NE
C
C       Process Events
C       ==============
1       SV(1,1) = 0.83
        SV(1,2) = 0.003
        SV(1,3) = 0.0001
        SV(1,4) = 0.0
        SV(1,5) = 0.0
        CALL BEGIN(1,*9999)
        RETURN
```

8.1.3 The Results

The Cedar Bog Lake model is to run for one year. Therefore the simulation will be ended when TEND = 2.

The input data for Cedar Bog Lake model is as follows:

```
TEXT; CEDAR BOG LAKE/
VARI; ICONT; 1/
VARI; IPRINT; 0/
VARI; TEND; 2./
VARI; EPS; 1.E-03/
INTI; 1;1;1.E-2;6;5;1.E-3;5.;1.E-03;10000/
PLO1; 1;0.;2.;0.02;21;001001;001002;001003;001004;001005;001006/
PLO3; 1;*P;PLANTS;*H;HERBIV;*C;CARNIV;*O;ORGANIC;*E;ENVIRON;*S;
SOLAR/
END/
```

The results show that the intensity of the solar radiation is periodic. The quantities of plants, herbivorous and carnivorous animals follow with a phase difference. The amount of dead organic material and the amount of energy transferred to the environment increase continuously.

Notes:

* The results include confidence intervals as well as mean values for the variables SV(1,1), SV(1,2), SV(1,3), SV(1,4) and SV(1,5).

* The confidence intervals and the end of the settling phase are only computed if the parameter ISTAT in the subroutine ENDPLO is set equal to one. Therefore these values are not printed for the Cedar Bog Lake model.

P L O T   NR   1

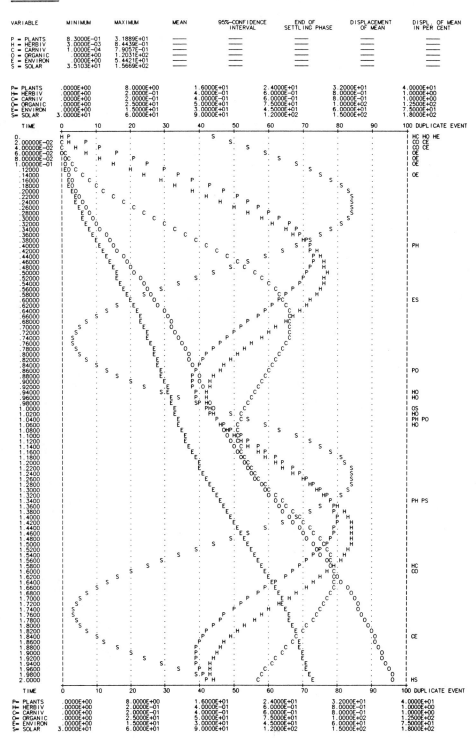

8.1.4 Problems

The problems demonstrate how the user must select the order of the equations in subroutine STATE.

* Problem 1

The simulation is to be repeated with the equations in the following order:

DV(1,2) = 0.48*SV(1,1) - 17.87*SV(1,2)
DV(1,3) = 4.85*SV(1,2) - 4.65*SV(1,3)
DV(1,4) = 2.55*SV(1,1) + 6.12*SV(1,2) + 1.95*SV(1,3)
DV(1,5) = 1.0*SV(1,1) + 6.90*SV(1,2) + 2.7*SV(1,3)
SV(1,6) = 95.9*(1. + 0.635*SIN(2.*3.14*T))
DV(1,1) = SV(1,6) - 4.03*SV(1,1)

The results must be the same as previously.

* Problem 2

The equation

DV(1,4) = 2.55*SV(1,1) + 6.12*SV(1,2) + 1.95*SV(1,3)

describes the rate of increase in dead organic material. It is assumed that DV(1,4) also depends on the rate with which energy is transferred to the environment. This is defined by the differential quotient DV(1,5).
DV(1,4) is given by:

DV(1,4) = 2.55*SV(1,1) + 6.12*SV(1,2) + 1.95*SV(1,3)
          + 0.1*DV(1,5)

The differential quotient DV(1,5) now appears on the right hand side of the equation for DV(1,4). Therefore DV(1,5) must be known when DV(1,4) is being calculated.

A possible order for the equations in the subroutine STATE is as follows:

SV(1,6) = 95.9*(1. + 0.635*SIN(2.*3.14*T))
DV(1,1) = SV(1,6) - 4.03*SV(1,1)
DV(1,2) = 0.48*SV(1,1) - 17.87*SV(1,2)
DV(1,3) = 4.85*SV(1,2) - 4.65*SV(1,3)
DV(1,5) = 1.0*SV(1,1) + 6.90*SV(1,2) + 2.7*SV(1,3)
DV(1,4) = 2.55*SV(1,1) + 6.12*SV(1,2) + 1.95*SV(1,3)
          + 0.1*DV(1,5)

8.2 Combination of Model Components to Structures

Model components are altered by subroutines in GPSS-FORTRAN Version 3. The index of the model component is transferred to the subroutine in the parameter list.

Example:

* The subroutine SEIZE causes a facility to be occupied. The index of the facility, NFA, is contained in the parameter list.

This allows models which contain many similar components to be constructed simply and quickly.

8.2.1 The Supermarket Model

The interarrival times of customers at a supermarket are exponentially distributed with mean = 1.0 . The mean time spent by a customer selecting goods is 25 time units.

The supermarket contains ten cash registers with a mean processing time of 9.5.

When the customer leaves the supermarket he chooses the cash register with the smallest queue. The mean queue and mean waiting time at each cash register is to be determined.

The simulation is to be ended when 10000 customers have been generated.

8.2.2 Structure of the Model

The customers are generated in the usual way. The time which a customer spends selecting goods is represented in the model by a call of the subroutine ADVANC.

The cash registers are represented by facilities. The customer goes to the cash register with the smallest queue length.

All ten facilities can be dealt with by the same call of SEIZE. The subroutine ACTIV is as follows:

```
C
C       Generate the transactions
C       =========================
1       CALL ERLANG(1.,1,0.032,5.,1,RAND1,*9999)
        CALL GENERA(RAND1,1.,*9999)
C
C       Time spent in supermarkt
C       ========================
        CALL ERLANG(25.,1,0.8,125.,2,RAND2,*9999)
        CALL ADVANC(RAND2,2,*9000)
```

```
C
C        Select cash register
C        =====================
2        XBIN = MIN(BIN(1,1),BIN(2,1),BIN(3,1),BIN(4,1),BIN(5,1),
        +BIN(6,1),BIN(7,1),BIN(8,1),BIN(9,1),BIN(10,1))
         IBIN = NINT(XBIN)
         DO 21 I = 1,10
         IF(IBIN.EQ.NINT(BIN(I,1))) GOTO 22
21       CONTINUE
         GOTO 9999
22       TX(LTX,9) = FLOAT(I)
C
C        Enter cash register
C        ===================
         NFA = NINT(TX(LTX,9))
         CALL ARRIVE(NFA,1)
3        NFA = NINT(TX(LTX,9))
         CALL SEIZE(NFA,3,*9000)
         CALL DEPART(NFA,1,0,*9999)
         CALL ERLANG(9.5,1,0.31,47.5,NFA + 2,RANDX,*9999)
         CALL WORK(NFA,RANDX,0,4,*9000,*9999)
4        NFA=NINT(TX(LTX,9))
         CALL CLEAR(NFA,*9999,*9999)
C
C        Eliminate transactions
C        ======================
         CALL TERMIN(*9000)
```

Notes:

*   Each transaction must specify at which cash register it is
to be serviced.   The number of the facility selected in the
section "Select a cash register" to deal with a transaction is
placed in the user attributes TX(LTX,9).

*   The repair workshop model already used the   possibilty of
selecting model components by their index.   The two bins used
for transactions of different priority are processed by calls
of the subroutines ARRIVE and DEPART in the section   "Processing of transactions."

*   It is possible to process the same station with different
subroutines by identifying the components of the model by parameters.   This has already been shown in chapter 3.4,   "The
Group Practice Model". The transactions call one of the subroutines MSEIZE or MPREEM, depending on their priority.

8.2.3 The Results

The results are shown in the output of the BIN matrix and the
BINSTA matrix.

T =   9984.6789   RT =   9984.6789

BIN ARRAY
=========

NBN	QTY	MAX	SUMIN	SUMOUT	ARRIVE	DEPART	TOTALWT	LAST
1	0	6	1018	1018	1018	1018	.1904E+05	9985.
2	0	6	1029	1029	1029	1029	.1825E+05	9985.
3	0	6	1102	1102	1102	1102	.1723E+05	9985.
4	0	6	1081	1081	1081	1081	.1632E+05	9985.
5	0	6	1061	1061	1061	1061	.1548E+05	9985.
6	0	6	989	989	989	989	.1473E+05	9985.
7	0	6	998	998	998	998	.1372E+05	9985.
8	0	6	975	975	975	975	.1252E+05	9985.
9	0	6	886	886	886	886	.1148E+05	9985.
10	0	5	861	861	861	861	.1043E+05	9985.

BINSTA ARRAY
============

NBN	DURATION TIME	NUM. OF TOKEN	CONF.INT. PER CENT	DISPLACEM. PER CENT	END OF SET-TLING PHASE
1	18.71	1.911	17.74	1.058	520.0
2	17.73	1.838	18.42	1.283	520.0
3	15.64	1.736	19.19	1.178	480.0
4	15.09	1.643	19.33	.9124	440.0
5	14.59	1.558	20.40	.9177	480.0
6	14.89	1.484	26.26	-7.221	640.0
7	13.75	1.383	23.59	1.481	520.0
8	12.84	1.267	27.86	-8.760	2800.
9	12.96	1.161	27.67	2.027	560.0
10	12.11	1.054	30.34	2.020	600.0

8.2.4 Problems

The problems show further possibilities for identifying the components of the model by parameters.

* Problem 1

The number of cash registers is to be reduced to 9.

* Problem 2

The number of cash registers is to be reduced to 9 and the interarrival time of the customers is to be increased to 1.1.

* Problem 3

The supermarket is to be given a second entrance. The interarrival time at each entrance is 2 time units. Each entrance is to represented by a source.

Note:

   * The subroutine GENERA generates transactions for all sources. The index of the source is therefore not included in the parameter list of GENERA.

The two entrances are only represented by the initiations of the sources in the main program:

```
     DO 5000   I = 1,2
     CALL START (I,0.,1,*9000)
5000    CONTINUE
```

The car telephone model in volume 2, chapter 5.3.1 showed the use of a single call of GENERA for several sources.

* Problem 4

Problem 3 is to altered so that each entrance has a different interarrival time.

Note:

   * The generation of random numbers used in the call of GENERA must be altered.
The arrival time of the next transaction is determined for each source in accordance with the distribution associated with the source. The number of a source which wishes to generate a transaction is known when ACTIV is called. It is contained in the variable LSL in the common area COMMON/SRC/.

The section "Generate transactions" is now as following:

```
C
C      Generate transactions
C      =====================
1      CALL ERLANG(RM(LSL,1),1,RM(LSL,2),RM(LSL,3),LSL,RAND1,
      +*9999)
       CALL GENERA(RAND1,1.,*9999)
```

Each row of the matrix RM contains the mean, the lower limit and upper limit of the interarrival time of each source. RM is assigned in the main program and made available to ACTIV in the common area COMMON/PRIV/.

8.3 The Representation of System Dynamics Models in GPSS–FORTRAN Version 3

System dynamics models change continuously with time. They are used to represent systems which can be represented as a set of feedback loops defining relations between levels and rates.

The simulation language DYNAMO was developed to deal with system dynamics models.

A very good introduction to system dynamics models and DYNAMO is to be found in /3/.

GPSS-FORTRAN Version 3 can be used to process system dynamics models. It provides, in general, similar facilities to DYNAMO. GPSS-FORTRAN Version 3 is more powerful than DYNAMO because it does not contain the many restrictions of DYNAMO.

8.3.1 System Elements and System Functions of System Dynamics and Their Representation in GPSS-FORTRAN Version 3

Rates and levels are the basic components of a system dynamics model.

The levels correspond to continuous variables. The rates represent the differential quotients with respect to time of the levels.

* Example

The level $x(t)$ is the stock level of completed cars. The rate of increase $dx(z)/dt$ is the rate at which cars are produced. The rate of decrease $dx(a)/dt$ is the rate at which cars leave the warehouses to be delivered to the customer.

System dynamics models can be represented dynamically. Five types of symbols and two types of connections are used. They are shown on the next page.

System Dynamics also supports delays in the model.

A rate of change dx/dt is a delay if the rate of change is proportional to the level:

$dx/dt = 1/D*x$

| level | State variable (e.g. quantity of goods, number of persons, amount of information or cash) |

| rate ◁ | Rate of change of a state variable |

| auxil-iary | Mathematical function to compute a rate |

| constant | Model constant |

| source or sink | Sources and sinks comprise the boundary between the model and its environment. Goods, persons, information, cash, etc., enter the model via a source and leave it via a sink. |

⟶ Direction of flow of quantities described by the state variables.

------------▶ Dependencies, effects, influences

This can be shown graphically:

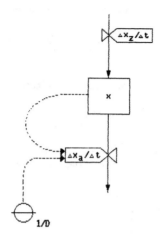

Note:

* A delay in System Dynamics must not be confused with a delayed variable in GPSS-FORTRAN Version 3. Delayed variables in
GPSS-FORTRAN Version 3 are defined in volume 2, chapter 2.2.6.

System Dynamics: Delay corresponds to first order delay
                            element

GPSS-FORTRAN Version 3:   Lag element

In System Dynamics, the variation of a level $x(t)$ with time is
computed using numerical integration by the trapezoidal rule:

Level(new) = level(old) + DT*(Rate(increase) - Rate(decrease))

DT is the time step selected by the user. It is the step size
used in integration.

The equation which describes the variation of the level with time
must be converted into a differential equation in GPSS-FORTRAN
Version 3. The latter does not distinguish between rates of
increase and rates of decrease. It deals only with the rate of
change:

DV(NSET,NV) = dx/dt = rate(increase) - rate(decrease)

The integration step size cannot be directly assigned by the user
in GPSS-FORTRAN Version 3. Its value is assigned automatically,
depending on the required accuracy.

Note:

* If the user of GPSS-FORTRAN Version 3 wishes to use a constant step size, then he must assign the same value to the
upper and lower limits of the integration step size. The
value of the accuracy must be assigned accordingly.

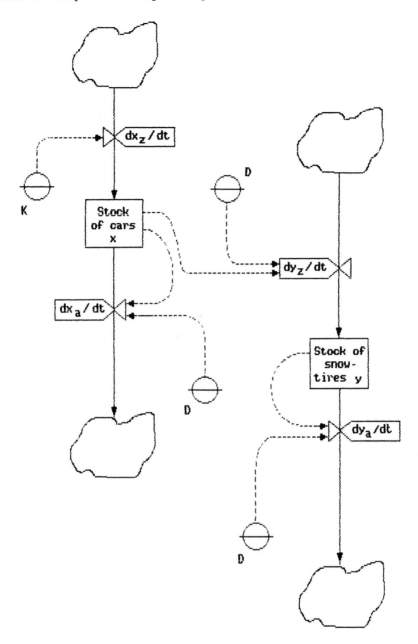

Figure 4   The snowtire supply model

8.3.2 The Snowtire Supply Model

This is an example to show how a system dynamics model can be constructed using GPSS-FORTRAN Version 3.
The snowtire supply model is taken from G. Niemeyer /4/.

A stock of cars x is increased at a constant rate dx(z)/dt and decreased at a rate dx(a)/dt. The rate of decrease of dx(a)/dt is a first order delay. The number of cars in stock is given by:

```
dx(z)/dt = 5.E + 06      rate of increase
dx(a)/dt = 1/D(1)*X      rate of decrease
D(1)     = 10.           delay of rate of decrease
```

The stock of cars influences the rate of increase of snowtires y with a time delay D(2). The rate of decrease of snowtires due to their wearing out, dy(a)/dt = 1/D(3)*y, is an output delay of the second order with rate of delay D(3). Figure 4 shows the structure of the model using the symbols of system dynamics.

The stock of snowtires is determined by:

```
dy(z)/dt = 1/D(2)*x      rate of increase
dy(a)/dt = 1/D(3)*y      rate of decrease
D(2) = 2.0               delay of rate of increase
D(3) = 5.                delay of rate of decrease
```

The initial conditions are as follows:

```
x(0) = 6 000 000  initial stock of cars
y(0) =   600 000  initial stock of snowtires
```

The simulation is to run for 50 years. The stock levels if cars and winter tyres are to be plotted.

The representation of the model in GPSS-FORTRAN Version 3 is extremly simple.

The following two differential equations for the two state variables, stock of cars and stock of snowtires, must be defined in the subroutine STATE:

```
        DV(1,1) = 5.E+06 - 0.1 * SV(1,1)
        DV(1,2) = 0.5*SV(1,1) - 0.2*SV(1,2)
```

The input data and the initial conditions must also be determined.

8.3.3 The Results

The plot shows how the number of cars and snowtires in stock approach their limits.

P L O T NR 1

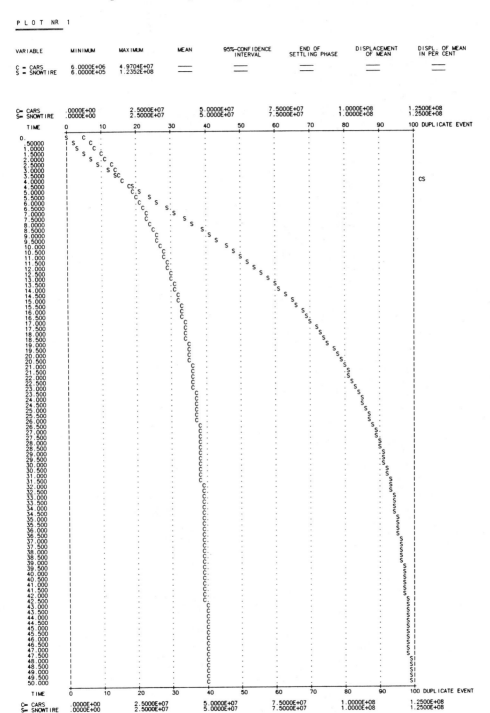

8.3.4 Problems

The   problems   show   how system dynamics models   can   easily   be
represented in GPSS-FORTRAN Version 3.

* Problem 2

Forrester   world model as described in chapter 3 of /5/ is to   be
programmed in GPSS-FORTRAN Version 3.

8.4 Differential Equations of Higher Order

GPSS-FORTRAN Version 3 can only deal with differential equations
of the first order. If differential equations of higher order
occur, the user must convert them to systems of differential
equations of the first order. Volume 1,   chapter 2.1.2,
"Formulation of Differential Equations" describes how this is
done. The wheel suspension model I is an example.

8.4.1 Wheel Suspension Model I

A mass M is attached to a fixed wall by a spring and a shock
absorber. Figure 5 shows this mechanical model.

The model is described by the following second order differential
equation:

$$Mx'' + Dx' + Kx = F(t)$$

The variables have the following meaning:

M   mass (kg)
D   damping constant (kg/s)
K   spring constant (kg/s**2)
x   coordinate of the center of gravity
F(t)   force at time t (N)

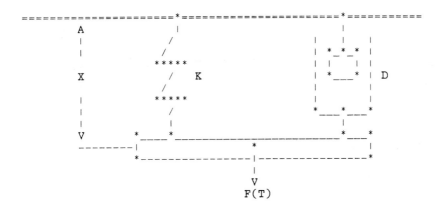

Figure 5   Model wheel suspension

The position and the velocity of the center of gravity are to be
plotted.

The initial conditions are as follows:

M   = 1 kg
D   = 0.3 kg/s
K   = 1.0 kg/s**2
F(t) = 1.0 N   for all t

The position of the center of gravity at time T=0. is given by x=0. and the velocity is given by x'=0.

The simulation is to end after 30 seconds.

8.4.2 Structure of the Model

The second order differential equation must be converted to two first order differential equations as described in volume 1, chapter 2.1.2.

A new variable x(1), given by

$$x(1) = x'$$

is introduced into the equation:

$$x'' = -K/M*x - D/M*x' + F/M$$

The two first order differential equations are:

$$x' = x(1)$$
$$x(1)' = - K/M*x - D/M*x(1) + F/M$$

Introducing the GPSS-FORTRAN Version 3 variables:

SV(1,1) = x(1)   DV(1,1) = x(1)'
SV(1,2) = x   DV(1,2) = x'

The equations become:

DV(1,2) = SV(1,1)
DV(1,1) = -K/M*SV(1,2) - D/M*SV(1,1) + F/M

These two equations must be placed in the subroutine STATE.

SV(1,1) is the velocity and SV(1,2) is the position of the center of gravity. SV(1,1) and SV(1,2) are to be plotted to show the variation with time of the velocity and position of the center of gravity.

The initial conditions are set in an event:

SV(1,1) = 0.
SV(1,2) = 0.

Note:

* The variables M and K must be declared as type REAL.

8.4.3 The Results

The following plot shows the velocity x' and the position x of the center of gravity.

The position is represented by the letter P and the velocity by the letter V.

It can be seen that the force F(t) which is applied from time T=0. onwards causes a damped oscillation of the system. The system settles to a steady state with:

V = 0.
P = 1.

The constant applied force produces a constant strain on the system. The velocity of the center of gravity in the final state is V=0. as expected. One can see from the plot that there is a phase difference between velocity and position.

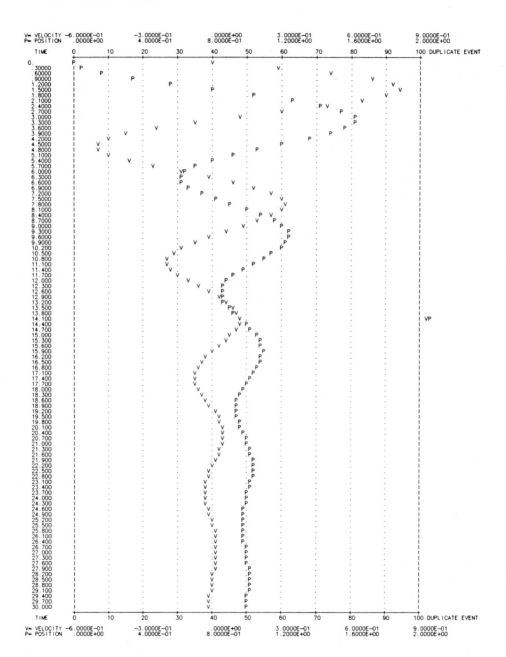

8.4.4 Problems

The problems show further examples of the treatment of differential equations of higher order.

* Problem 1

The equation of harmonic motion:

$$x'' + A*x = 0$$

is to be plotted.

Initial conditions:

$$x'(0) = 0.$$
$$x(0) = 1.$$

The result is a sine curve with period T =2*3.14/A.

* Problem 2

The wheel suspension model is to be altered so that the force F = 1. N is to be applied for two time units at intervals of 15 time units.
The value of the force is represented by the continuous variable SV(1,3) so that it can be plotted. The graphical representation shows then with particular clarity the influence of the applied force. See volume 2, chapter 8.1, "Variables and Their Graphical Representation".
Two plots are to be produced: one of position and force and the other of velocity and force.

Note:

> * Two events are necessary. One to switch on the force and one to switch off the force. Each event must schedule its next occurrence.

* Problem 3

A force is applied starting every 25 time units and lasting eight time units. The amplitude of the force is given by a sine function:

$$F(t) = F1*sin(a*T)$$
$$F1 = 1.$$
$$A = 3.14/8.$$

Note:

   * The force F(t) is a function of time in the current   example.
   The differential equations in the subroutine STATE are as
   follows:

```
F = F1*sin(3.14/8.*T - PHI)
DV(1,2) = SV(1,1)
DV(1,1) = -K/M*SV(1,2) - D/M*SV(1,1) + F/M
SV(1,3) = F
```

The switching on and switching off of the force is performed by
two events which set F1 = 1. and F1 = 0.

The phase PHI must be such that at time T at which the force is
switched on, its initial value is given by F(T) = 0. It follows
that:

PHI = (3.14*T)/8.

The two additional events are as follows:

```
C
C       Switch on the force
C       ===================
2       CALL MONITR(1)
        F1 = 1.
        PHI = AMOD(T,2.*3.14)
        CALL BEGIN(1,*9999)
        CALL ANNOUN(2,T + 25.,*9999)
        CALL ANNOUN(3,T + 8.,*9999)
        CALL MONITR(1)
        RETURN
C
C       Switch off the force
C       ====================
3       CALL MONITR(1)
        F1 = 0.
        CALL BEGIN(1,*9999)
        CALL MONITR(1)
        RETURN
```

It is to be noted that F1 and PHI must be made available to the
subroutine STATE in the common area COMMON/PRIV/.

Two plots are to be produced, one of the position and the force,
and the other with the velocity and the force.

Notes:

   * The simulation should run until T = 100. to provide an adequate picture with time. The recommended monitor step is 0.5.

   * The value of the variable F(t) must be stored in SV(1,3), so
   that it can be plotted.

8.5 Stochastic, Continuous Systems

All subroutines used to generate random numbers and to evaluate statistical material can also be used in modelling continuous systems. The wheel suspension model II is a simple example of this.

8.5.1 The Wheel Suspension Model II

The wheel suspension model I, described in problem 2 of volume 2, chapter 8.4.4 is to be altered so that the impulses occur at random intervals rather than regularly. The time interval between 2 successive impulses is a random sample with normal distribution, MEAN = 15.0 and SIGMA = 2.0, lower limit RMIN = 10. and upper limit RMAX = 20.0.

The position and velocity of the center of gravity are to be plotted for 50.0 time units. In addition, the impulses are to be shown on both plots.

8.5.2 The Results

The only change in the wheel suspension model I (Problem 2) refers to the rescheduling of the event NE = 2 which causes the impulse. The time interval is now randomly distributed instead of having the constant value of 15.0. The new time interval until the next impulse is a random number generated by the subroutine GAUSS.

The subroutine EVENT is now as follows:

```
C
C       Label selector
C       ==============
        GOTO(1,2,3),NE

C
C       Initialise
C       ==========
1       SV(1,1) = 0.
        SV(1,2) = 0.
        SV(1,3) = 0.
        CALL BEGIN(1,*9999)
        RETURN

C
C       Switch on the force
C       ===================
2       CALL MONITR(1)
        SV(1,3) = 1.
        CALL BEGIN(1,*9999)
        CALL MONITR(1)
        CALL GAUSS(15.,2.,10.,20.,1,RANDOM)
        CALL ANNOUN(2,T + RANDOM,*9999)
        CALL ANNOUN(3,T + 2.,*9999)
        RETURN
```

```
C
C       Switch off the force
C       ====================
3       CALL MONITR(1)
        SV(1,3) = 0.
        CALL BEGIN(1,*9999)
        CALL MONITR(1)
        RETURN
        END
```

The plot shows behaviour similar to that seen in the wheel suspension model I (problem 1). The difference is in the random time interval between impulses.

Plot 1 shows the position and the impulses, and plot 2 shows the velocity and the impulses.

P L O T NR 1

VARIABLE	MINIMUM	MAXIMUM	MEAN	95%-CONFIDENCE INTERVAL	END OF SETTLING PHASE	DISPLACEMENT OF MEAN	DISPL. OF MEAN IN PER CENT
V = VELOCITY	-1.2321E+00	1.0542E+00	——	——	——	——	——
F = FORCE	.0000E+00	1.0000E+00	——	——	——	——	——

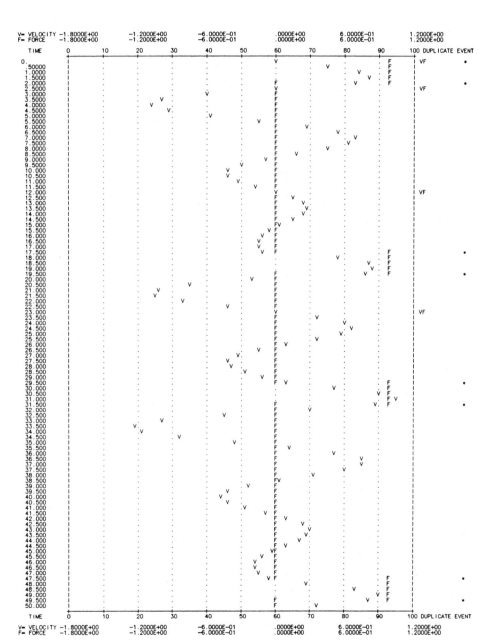

PLOT NR 1

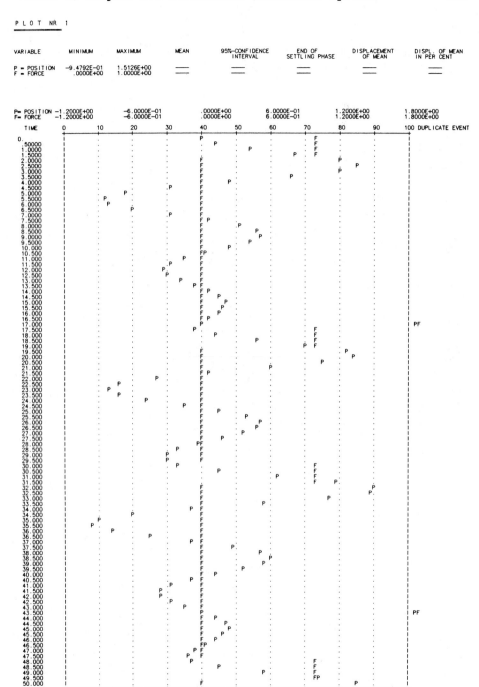

8.5.3 Problems

The problems show additional use of subroutines for generating random numbers.

* Problem 1

The wheel suspension model II is to be altered so that the impulses can overlap. This means that a new impulse can start before the previous one has finished. In this case, the total impulse is the sum of the two single impulses.

The length of the impulse is increased from its previous value of 2.0 to 12.0.

* Problem 2

Both the length and the force of the impulse are to be randomly distributed inside realistic limits.

* Problem 3

In addition to positive impulses, negative impulses are to occur with probability 0.4. In this way a test track for the wheel suspension of vehicles which contains holes as well as bumps can be simulated.

Note:

  * The direction of the impulse is determined by using a random number with uniform distribution between 0 and 1. The code is:

```
F = 1.
CALL UNIFORM(0.,1.,4,RAND)
IF(RAND.LE.0.4)F = -1.
```

8.6 Delayed Variables

The values SV and DV are also available for delayed variables for
times between the current simulation time T and the previous
T-TAUMAX. In this way models can be described in which the value
of a continuous variable or a differential quotient is dependent
on the value of a state variable or differential quotient at a
previous time T - TAU where O.LE.TAU.LE.TAUMAX.

Examples:

* An increase in the stock of capital goods influences the rate
of production of a firm. The increase in the amount of capital
goods is only effective after a delay reflecting the time needed
to construct the new capital goods. This means that the rate of
change of production dx/dt at time t is a function of the
quantity of capital goods y at a previous time:

dx(T)/dt = f(y(T - TAU))

* The level of water in a river at time T depends on the amount
of rain at time T - TAU. The delay TAU corresponds to the time
the water needed to collect and reach this point in the river.

* The probabilty that a parasite attacks a host is proportional
to the number of hosts and the number of parasites in the host
parasite model. If one assumes a period of incubation, then the
part of the rate of change dependent on these attacks is
dependant on the number of hosts and the number of parasites at
time T - TAU, where TAU is the period of incubation.

8.6.1 The Host Parasite Model VI

The host parasite model VI is based on the simple host parasite
model described in volume 2, chapter 1.1. However, it includes a
period of incubation.

The invasion of a host by a parasite leads to the death of the
host and so to the birth of a new parasite after a period of
incubation TAU.

The equations which describe the host parasite model VI are as
follows:

dx(T)/dt = a*x(T) - c*x(T - TAU)*y(T - TAU)
dy(T)/dt = -b*y(T) + c*x(T - TAU)*y(T - TAU)

The details given in volume 2, chapter 1.1 apply to the running
of the host parasite model VI. TAU is assigned the value 10.

8.6.2 Implementation

The calculation of the differential quotient DV at time T
requires the value of the state variable SV at time T and at time
T - TAU. The value of the state variable SV at time T - TAU is
obtained using the subroutine DELAY. The differential equations
in the subroutine STATE are as follows:

```
1        CALL DELAY(1,1,10.,SVD1,*9999)
         CALL DELAY(1,2,10.,SVD2,*9999)
         DV(1,1) = 0.005*SV(1,1) - 0.000006*SVD1*SVD2
         DV(1,2) = -0.05*SV(1,2) + 0.000006*SVD1*SVD2
         RETURN
```

The initial conditions must be set in an event NE=1, as in previous examples.

First of all the initial values at time T=0. must be assigned. As in chapter 1.1 we have:

```
         SV(1,1) = 10000.
         SV(1,2) = 1000.
```

In addition at least two previous states must be given. One must be available at the time of the maximum delay T = -10. The second is required at the time of the beginning of the simulation, i.e. T = 0. In the current example, three previous values should be available. They are stored in the matrix XD1:

```
XD1(1,1) = 10000.
XD1(2,1) = -10.
XD1(1,2) = 10000.
XD1(2,2) = -6.
XD1(1,3) = 10000.
XD1(2,3) = 0.
```

The previous values for the parasites must be placed in the matrix XD2:

```
XD2(1,1) = 1000.
XD2(2,1) = -10.
XD2(1,2) = 1000.
XD2(2,2) = -6.
XD2(1,3) = 1000.
XD2(2,3) = 0.
```

The subroutine DEFILL is used to place the previous values of SV(1,1) and SV(1,2) in the corresponding data areas for later retrieval.
The subroutine EVENT is as follows:

```
C        Events
C        ======
1        SV(1,1) = 10000.
         SV(1,2) = 1000.
C
         XD1(1,1) = 10000.
         XD1(2,1) = -10.
         XD1(1,2) = 10000.
         XD1(2,2) = -6.
         XD1(1,3) = 10000.
         XD1(2,3) = 0.
C
         XD2(1,1) = 1000.
         XD2(2,1) = -10.
         XD2(1,2) = 1000.
         XD2(2,2) = -6.
         XD2(1,3) = 1000.
         XD2(2,3) = 0.
```

```
C
        CALL DEFILL(1,1,XD1,3,*9999)
        CALL DEFILL(1,2,XD2,3,*9999)
        CALL BEGIN(1,*9999)
        CALL REPRT7
        RETURN
```

Notes:

   * The call of REPRT7 is used to check that the previous   initial values have been transferred correctly.

   * It is to be noted that the arrays XD1 and XD2 must be dimensioned by the user in the subroutine EVENT:

   DIMENSION XD1(2,3), XD2(2,3)

   * The matrix which contains previous initial values consists
   of two rows and a number of columns equal to the number of
   previous values.   The first row of the array contains the
   values of SV and DV to be retrieved, and the second row the
   corresponding times.

Negative times are normally not allowed in the   simulator GPSS-
FORTRAN Version 3.

The exception is the initialisation of delay variables.   The
reason for this exception is that it allows the simulation to
begin at T = 0., independent of the delay times. This means that,
as usual, the event NE = 1 can be scheduled at time T = 0.:

   CALL ANNOUN(1,0.,*9999)

The variables SV(1,1) and SV(1,2) must be declared as delay
variables if previous system states are to be recorded. This is
done by including two additional records in the input data file.
In the example host parasite model VI, they are as follows:

DELA; 1; 1; 10./
DELA; 1; 2; 10./

8.6.3 Combining the Data Areas for Delayed Variables

The data area for recording the previous values during a
simulation has fixed dimensions for all delayed variables.

The dimension can be changed by the user by modifiying the array
bound 'LDEVAR'. See appendix A4 "Array bounds". It is possible
that the size of the data areas is not sufficient to record the
previous states during a simulation. This can happen when the
activation of many discrete activities leeds to the inclusion of
additional variables.

If the data area for recording previous states is full, the
values for neighbouring states are replaced by an average value.

Two values which represent a discontinuity and have occurred at
the same time are not combined and remain unchanged. Both values
are necessary to interpolate correctly near a discontinuity. See
volume 1, chapter 2.2.6 "Delays".

The data areas for recording previous states are arranged as a ring buffer. All states which are older than T - TAUMAX can be overwritten.

It is therefore only necessary to combine values if more states are computed during the time interval T - TAUMAX than can be stored in the data areas with size LDEVAR.

The process of combining values can be repeated during a simulation until there are only values stored which cannot be combined.

Note:

  * The combining of previous values can be traced. This is controlled by the variables IPRINT or JPRINT (22). See volume 1, chapter 5.3.2, "The Use of IPRINT and JPRINT to Control the Protocol".

8.6.4 Initialisation of the Delayed Variables

It is best to initalise the delayed variables with the values which occurred at the previous times.

The accurate initial values are often not known. The use of the initial values of the continuous variables at the time of the simulation should be used to initialise the delayed variables. This is done in the host parasite model VI.

Example:

* The following is a possible initialisation of the delayed variables:

SV(1,1) = 10000.
SV(1,2) = 1000.

XD1(1,1) = 10000.
XD1(2,1) = -10.
XD1(1,2) = 10000.
XD1(2,2) = 0.

XD2(1,1) = 1000.
XD2(2,1) = -10.
XD2(1,2) = 1000.
XD2(2,2) = 0.

A discontinuity in the values of the delayed variables normally leads to a discontinuity in the value of a differential quotient at a later time. As this discontinuity of the differential quotient is normally inside an integration step, the relative error becomes very large. It is therefore arranged that the integration step ends at such a discontinuity.

The simulator is responsible for discontinuities in the value of delayed variables which are caused by events during the simulation. It prevents integration past such a discontinuity. The user must prevent discontinuities which can be caused by initialisation.

Note:

* It is recommended that the course of the integration in the
region of time around

T = simulation start time + TAU

is checked very carefully using the trace control variable
IPRINT. It should be rememebered that the values at the beginning of the simulation must occur twice: firstly as the initial values of the variables SV and secondly it must be recorded using the array XD1 or XD2.

8.6.5 The Results

The plot below shows the variation with time of the number of
hosts or parasites. It can be seen that it differs from the host
parasite model I in that the period of the oscillations is longer
and that the system is no longer stable. Because of the delays
the system continues to oscilate.

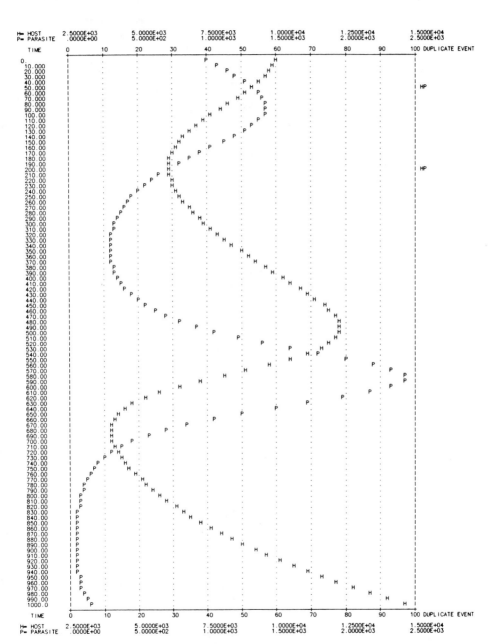

8.6.6 Examples

The examples show the use of delayed variables.

* Example 1

It is assumed in the host parasite model VI that the delay TAU is
the same for hosts and parasites. This means that a parasite is
born at the same time as a host dies.
The model can be extended by allowing different time delays for
hosts and parasites. This means that a host lives for some time
after the birth of a new parasite from that which has attacked
it.   The complementary case is also possible: Some time after
the death of a host, a new parasite is born.
The host parasite model VI is to be extended so that:

delay for hosts: TAUX = 15.
delay for parasites: TAUY = 8.

* Example 2

The data areas for the recorded values of the continuous
variables SV(1,1) and SV(1,2) are to be printed at intervals of
200. time units.

Note:

   * A second event NE = 2 is required which calls the subroutine REPRT7 and reschedules itself at time T + 200.

* Example 3

Example 2 is to repeated with a constant step size of 1.01.   The
simulation is to end at TEND = 200.

Note:

   * A constant step size is achieved by setting the allowable
   relative error to a very large value and the maximum step
   size for integration to 1.01.

* Example 4

Example 3 is to be repeated, however including the reduction of
the hosts by 100 every 50. time units.

Note:

   * The additional events have actually no great effect. They are
   only intended to show how recorded pairs of values are treated
   at discontinuities.

* Example 5

Example 4 is to be repeated including the call of REPRT7
immediately before and immediately after combining the recorded
values instead of calling it every 200. time units.
In addition, the trace indicator will be set as follows:
     JPRINT(22) = 1

References

/1/ Pritsker, A.; The GASP IV Simulation Language,
John Wiley & Sons, 1974

/2/ Williams, R. B.; System Analysis and Simulation in Ecology,
Academic Press, 1971

/3/ Roberts, Nancy; Introduction to Computer Simulation, A
System Dynamics Modelling Approach,
Addison Wesley, 1983

/4/ Niemeyer, B.; System Simulation, Akademische
Verlagsgesellschaft, 1975

/5/ Forrester, Jay W.; World Dynamics,
Wright Allen Press, Inc.

Appendix

A 1   FORTRAN Features 194

A 1.1   File Handling. 194
A 1.2   Computed GOTO. 196
A 1.3   Treatment of Characters. 196
A 1.4   Multiple Exits from Subroutines. 197

A 2   Handling the Simulator 198

A 3   Data Areas 201

A 3.1   Alphabetic List of Variables in the Common List. 201
A 3.2   Multidimensional Arrays. 212

A 4   Array Bounds 225

A 4.1   Array Bounds 225
A 4.2   Notes. 228
A 4.3   Replacement of the Variables 229

A 5   Random Numbers 230

A 5.1   The Double Word Random Number Generator. 230
A 5.2   The Version with Small Multipliers 233
A 5.3   The Version with Large Multipliers 234

A 6   User Programs. 236

A 7   Subroutines. 256

A 1 FORTRAN Features

GPSS-FORTRAN Version 3 uses certain advanced facilities of the FORTRAN language which are described below. The reader is advised to refer to the appropiate sections of a FORTRAN text book.

A 1.1 File Handling

FORTRAN 77 provides statements for handling files. GPSS-FORTRAN Version 3 uses OPEN and CLOSE commands to open and close files.

The OPEN statement has the following form:

    OPEN (olist)

where olist can contain the following parts:

[UNIT=] u   The file number u (a non-negative INTEGER expression is defined. The phrase UNIT= can be omitted if u is the first element in the list.

IOSTAT = ios   The INTEGER variable ios is assigned the value 0 if the open statement has been executed without error, otherwise a machine dependent value larger than zero is assigned.

ERR = n   If an error occurs when opening a file, then control is transferred to the statement with label n.

FILE = fn   The CHARACTER expression fn is the name of the file with number u.

STATUS = sta   The CHARACTER expression sta is the current status of the file. Possible values are:
                 OLD   an already existing file
                 NEW   a new file
                 SCRATCH   an unnamed scratch file which is no longer available after completion of the program or after a CLOSE statement.
                 UNKNOWN   the status of the file is unknown and is to be determined by the system.

ACCESS = acc   The CHARACTER expression acc determines whether access is direct or sequential.
                 Possible values are:
                 DIRECT: direct access
                 SEQUENTIAL: sequential access

FORM = fm   The CHARACTER expression fm determines whether the file access is formatted or has free format.
                 Possible values are:
                 FORMATTED: formatted data transfer
                 UNFORMATTED: free format data transfer

RECL = rl   The nonegative INTEGER expression rl is the record length of a direct access file.

BLANK = blnk   The CHARACTER expression blnk defines how a blank
               character in a numeric record is to be interpreted.
               NULL: blank characters are ignored
               ZERO: blank characters are interpreted as zeros

The file number u must be given. The record length must be given
for direct access files. All other attributes are optional.

The default settings for parameters STATUS, ACCESS, FORM and
BLANK are:

     STATUS = 'UNKNOWN'
     ACCESS = 'SEQUENTIAL'
     FORM   = 'FORMATTED'
     BLANK = 'NULL'

The default setting for files with direct access (ACCESS =
'DIRECT') is:

     FORM = 'UNFORMATTED'

The length of a formatted record is identical to the number of
characters which the record, as described, contains. The record
length of unformatted length is provided in maschine dependent
units e.g. machine words.

Example:

a) OPEN (5,FILE='XYZ',BLANK='ZERO',STATUS='OLD')
The already existing file XYZ is assigned the file number 5.   The
file is sequential and formatted. Blanks are interpreted as zeros
when inputting numeric data.

b) OPEN (8,STATUS='SCRATCH', FORM='UNFORMATTED')
An unformatted scratch file with file number 8 is opened. Access
to the file is sequential. The file is erased at the latest upon
termination of the program.

c) OPEN (6, FILE='OTTO', ACCESS='DIRECT', RECL=80,
         STATUS='NEW', FORM='FORMATTED')
A new file called OTTO is defined. It allows direct access to
records with a maximum length of 80 characters. The data
transferred is formatted.

A CLOSE statement is used to close the connection between a file
and file number during program execution. The file number can
subsequently be assigned to another file. The file (if it still
exists) can also be subsequently assigned a new number.

A CLOSE statement is as follows:

     CLOSE (clist)

where clist can contain the following:

[UNIT=] u   !
                  !
IOSTAT = ios   >   These parameters have the same meaning as
                  !   in the open statement.
ERR = n   !

STATUS = sta   The   CHARACTER expression sta can have the
               following values:
               KEEP: The file remains in existence.
               DELETE: The file is deleted.

If the close list does not contain a status clause, then:

               STATUS = 'DELETE'   for SCRATCH files
               STATUS = 'KEEP'   for all other files

STATUS = 'KEEP' is not allowed for SCRATCH files.

Example: CLOSE (5, STATUS = 'DELETE')

The file with file number 5 is deleted.

Examples of the files which are required in GPSS-FORTRAN Version
3 can be found in appendix A2 "Model construction".

A 1.2 Computed GOTO

The computed GOTO statement transfers control to one of a number
of statements depending on the value of the integer I.

     GOTO (S1,S2,S3,....,SN), I
     S1,S2,S3,....,SN are statement labels

If I has the value 1, control is transfered to the statement
whose label number is the first value in the list.

In GPSS-FORTRAN Version 3 the integer variable I contains the
label of the statement to which control will be transferred. This
is possible using a computed GOTO statement, if the number I is
placed in the i'th position in the list of statement numbers.

In GPSS-FORTRAN Version 3 the list of statement labels must
consist of consecutive integers starting with 1.

A 1.3 Treatment of Characters

FORTRAN 77 allows variables of type CHARACTER. This allows
character strings to be dealt with conveniently. However, older
versions of FORTRAN do not contain the variable type CHARACTER.
Characters must be stored rather awkwardly in variables of type
REAL or INTEGER. There are two ways to store a character string
in a variable of type REAL.

a) using a DATA statement
b) reading the variables

GPSS-FORTRAN Version 3 uses FORTRAN 77 which accepts the type
CHARACTER. To facilitate the conversion of the simulator to older
FORTRAN Compilers all variables of type CHARACTER contain 4
characters.

Example:
CHARACTER*4 TEXT

A 1.4 Multiple Exits from Subroutines

Normally the statement following a subroutine call is the statement to which control is to be transferred on exit from the subroutine.
It is possible to include specially marked statement labels in the parameter list to which control will be returned on exit from the subroutine.

The selection of the address to which control is transferred on exit from the subroutine is made by special RETURN statements.

* Example:

The parameters of the subroutine SEIZE is as follows:

        CALL SEIZE(NFA,ID,*9000)

If a transaction can occupy a facility, the section 'Occupy' of the subroutine SEIZE, which is ended by the return statement, is executed. This causes exit from the subroutine. Control is transferred to the statement following the subroutine call CALL SEIZE.

If a transaction is to be placed in a queue because the facility is occupied, the section 'Block' of the subroutine SEIZE is executed. The statement RETURN1 transfers control to the statement in the calling program which has the first specially marked statement label in the parameter list. In the previous example, this means that control is transferred to the statement with label 9000.

A 2 Handling the Simulator

The following steps are necessary to prepare a model so that it can be run on a computer using GPSS-FORTRAN Version 3:

* Model implementation

GPSS-FORTRAN Version 3 consists of two parts: the user programs and the system subroutines. The user programs contain the model. They include the FORTRAN main program and the six subroutines ACTIV, CHECK, EVENT, STATE, DETECT and TEST.

The user programs can be extended by further subroutines which are provided by the user, e.g. DYNPR which determines the dynamic priorities or the subroutines PLANI, PLANO, POLI, STRATA, STRATF and INTE.

The user must write the statements in the user programs which describe the model.

* Compilation

Then the user program must be translated by a FORTRAN compiler. Since the system subroutines are not normally altered by the user and are the same for all models, it is recommended that the system subroutines by compiled separately. The compiled user programs and the compiled system subroutines must then be linked.

* Logical device numbers for input and output

The device numbers for input and output must be defined. There is a difference here between batch and interactive operation, see volume 2, chapter 7.4, "Modes of operation".

In batch mode (XMODUS = 0), the data records are read in from a file with the name DATAIN.
In batch mode, the data is written to a file with the name DATAOUT.

The logical device numbers used to access these two files can be selected by the user. How this is done is described in section 1 under the heading 'Setting channel numbers for input and output'.

The default values are as follows:

input: UNIT1 = 14
output: UNIT2 = 15

In dialogue, the terminal is used for input and output. The logical numbers for terminal input and output must be determined. This is done using the variables XUNIT1 and XUNIT2.
The default values are as follows:

XUNIT3 = 5
XUNIT4 = 6

In addition, the interactive user can request that the results
are written to a file from which they can subsequently be
printed. In this case, the data is output as in batch operation
in accordance with the default setting, to the file DATAOUT with
the logical device number UNIT2 = 15.

The data representing pictures to be displayed on a graphical
output device are written to a file with the name GRAPHDAT and
the logical device number UNIT5. The default setting is:

UNIT5 = 7   (file for graphical output)

The logical device numbers for the scratch files are similarly
specified. The default values are as follows:

UNIT6 = 11   (Scratch file)
UNIT7 = 12   (Save file)
UNIT8 = 20   (Scratch file)

Each file must be opened with the corresponding logical device
number.

Note:

   * The correspondence between file and logical device number can
   be altered by the user. To do this, the values of the variables
   in the section 'Setting channel numbers for input and output'
   must be modified.

* Declaring the files

All necessary files must be opened in section 1 of the framework.
There are three types of files:
Input and output files
Scratch and save files
Plot files

When input or output files are opened, files are declared
corresponding to the logical device numbers selected by the user
for input and output. The default setting is as follows:

```
C
C     OPEN INPUT AND OUTPUT FILES
C     ===========================
      OPEN(UNIT1,FILE = 'DATAIN',ACCESS = 'SEQUENTIAL',
     +FORM = 'FORMATTED')
      OPEN(UNIT2,FILE = 'DATAOUT',ACCESS = 'SEQUENTIAL',
     +FORM = 'FORMATTED')
C
      OPEN(XUNIT3,FILE = 'INPUT')
      OPEN(XUNIT4,FILE = 'OUTPUT')
```

Example:

* The logical device number XUNIT3 = 5 for terminal input is assigned in section 1 under the heading "Setting of channel numbers for input and output". The corresponding file should be given the following name "INPUT".

The file GRAPHDAT contains data representing pictures to be displayed on a graphical terminal.

```
C
C      OPEN FILE FOR GRAPHICS
C
       OPEN(UNIT5,FILE=GRADAT,ACCESS='SEQUENTIAL',FORM=
      +'FORMATTED')
```

In addition, 2 scratch files and a save file are required.

The scratch files are used for intermediate storage of data. The user can store the state of simulation model in the save file, in order to read it in later and continue with the simulation run.

The default values are as follows:

```
C
C      OPEN SCRATCH AND SAVE FILES
C      ===========================
       OPEN(UNIT6,FILE = 'SCRAT2',ACCESS = 'DIRECT',FORM =
      +'UNFORMATTED',RECL = 101)
       OPEN(UNIT7,FILE = 'SAVED',ACCESS = 'SEQUENTIAL',
      +FORM = 'UNFORMATTED')
       OPEN(UNIT8,FILE = 'SCRAT3',ACCESS = 'SEQUENTIAL',
      +FORM = 'UNFORMATTED')
```

Plot files are opened to store plots. Data is collected during the simulation run in these files and can be plotted later.

The PLO1 record is used to specify the logical device number for each plot. See volume 2, chapter 7.1.1, "The input data records".

The default setting defines two files for plots. If the user requires further plots, the files used must also be opened.

The default setting is as follows:

```
C      OPEN PLOT FILES
C      ===============
       OPEN(21,FILE = 'PLOT1',ACCESS = 'SEQUENTIAL',
      +FORM = 'UNFORMATTED')
       OPEN(22,FILE = 'PLOT2',ACCESS = 'SEQUENTIAL',
      +FORM = 'UNFORMATTED')
```

Note:

* The scratch files and the save file are used by GPSS-FORTRAN Version 3. They should not be called by the user.

If the user requires his own scratch files, then he should declare them.

A 3 Data Areas

The most important variables are described here.

Note:

  * The user may only use variables in the user programs which have not already been declared in GPSS-FORTRAN Version 3.

The variables declared in GPSS-FORTRAN Version 3 are listed in the COMMON blocks. In addition the variable ICONT is used in the main program. All other variables in the main program and subprograms are local. These names are available to the user.

A 3.1 Alphabetic List of Variables in the COMMON List

ACTIVL("TX1",2) transaction activation array
COMMON/TXS/
The transaction activation array contains the state of the transaction and the number of the label to which control is to be transferred when the transaction is activated.

ASM("FAM","ASM") assembly array
COMMON/FAM/
The assembly array contains the counters for the assembly stations which record how many members of a family have already been eliminated.

BHEAD("STAT") head of queue of blocked transactions
COMMON/TYP/
All transactions which are blocked at a station form a queue. BHEAD contains the index of the head of the queue. The chaining of the transactions is recorded in CHAINA.

BIN("BIN",8) bin array
COMMON/BIN/
The bin array contains all information required for statistical analysis of the behauviour of the queues.

BINST("BIN",5) bin statistics array
COMMON/BIN/
BINST contains the current values of the mean queue length, mean waiting time, confidence interval and settling time for each bin.

CHAINA("TX1",2) chaining of the transaction schedule
COMMON/TXS/
Transactions can be in the queue of scheduled transactions or the queue of blocked transactions. The array CHAINA contains the pointers belonging to both queues.

CHAINC("BIN") chaining of the bin schedule
COMMON/CON/
For every bin there is a time at which statistical material is to
be collected for the determination of the confidence interval.
The bins are chained according to the chronological order of
their processing. The pointers are stored in CHAINC.

CHAINE("NSET") chaining of the set schedule
COMMON/EQU/
For each set there is a time at which the next integration step
is to be performed. The sets are chained in the corresponding
chronological order. The pointers are held in CHAINE.

CHAINM("NPLO") chaining of the monitor schedule
COMMON/PLO/
There is a time for each plot at which the values of the
variables to be plotted are to be recorded. The monitor calls
required are chained in chronological order. The pointers are
held in CHAINM.

CHAINS("SRC") chaining of the source schedule
COMMON/SRC/
For each source there is a time at which a new transaction is to
be generated. The sources are chained on the corresponding
chronological order. The pointers are held in CHAINS.

CHAINV("EVT") chaining of the event schedule
COMMON/EVT/
For every event there is a time at which it is to be activated.
The events are chained in chronological order. The pointers are
held in CHAINV.

CLEV confidence index
COMMON/CON/
The confidence index is the probability that the required mean is
within the required interval.

CON("BIN",500) confidence array
COMMON/CON/
500 components are reserved in the confidence array for each bin.
The components contain the samples used to determine the mean and
the confidence interval.

CONFL("BIN,5) bin schedule array
COMMON/CON/
Samples are obtained at regular intervals for each bin in order
to calculate the mean and the confidence interval. The bin
schedule array contains the information necessary for this.

DCONST("30") array of additive constants for random numbers
COMMON/DRN/
Each random number generator contains an additive constant for
the multiplicative congruence method.

DEVAR("NDVAR",2,"LDVAR") storage for delayed variables
COMMON/DEL/
Past values of delay variables are stored in DEVAR.

DFACT("30") array of multipliers for random numbers
COMMON/DRN/
Each random number generator contains a multiplier for the
multiplicative congruence method.

DMODUL   base for random numbers
COMMON/DRN/
All random number generators have the common base DMODUL.

DRN("30") array of random numbers
COMMON/DRN/
Each random number generator possesses an element which contains
the last random number generated.

DV("NSET","NV") current value of the differential coefficients
COMMON/EQU/
DV contains the differential coefficients of the continuous
variables SV with respect to time.

DVLAST("NSET","NV") previous differential coefficient
COMMON/EQU/
DVLAST contains the differential coefficient of the continuous
variables SV at the end of the previous set.

EPS   discriminant
COMMON/TIM/
EPS is a very small number which defines the width of an
interval. All numbers of type real within the interval EPS are
represented in the computer by the same number. This is due to
the way in which numbers are represented in the computer. Two
numbers whose difference is less than EPS are treated as equal.

EQUL("NSET",4) set schedule array
COMMON/EQU/
The set schedule array contains the information necessary to
perform the next integration step for each set.

EVENTL("EVT") event activation time
COMMON/EVT/
The event list contains the scheduled activation time of each
event in the event schedule.

FAC("FAC",3) facility array
COMMON/FAC/
Each facility is represented by a row in the facility array. This
contains information about the state of the facility.

FAM("FAM",2) family array
COMMON/FAM/
The family array contains the information necessary to describe a
family.

GATHT("GATT") gather array for transactions
COMMON/GAT/
There is a counter for each gather station for transactions which
records how many transactions have already reached it.

GATHF("FAN","GATF") gather array for families
COMMON/GAT/
There is a counter for each gather station and each family, which
records how many members of a family have already arrived.

ICONT continuous simulation
COMMON/EQU/
ICONT indicates whether the model has a continuous part.

IDELAY delay indicator
COMMON/DEL/
IDELAY indicates whether the model contains delayed variables. It
is set in subroutine INPUT if there is a DELA record.

IDEMA("NDVAR",2) delay array
COMMON/DEL/
IDEMA indicates where delayed variables are recorded in DEVAR.

IDPNTR("NDVAR",2) delay pointers
COMMON/DEL/
Two pointers are used to record delayed variables in the array
DEVAR or to access values from an earlier time.

IFLAG("NSET","NCRO") crossing flag
COMMON/EQU/
IFLAG(NSET,NCRO) is assigned the value 1 when a crossing has been
found in an integration step.

IFLAGP("NSET","NCRO") traces indicator for crossing flags.
COMMON/EQU/
IFLAGP records which flags have already been dealt with for
output trace by IPRINT or JPRINT.

INTMA("NSET",8) integration array
COMMON/EQU/
The integration array contains information required for
integration. This is provided by the user via the input data
record INTI.

INTSTA("NSET",4) array for integration statistics
COMMON/EQU/
Statistical information about the integration of the sets is
collected in INTSTA. INTSTA can be output using the subroutine
REPRT6.

IPRINT general trace control
COMMON/TIM/
A trace is output for every state transition if IPRINT is equal
to one.

ITXT number of rows of text
COMMON/INP/
Number of rows of text in the title of the simulation run.

IV("VAR") value of an integer variable
COMMON/VAR/
IV contains the value of an integer variable which has been input
in free format.

JEPS EPS indicator
COMMON/INP/
JEPS indicates whether the value of the disciminant EPS has been
input by the user or assigned by the simulator.

JFLAG("NSET","NCRO") crossing position flag
COMMON/EQU/
JFLAG indicates whether a variable is above or below the crossing
boundary.

JFLAGL("NSET","NCRO") previous crossing position flag
COMMON/EQU/
JFLAG records the value of the crossing position flag during the
previous integration step. It is used to locate a crossing.

JPRINT(25) selective trace control
COMMON/TIM/
JPRINT is used to cause a trace of a particular state transition
to be output.

LHEAD(6) heads of linked lists of the flow control
COMMON/TYP/
The six flow control lists are chained in chronological order.
LHEAD contains the heads of each list.

LSE row index in the multifacility array
COMMON/MFA/
Each element of a multifacility is assigned one row of the
multifacility element array. LSE selects the row which is being
currently processed.

LSL   row index in the source array
COMMON/SRC/
LSL contains the row number in the source array of a source which
generates a transaction.

LSM   row index of the segment array
COMMON/STO/
LSM contains the index of a row in the segment array.

LTX   row index of the active transaction
COMMON/TXS/
LTX is the row index in the transaction array and the activation
list of the currently active transaction.

MBV("MFAC")   multifacility basis array
COMMON/MFA/
MBV contains the row index of the first element of each
multifacility in the SE array.

MFAC("MFAC",2)   multifacility array
COMMON/MFA/
MFAC records the capacity and the level of occupation of the
multifacilities.

MONITL("NPLO") monitor activation times
COMMON/PLO/
The MONITL contains the times at which the values of the
continuous variables are recorded for plotting.

NCOMP("NDVAR") number of times delayed variables have been
compressed.
COMMON/DEL/
The data area used to store delayed variables is reduced by
combining neighbouring values if its size is insufficient. NCOMP
records how many times this has happened during a simulation run.

NDELAY number of delayed variables
COMMON/INP/
NDELAY is the number of delay data records read.

NTXC transaction counter
COMMON/SRC/
NTXC counts the number of transactions generated.

NUNIT1 logical device number for input
COMMON/FIL/
The actual logical device number for input is determined by UNIT1
or XUNIT1.

NUNIT2 logical device number for output
COMMON/FIL/
The actual logical device number for output is determined by
UNIT2 or XUNIT4.

PLAMA("MFAC",2) plan array
COMMON/PLA/
The plan array contains the index of the plans according to which
the elements of a multifacility are occupied or freed.

PLOMA1("NPLO",16) plot array 1
COMMON/PLO/
PLOMA1 contains information about the variables to be plotted.
Its elements are assigned by the user via the input data record
PLO1.

PLOMA2("NPLO",5) plot array 2
COMMON/PLO/
PLOMA2 contains information about the format of the plots, e.g.
the scaling of the x and y axes. Its elements are assigned by the
user via the input data record PLO2.

PLOMA3("NPLO",18) plot array 3
COMMON/PLO/
PLOMA3 defines the symbols which represent the variables in the
plots. Its elements are assigned by the user via the input data
record PLO3.

POL("POL",3) policy array
COMMON/POL/
POL defines the policy according to which the queue at a station
is processed.

POOL("POOL",2) pool array
COMMON/POO/
POOL contains the capacity and the current level of occupation of
all non-addressable storages.

RT user clock
COMMON/TIM/
RT is a clock which can be reset by the user to measure time
intervals during the simulation run.

RV("VAR") real variable value
COMMON/VAR/
RV contains the value of a real variable which has been input
in free format.

SBM("STO",2)
COMMON/STO/
Each addressable storage occupies a section in the segment array.
SBM contains the row index of the first location of a storage and

its capacity.

SE("SE",3) service element array
COMMON/MFA/
The SE array records the state of every service element.

SM("SM",2) segment array
COMMON/STO/
Each row of the segment array records the occupation of a
location of an addressable storage.

SOURCL("SRC",3) source array
COMMON/SRC/
The source array contains the characteristics of a source.

STRAMA("STO",2) strategy array
COMMON/STR/
STRAMA defines how an addressable storage is to be allocated or
freed.

SV("NSET","NV") continuous variables
COMMON/EQU/
SV contains the values of the continuous variables at time T.

SVIN input of the state of the system
COMMON/MOD/
The user specifies whether the values of the system variables are
to be read in after an interruption.

SVLAST("NSET","NV") previous values of continuous variables
COMMON/EQU/
SVLAST contains the values of the continuous variables SV after
the previous integration step.

SVOUT save the system state
COMMON/MOD/
The user specifies whether the system variables are to be output
to a file so that they can be subsequently read in again.

T simulation clock
COMMON/TIM/
T is the current value of the simulation clock.

TAB("TAB",4,"NTAB") frequency array
COMMON/TAB/
Frequency arrays can be declared by the user to collect
statistical data.

TAUMAX("NDVAR") maximum delay
COMMON/DEL/
The maximum delay must be specified for every delayed variable.
The values of delayed variables held are all past values
occurring since the current time T minus TAUMAX, the maximum
delay.

TBUSY   continuation indicator
COMMON/TIM/
TBUSY indicates whether further state transitions other than
calls of CONF and MONITR are scheduled for execution by FLOWC.

TCLEAR   empty indicator for DEVAR
COMMON/DEL/
All elements of the array DEVAR which are unused and therefore
available for the storage of past values of continuous variables
are initialised with TCLEAR.

TCOND("NCOND") condition indicator
COMMON/TIM/
The condition indicator is used to ensure that a condition is
only checked once at a particular time. The time at which the
condition was last checked is entered for each condition.

TDELA("NSET") indicator of a discontinuity of a delayed variable
COMMON/DEL/
If a discontinuity of a delayed variable occurs within an
integration step, the indicator TDELA is set.

TEND end of simulation time
COMMON/TIM/
TEND is the time at which the simulation run is to be ended.

THEAD(6) time of next activation of flow control schedules
COMMON/TYP/
The six flow control schedules contain elements which are chained
in the order in which they are to be activated. THEAD contains
the times at which the first element of each schedule is to be
activated.

TTEST test indicator
COMMON/TYP/
The test indicator shows when the conditions are to be tested. If
TTEST is set the flow control calls the subroutine TEST.

TX("TX1","TX2") transaction array
COMMON/TXS/
Each transaction occupies one row in the transaction array which
contains all the attributes which characterise the transaction.

TXMAX   maximum number of transactions
COMMON/SRC/
TXMAX is the maximum number of transactions which can be
generated during a simulation run. The simulation run is ended
when TXMAX is reached.

TXT(3,19) rows of text
COMMON/TXT/
TXT contains the rows of text for the title of the simulation
run.

TYPE(15) type array
COMMON/TYP/
TYPE is used to calculate the station index K.

UNIT1 logical device number for input
COMMON/FIL/
UNIT1 is the logical device number with which the file DATAIN
containing the input data records is accessed.

UNIT2 logical device number for output
COMMON/FIL/
UNIT2 is the logical device number under which the file DATAOUT
containing the results is accessed.

UNIT5 logical device number for GRADAT file
COMMON/FIL/
UNIT5 is the logical device number under which the file GRADAT
can be accessed. The logical device numbers UNIT6, UNIT7 and
UNIT8 are similarly used to access the files SCRAT2, SAVED and
SCRATCH4. See volume 2, appendix A 2, "Model construction: Logi-
cal device numbers for input and output".

USERCT("UCHT",2) user chain array
COMMON/UCH/
The user chain array contains for each user chain the number of
transactions which have already arrived and the number which have
been removed.

USERCF("FAM","UCHF",2) User chain array for families
COMMON/UCH/
The user chain array for families contains for each user chain
the number of members of each family which have already arrived
and the number which have been removed.

VNAMEI("ZVAR") identifier array of type integer
COMMON/SYM/
The identifier of variables of type integer which have been read
in in free format are stored in VNAMEI.

VNAMER("ZVAR") name array of type real
COMMON/SUM/
The identifier of variables of type real which have been read in
in the free format are stored in VNAMER.

XFORM   format indicator
COMMON/FIL/
XFORM indicates whether the width of the output is 80 or 132
characters.

XMODUS operational mode
COMMON/MOD/
XMODUS is assigned by the user to indicate if batch or
interactive operation is required.

XUNIT3 logical device number for interactive input
COMMON/FIL/
XUNIT3 is the logical device number with which the input file
INPUT is accessed. Input from the terminal is obtained from
INPUT.

XUNIT4 logical device number for interactive output
COMMON/FIL/

XUNIT4 is the logical device number with which the file OUTPUT is
accessed. Output to the terminal is sent to OUTPUT.

YMODUS mode of operation
COMMON/MOD/
YMODUS is set by the user to indicate if real time operation is
required by the user.

Notes:

   * All variables from COMMON/SYS/ begin with Z. They are used to
   dimension the model. Their main function is to provide the
   upper bounds of the controlled variables used in loops. They
   are assigned values in the subroutine SYSVAR.

   * The type of some variables is explicitly declared. Explicit
   type declarations occur in the main program and in the subroutines in which these variables occur. If the type of a variable
   is not explicitly declared, then its type is implicit in the
   first letter of the name of the variable.

A 3.2 Multidimensional Arrays

Appendix A 3.2 lists the most important multidimensional arrays.

These are:

* Flow control
Head of scheduled lists THEAD, LHEAD
Event schedule EVENTL, CHAINV
Source schedule SOURCL, CHAINS
Transaction schedule ACTIVL, CHAINA
Bin schedule CONFL, CHAINC
Monitor schedule MONITL, CHAINM
Set schedule EQUL, CHAINE

* Transactions and families
Transaction array TX
Family array FAM

* Queue management
Type array TYP
Policy array POL

* Facilities
Facility array FAC

* Pools
Pool array POOL

* Storages
Storage basis array SBM
Segment array SM
Strategy array STRAMA

* Multifacilities
Multifacility array MFAC
Multifacility element array SE
Plan array PLANA

* Gather stations
Gather counter for transactions GATHT
Gather counter for families GATHF

* User chains
User chains for transactions USERCT
User chains for families USERF

* Assembly stations
Assembly array ASM

* Bins
Bin array BIN
Bin statistics BINSTA
Confidence array CON

* Integration of continuous systems
Integration array INTMA
Integration statistics INTSTA

* Plots
Plot arrays PLOMA1, PLOMA2, PLOMA3

* Trace control
Trace array JPRINT

HEAD INDICATORS OF THE SCHEDULES

```
THEAD(6)                      LHEAD(6)
---------------------         ---------------------
  | TIME OF NEXT      |       |                     |
1 | EVENT             |       | POINTER TO EVENTL   |
  |                   |       |                     |
---------------------         ---------------------
  | TIME OF NEXT      |       |                     |
2 | SOURCE            |       | POINTER TO SOURCL   |
  | ACTIVATION        |       |                     |
---------------------         ---------------------
  | TIME OF NEXT      |       |                     |
3 | TRANSACTION       |       | POINTER TO ACTIVL   |
  | ACTIVATION        |       |                     |
---------------------         ---------------------
  | TIME OF NEXT      |       |                     |
4 | CALL OF CONF      |       | POINTER TO CONFL    |
  |                   |       |                     |
---------------------         ---------------------
  | TIME OF NEXT      |       |                     |
5 | MONITOR CALL      |       | POINTER TO MONITL   |
  |                   |       |                     |
---------------------         ---------------------
  | TIME OF NEXT      |       |                     |
6 | INTEGRATION       |       | POINTER TO EQUL     |
  | CALL OF EQUAT     |       |                     |
---------------------         ---------------------
```

EVENT ACTIVATION TIMES   SOURCE ARRAY

```
EVENTL("EVT")                       SOURCL ("SRC",3)
---------------------               ---------------------
  |                 |                 |                    |
  | TIME OF         |               1 | TIME OF            |
  | ACTIVATION      |                 | GENERATION         |
---------------------               ---------------------
                                      |                    |
EVENT CHAINING                      2 | LABEL              |
CHAINV ("EVT1")                       |                    |
---------------------               ---------------------
  | POINTER TO NEXT |                 | NUMBER OF          |
  | EVENT           |               3 | TRANSACTIONS TO BE |
  |                 |                 | GENERATED          |
---------------------               ---------------------
```

```
                                    SOURCE CHAINING
                                    CHAINS ("SRC")
                                    ---------------------
                                      | POINTER TO NEXT    |
                                      | SOURCE             |
                                      | ACTIVATION         |
                                    ---------------------
```

```
        TRANSACTION SCHEDULE              BIN SCHEDULE
        ACTIVL ("TX1",2)                 CONFL ("BIN",5)
        --------------------             --------------------
        | TIME OF ACTIV-    |            | TIME OF NEXT      |
     1  | ATION / BLOCKING  |        1   | CALL OF CONF      |
        | INDICATOR         |            |                   |
        --------------------             --------------------
        |                   |            |                   |
     2  | LABEL             |        2   | LENGTH OF INTER-  |
        |                   |            | VAL               |
        --------------------             --------------------
                                         | TOTAL TIME OF     |
        CHAINA ("TX1",2)             3   | TOKEN IN INTER-   |
        --------------------             | VAL (I-1)         |
        | POINTER TO        |            --------------------
     1  | NEXT              |            |                   |
        | ACTIVATION        |        4   | POINTER TO CON    |
        --------------------             |                   |
        | POINTER TO NEXT   |            --------------------
     2  | BLOCKED TRANS-    |            | INDICATOR OF      |
        | ACTION IN QUEUE   |        5   | AUTOMATIC         |
        --------------------             | DETERMINATION OF  |
                                         | INTERVALS         |
                                         --------------------


                                         BIN CHAINING
                                         CHAINC ("BIN")
        SET ARRAY                        --------------------
        EQUL ("NSET",4)                  | POINTER TO NEXT   |
        --------------------             | CALL              |
        | TIME OF NEXT      |            |                   |
     1  | INTEGRATION       |            --------------------
        |                   |
        --------------------
        |                   |
     2  | STEP SIZE         |            MONITOR SCHEDULE
        |                   |            MONITL ("NPLOT")
        --------------------             --------------------
        |                   |            | TIME OF NEXT      |
     3  | LOOK AHEAD        |            | ACTIVATION OF     |
        | INDICATOR         |            | MONITR            |
        --------------------             --------------------
        | TIME OF LAST      |
     4  | INTEGRATION       |            CHAINM ("NPLOT")
        |                   |            --------------------
        --------------------             | POINTER TO        |
                                         | NEXT CALL         |
        CHAINE ("NSET")                  |                   |
        --------------------             --------------------
        | POINTER TO        |
        | NEXT CALL         |
        |                   |
        --------------------
```

```
         TRANSACTION ARRAY              FAMILY ARRAY
         TX ("TX1","TX2")               FAM ("FAM",2)
         ---------------------          ---------------------
         | NUMBER OF         |          | NUMBER OF         |
      1  | TRANSACTIONS      |       1  | MEMBERS           |
         |                   |          |                   |
         ---------------------          ---------------------
         |                   |          | NUMBER OF LAST    |
      2  | DUPLICATE         |       2  | GENERATED         |
         | INDEX             |          | DUPLICATED        |
         ---------------------          ---------------------
         |                   |
      3  | LFAM              |
         |                   |
         ---------------------
         |                   |
      4  | PRIORITY          |
         |                   |
         ---------------------
         |                   |
      5  | LABEL FOR         |
         | PREEMPTION        |
         ---------------------
         |                   |
      6  | PROCESSING TIME   |
         | REMAINING         |
         ---------------------
         |                   |
      7  | RETURN INDICATOR  |
         |                   |
         ---------------------
         |                   |
      8  | TIME OF BLOCKING  |
         |                   |
         ---------------------
         |                   |
      9  | USER ATTRIBUTES   |
         |                   |
         ---------------------
         |                   |
         |         *         |
         |                   |
         |         *         |
         |                   |
         |         *         |
         |                   |
         ---------------------
         |                   |
  "TX2" | USER ATTRIBUTES   |
         |                   |
         ---------------------
```

```
      TYPE ARRAY                        POLICY ARRAY
      TYP(12)                           POL ("POL",3)
      ----------------------            ----------------------
      |                    |            |                    |
   1  | FIRST FACILITY     |         1  | TYPE OF STATION    |
      |                    |            |                    |
      ----------------------            ----------------------
      |                    |            |                    |
   2  | FIRST MULTI-       |         2  | INDEX OF TYPE      |
      | FACILITY           |            |                    |
      ----------------------            ----------------------
      |                    |            |                    |
   3  | FIRST POOL         |         3  | INDEX OF POLICY    |
      |                    |            |                    |
      ----------------------            ----------------------
      |                    |
   4  | FIRST STORAGE      |
      |                    |
      ----------------------
      |                    |
   5  | FIRST GATE         |            FACILITY ARRAY
      |                    |            FAC ("FAC",3)
      ----------------------            ----------------------
      | FIRST GATHER       |            | OCCUPATION         |
   6  | STATION OF TYPE 1  |         1  | INDICATOR          |
      |                    |            |                    |
      ----------------------            ----------------------
      | FIRST GATHER       |            | PREEMPTION         |
   7  | STATION OF TYPE 2  |         2  | INDICATOR          |
      |                    |            |                    |
      ----------------------            ----------------------
      | FIRST USER CHAIN   |            | PROCESSING         |
   8  | OF TYPE 1          |         3  | PHASE              |
      |                    |            |                    |
      ----------------------            ----------------------
      | FIRST TRIGGER      |
   9  | STATION OF TYPE 1  |
      |                    |
      ----------------------
      | FIRST USER CHAIN   |
  10  | OF TYPE 2          |            POOL ARRAY
      |                    |            POOL ("POOL",2)
      ----------------------            ----------------------
      | FIRST TRIGGER      |            |                    |
  11  | STATION OF TYPE 2  |         1  | LEVEL              |
      |                    |            |                    |
      ----------------------            ----------------------
      | FIRST MATCH        |            |                    |
  12  | STATION OF TYPE 2  |         2  | CAPACITY           |
      |                    |            |                    |
      ----------------------            ----------------------
```

```
    STORAGE BASE ARRAY              SEGMENT ARRAY
    SBM ("STO",2)                   SM ("SM",2)
    ---------------------           ---------------------
    | BEGINNING OF A    |           |                   |
1   | SEGMENT           |        1  | LENGTH            |
    |                   |           |                   |
    ---------------------           ---------------------
    | CAPACITY OF THE   |           |                   |
2   | STORAGE           |        2  | INDICATOR         |
    |                   |           |                   |
    ---------------------           ---------------------


    STRATEGY ARRAY
    STRAMA ("STO",2)
    ---------------------
    | OCCUPATION        |
1   | STRATEGY          |
    |                   |
    ---------------------
    | FREEING           |
2   | STRATEGY          |
    |                   |
    ---------------------


    MULTIFACILITY-ARRAY            SERVICE ELEMENT-ARRAY
    MFAC ("MFAC",2)                SE ("SE",3)
    ---------------------           ---------------------
    | NUMBER OF         |           | OCCUPATION        |
1   | OCCUPIED ELEMENTS |        1  | INDICATOR         |
    |                   |           |                   |
    ---------------------           ---------------------
    |                   |           | PREEMPTION        |
2   | CAPACITY          |        2  | INDICATOR         |
    |                   |           |                   |
    ---------------------           ---------------------
                                    | PROCESSING        |
                                 3  | PHASE             |
    PLAN-ARRAY                      |                   |
    PLANA ("MFAC",2)                ---------------------
    ---------------------
    | OCCUPATION        |
1   | PLAN              |
    |                   |
    ---------------------
    | FREEING           |
2   | PLAN              |
    |                   |
    ---------------------
```

```
                                       USER ARRAY FOR
        USER ARRAY                     FAMILIES
        USERCT ("UCHT",2)              USERCF ("FAM","UCHF",2)
        --------------------          --------------------
        | NUMBER OF TRANS- |          | NUMBER OF         |
      1 | ACTIONS IN USER  |        1 | TRANSACTIONS IN   |
        | CHAIN            |          | USER CHAIN        |
        --------------------          --------------------
        | COUNTER OF TRANS-|          | COUNTER OF        |
      2 | ACTIONS FETCHED  |        2 | TRANSACTIONS      |
        |                  |          | FETCHED           |
        --------------------          --------------------


                                       GATHER COUNTER FOR
        GATHER COUNTER                 FAMILIES
        GATHT ("GATT")                 GATHF ("FAM","GATF")
        --------------------          --------------------
        | NUMBER OF        |          | NUMBER OF TRANS-  |
      1 | TRANSACTIONS     |        1 | ACTIONS ARRIVED   |
        | ARRIVED          |          | FOR STATION 1     |
        --------------------          --------------------
                                      |                   |
                                      |         *         |
                                      |                   |
                                      |         *         |
                                      |                   |
                                      --------------------
                                      | NUMBER OF TRANS-  |
                              "GATF"  | ACTIONS ARRIVED   |
                                      | FOR STATION "GATF"|
                                      --------------------


                                       ASSEMBLY ARRAY
                                       ASM ("FAM","ASM")
                                      --------------------
                                      | NUMBER OF TRANS-  |
                                    1 | ACTIONS ARRIVED   |
                                      | FOR STATION 1     |
                                      --------------------
                                      |                   |
                                      |         *         |
                                      |                   |
                                      |         *         |
                                      |                   |
                                      --------------------
                                      | NUMBER OF TRANS-  |
                               "ASM"  | ACTIONS ARRIVED   |
                                      | FOR STATION "ASM" |
                                      --------------------
```

```
    BIN ARRAY                           BIN STATISTICS
    BIN ("BIN",8)                       BINSTA ("BIN",5)
    ---------------------              ---------------------
    |                   |              | MEAN TIME OF      |
 1  | CURRENT LENGTH    |           1  | OCCUPATION        |
    |                   |              |                   |
    ---------------------              ---------------------
    |                   |              | MEAN NUMBER OF    |
 2  | MAXIMUM LENGTH    |           2  | TOKENS IN BIN     |
    |                   |              |                   |
    ---------------------              ---------------------
    | NUMBER OF         |              | CONFIDENCE        |
 3  | ARRIVALS          |           3  | INTERVAL IN %     |
    |                   |              |                   |
    ---------------------              ---------------------
    | NUMBER OF         |              | DEVIATION DUE TO  |
 4  | DEPARTURES        |           4  | THE SETTLING      |
    |                   |              | PHASE             |
    ---------------------              ---------------------
    | NUMBER OF CALLS   |              | END OF SETTLING   |
 5  | OF ARRIVE         |           5  | PHASE             |
    |                   |              |                   |
    ---------------------              ---------------------
    |                   |
 6  | NUMBER OF CALLS   |
    | OF DEPART         |              CONTENT ARRAY
    ---------------------              CON ("BIN",500)
    |                   |              ---------------------
 7  | TOTAL OCCUPATION  |              | TOTAL TIME OF     |
    |                   |           1  | OCCUPATION        |
    ---------------------              | FOR INTERVAL 1    |
    | TIME OF LAST      |              ---------------------
 8  | ALTERATION        |              |                   |
    |                   |              |         *         |
    ---------------------              |                   |
                                       |         *         |
                                       |                   |
                                       |         *         |
                                       |                   |
                                       ---------------------
                                       | TOTAL TIME OF     |
                                 500   | OCCUPATION FOR    |
                                       | INTERVAL 500      |
                                       ---------------------
```

```
        INTEGRATION ARRAY              INTEGRATION STATISTICS
        INTMA ("NSET",8)               INTSTA ("NSET",4)
      ---------------------------    ---------------------------
      |                         |    | NUMBER OF               |
  1   | INTEGRATION METHOD      |  1 | INTEGRATION STEPS       |
      |                         |    | CARRIED OUT             |
      ---------------------------    ---------------------------
      |                         |    |                         |
  2   | INITIAL STEP SIZE       |  2 | MEAN STEP SIZE          |
      |                         |    |                         |
      ---------------------------    ---------------------------
      | NUMBER OF CONTINUOUS    |    |                         |
  3   | VARIABLES SV            |  3 | NUMBER OF CROSSINGS      |
      |                         |    |                         |
      ---------------------------    ---------------------------
      | NUMBER OF               |    | NUMBER OF STEPS         |
  4   | DERIVATIVES DV          |  4 | NEEDED TO LOCATE        |
      |                         |    | CROSSING                |
      ---------------------------    ---------------------------
      |                         |
  5   | MINIMUM STEP SIZE       |
      |                         |
      ---------------------------
      |                         |
  6   | MAXIMUM STEP SIZE       |
      |                         |
      ---------------------------
      | MAXIMUM RELATIVE        |
  7   | ERROR                   |
      |                         |
      ---------------------------
      | MAXIMUM NUMBER          |
  8   | OF INTEGRATION STEPS    |
      |                         |
      ---------------------------
```

```
         PLOT-ARRAY 1                        PLOT-ARRAY 2
         PLOMA1 ("NPLO",16)                  PLOMA2 ("NPLO",5)
         ----------------------             ----------------------
         | TIME OF START OF   |             |                    |
      1  | PLOT               |          1  | PLOT STEP SIZE     |
         |                    |             |                    |
         ----------------------             ----------------------
         | TIME OF END OF     |             |                    |
      2  | PLOT               |          2  | PRINT INDICATOR    |
         |                    |             |                    |
         ----------------------             ----------------------
         | STEP SIZE FOR      |             |                    |
      3  | RECORDING PLOT     |          3  | SCALING            |
         | DATA               |             |                    |
         ----------------------             ----------------------
         | INDEX OF FILE USED|              |                    |
      4  | FOR INTERMEDIATE   |          4  | MINIMUM Y VALUE    |
         | STORAGE OF PLOT    |             |                    |
         | DATA               |             ----------------------
         ----------------------             |                    |
         | INDEX IN SET       |          5  | MAXIMUM Y VALUE    |
      5  | OF FIRST PLOT      |             |                    |
         | VARIABLE           |             ----------------------
         ----------------------
         | INDEX IN SET OF    |
      6  | FIRST PLOT         |
         | VARIABLE           |
         ----------------------
         |                    |
         |           *        |
         |                    |
   7-14  |           *        |
         |                    |
         |           *        |
         |                    |
         ----------------------
         | INDEX OF SET OF    |
     15  | SIXTH PLOT         |
         | VARIABLE           |
         ----------------------
         | INDEX IN SET OF    |
     16  | SIXTH PLOT         |
         | VARIABLE           |
         ----------------------
```

```
        PLOT-MATRIX 3
        PLOMA3 ("NPLO",18)
        --------------------
        | SYMBOL USED FOR   |
   1    | FIRST PLOT        |
        | VARIABLE          |
        --------------------
        | FIRST 4 CHARACTERS|
   2    | OF IDENTIFIER OF  |
        | FIRST PLOT        |
        | VARIABLE          |
        --------------------
        | 2ND 4 CHARACTERS  |
   3    | OF IDENTIFIER OF  |
        | FIRST PLOT        |
        | VARIABLE          |
        --------------------
        |                   |
        |         *         |
        |                   |
 4-15   |         *         |
        |                   |
        |         *         |
        |                   |
        --------------------
        | SYMBOL USER FOR   |
  16    | SIXTH PLOT        |
        | VARIABLE          |
        --------------------
        | FIRST 4 CHARACTERS|
  17    | OF IDENTIFIERS OF |
        | SIXTH PLOT        |
        | VARIABLE          |
        --------------------
        | 2ND 4 CHARACTERS  |
  18    | OF IDENTIFIERS OF |
        | SIXTH PLOT        |
        | VARIABLE          |
        --------------------
```

```
      TRACE ARRAY
      JPRINT (25)
   -----------------------------------------------------------
 1 | FACILITIES                                              |
   -----------------------------------------------------------
 2 | MULTIFACILITIES                                         |
   -----------------------------------------------------------
 3 | POOLS                                                   |
   -----------------------------------------------------------
 4 | STORAGES                                                |
   -----------------------------------------------------------
 5 | GATES                                                   |
   -----------------------------------------------------------
 6 | GATHER STATIONS OF TYPE 1                               |
   -----------------------------------------------------------
 7 | GATHER STATIONS OF TYPE 2                               |
   -----------------------------------------------------------
 8 | USER CHAINS OF TYPE 1                                   |
   -----------------------------------------------------------
 9 | TRIGGER STATIONS OF TYPE 1                              |
   -----------------------------------------------------------
10 | USER CHAINS OF TYPE 2                                   |
   -----------------------------------------------------------
11 | TRIGGER STATION OF TYPE 2                               |
   -----------------------------------------------------------
12 | MATCH STATIONS                                          |
   -----------------------------------------------------------
13 | SCHEDULING SOURCE ACTIVATIONS                           |
   -----------------------------------------------------------
14 | GENERATION AND ELIMINATION OF TRANSACTIONS              |
   -----------------------------------------------------------
15 | SUBROUTINE ADVANC AND TRANSF                            |
   -----------------------------------------------------------
16 | BINS                                                    |
   -----------------------------------------------------------
17 | CONFIDENCE INTERVALS                                    |
   -----------------------------------------------------------
18 | OUTPUT OF FREQUENCY TABLES                              |
   -----------------------------------------------------------
19 | TRACE OF EVENTS                                         |
   -----------------------------------------------------------
20 | TRACE OF INTEGRATION                                    |
   -----------------------------------------------------------
21 | OVERFLOW IN SUBROUTINE FUNCT                            |
   -----------------------------------------------------------
22 | TRACE OF COMBINING OF DELAYED VARIABLES                 |
   -----------------------------------------------------------
23 | AVAILABLE TO USER                                       |
   -----------------------------------------------------------
24 | AVAILABLE TO USER                                       |
   -----------------------------------------------------------
25 | AVAILABLE TO USER                                       |
   -----------------------------------------------------------
```

A 4 Array Bounds

The user of GPSS-FORTRAN Version 3 can himself decide the size of
the simulator. He can specify how many events and how many
transactions can exist simultaneously and how many stations of
each type can be used.

The size of the simulator is determined by specifying the size of
the data areas in the escape character version. This is done by
the user by means of an editor. The editor searches for the
appropriate identifier which determines the array bound. It is
uniquely identified by being enclosed in apostrophes. The editor
replaces it by an actual numerical value.

* Example

The data area for the facility array in the escape character
version of the simulator is FAC("FAC",3). "FAC" must be replaced
by a value which determines the size of the facility table before
the program can be compiled and executed.

The following section describes the array bounds in alphabetic
order. The names of the variables which are affected by the array
size parameters are listed. In addition proposed array sizes are
given. In this proposal the simulator is so large that it should
suffice for very large models.

The user of GPSS-FORTRAN Version 3 is advised to set the bounds
of the arrays in accordance with his own requirements. This
allows a substantial reduction in the memory requirements.

Note:

   * At least one of every object in GPSS-FORTRAN Version 3 must
   be present. None of the array bounds may be less than one.

A 4.1 Array Bounds

"ASM"   Number of assembly stations
variable: ASM("FAM","ASM")
"ASM" = 1
One assembly station is allowed model. If more assembly stations
are required the bounds of the simulator must be redefined.

"BIN"   Number of bins
variables: BIN("BIN",8), BINSTA("BIN",5), CONFL("BIN",5),
           CHAINC("BIN"), CON("BIN",500)
"BIN"=10
10 bins are allowed. Bins should be used sparingly because the
confidence table CON("BIN",500) occupies a lot of memory.

"EVT"   Number of events
Variables: EVENTL("EVT",4), CHAINV("EVT")
"EVT"=50
A model can contain up to 50 different events.

"FAC"   Number of facilities
Variables: FAC("FAC",3)
"FAC"=10
10 facilities are allowed.

"FAM"   Number of families
Variables: FAM("FAM",2), ASM("FAM","ASM"), GATHF("FAM","GATF")
"FAM"=200
The number of families is 200. It is possible that each
transaction belongs to a separate family. This occurs when each
family has only a single member. For this reason "FAM" should be
set equal to "TX1".

"GATE"   Number of gates
Gates do not have their own data area. "GATE" occurs only as the
program variable ZGATE. See note at the end of appendix A 3.1.
"GATE"=20
20 different gates are allowed.

"GATF"   Number of gather stations for families
Variables: GATHF("FAM","GATF")
"GATF"=1
1 gather station for families is allowed.

"GATT"   Number of gather stations for transactions
Variable: GATHT("GATT")
"GATT"=5
5 gather stations for transactions, i.e. gather stations which do
not take into account membership of a family, are allowed.

"LDVAR"   Number of values of each delayed variable stored
Variables: DEVAR("NDVAR",2,"LDVAR")
"LDVAR"=100
100 values of each delayed variable can be stored.

"MFAC"   Number of multifacilities
Variables: MFAC("MFAC",2), MBV("MFAC"), PLAMA("MFAC",2)
"MFAC"=2
2 multifacilities are allowed.

"NCOND"   Number of conditions
Variables: TCOND("NCOND")
"NCOND"=150
150 different conditions are allowed.

"NCRO"   Number of crossings
Variables: IFLAG("NSET","NCRO"), IFLAGL("NSET","NCRO")
"NCRO"=50
50 different crossings are allowed for each set. It is not
possible to specify the number of possible crossings for each set
individually.

"NDVAR"   Number of delayed variables
Variables: DEVAR("NDVAR",2,"LDVAR")
          IDEMA("NDVAR",2), IDPTR("NDVAR",2)
          NCOMP("NDVAR"), TAUMAX("NDVAR")
"NDVAR"=2
2 delayed variables are allowed.

"NPLO"   Number of plots
Variables: MONITL("NPLO"), CHAINM("NPLO"), PLOMA1("NPLO",16),
           PLOMA2("NPLO",5), PLOMA3("NPLO",18), PLOFIL("NPLO")
"NPLO"=10
10 plots are allowed.

"NSET"   Number of sets
Variables: EQUL("NSET",4), CHAINE("NSET"), INTMA("NSET",8),
           INTSTA("NSET",4), IFLAG("NSET","NCRO"),
           IFLAGL("NSET","NCRO"), TDELA("NSET")
           DV("NSET","NV"), DVLAST("NSET","NV"),
           SV("NSET","NV"), SVLAST("NSET","NV")
"NSET"=3
3 sets are allowed.

"NTAB"   Number of frequency tables
Variable: TAB("TAB",4,"NTAB")
"NTAB"=7
7 frequency tables are allowed.

"NV"   Number of continuous variables
Variables: SV("NSET","NV"), SVLAST("NSET","NV"),
           DV("NSET","NV"), DVLAST("NSET","NV")
"NV"=100
100 continuous variables are allowed.

"POL"   Number of policies
Variable: POL("POL",3)
"POL"=10
10 policies are allowed.

"POOL"   Number of pools
Variable: POOL("POOL",2)
"POOL"=5
5 pools are allowed.

"SE"   Number of service elements
Variable: SE("SE",3)
"SE"=20
20 service elements are allowed. They must be assigned to the
multifacilities by the user.

"SM"   Number of locations
Variable: SM("SM",2)
"SM"=1024
Up to 1024 locations are allowed. These 1024 locations must be
assigned to the storages by the user.

"SRC"   Number of sources
Variables: SOURCL("SRC",3), CHAINS("SRC")
"SRC"=10
10 sources are allowed.

"STAT"   Total number of stations
Variable: BHEAD("STAT")
"STAT"=656
"STAT" is the total number of stations of all kinds. "BSTAT" is
the total number of all stations at which transactions can be
blocked. "STAT" must be calculated by the user. See the notes at
the end of appendix A 4 for the calculation of "STAT".

"STO"   Number of storages
Variables: SBM("STO",2), STRAMA("STO",2)
"STO"=5
5 storages are allowed.

"TAB"   Number of components in the frequency tables
Variable: TAB("TAB",4,"NTAB")
"TAB"=100
Each frequency table contains 100 components.

"TX1"   Number of transactions
Variables: TX("TX1","TX2"), ACTIV("TX1",2), CHAINA("TX1")
"TX1"=200
The model can contain at most 200 transactions simultaneously.

"TX2"   Number of attributes of the transactions
Variable: TX("TX1","TX2")
"TX2"=16
The transaction can have up to 16 attributes. The attributes 1 to
eight are fixed attributes which are already defined by the
simulator. The remaining eight attributes 9-16 are freely
available to the user.

"UCHF"   User chain for families
Variable: USERCF("FAM","UCHF",2)
"UCHF"=1
1 user chain for families is allowed.

"UCHT"   Number of simple user chains
Variable: USERCT("UCHT",2)
"UCHT"=2
2 user chains for transactions are allowed. These do not take
family membership into account.

"VAR"   Number of free format input variables
Variables: IV("VAR"), RV("VAR")
"VAR"=50
50 variables of type integer and 50 variables of type real which
can be read in free format are allowed.

A 4.2   Notes

* The choice of the size of the data arrays also determines the
upper bounds of the controlled variables in some DO loops.
Variables which depend on the size of the arrays begin with the
letter "Z".

Example: The subroutine RESET clears all arrays. The controlled
variables of the DO loops which clear the arrays BIN and BINSTA
take values from 1 to ZBIN.
Program variables which begin with Z are initalised in the
subroutine SYSVAR in accordance with the size of the arrays.

* The user must calculate the quantity "STAT" which determines
the size of the array BHEAD. Particular care is needed here.
"STAT" is the number of stations at which transactions can be
blocked. The following points are to be taken into account when
calculating "STAT":

For stations with families (gather stations for families and user chains for families) an element must be reserved in BHEAD for each family.

User chains require two components, one for the user chain itself and one for the corresponding trigger station.

Match stations are similar to gates in that they do not have their own data areas. There are no program variables needed for match stations. The number of possible match stations is only significant through its contribution to "STAT". In the given example with "STAT" = 656   NMATCH has the value 5.

"STAT" = "FAC" + "MFAC" + "POOL" + "STO" + "GATE" + "GATT" +
       + "GATF" + "FAM" + "UCHT"*2 + "UCHF"*FAM"*2 + NMATCH

The following applies to the array sizes proposed in appendix A4.

"FAC"	= 10	"GATT"	= 5	
"MFAC"	= 2	"GATF"	= 1	"GATF"*"FAM"=200
"POOL"	= 5	"UCHT"	= 2	
"STO"	= 5	"UCHF"	= 1	"UCHF"*"FAM"=200
"GATE"	= 20	NMATCH	= 5	

It follows that "STAT" = 656.

A 4.3 Replacement of the Variables

The version of the simulator using escape characters must be modified to obtain a version which can be compiled and run. All variables enclosed in apostrophes must be replaced by numbers using an editor. This applies both to user programs and to system programs as well.

A 5 Random Numbers

It is intended that the program structures in GPSS-FORTRAN
Version 3 should be as transparent as possible to the user. For
this reason, techniques which save computer time or memory are
not used if they are difficult to understand. This applies to the
generation of random numbers. If the GPSS-FORTRAN Version 3 user
feels that he sufficiently understands the techniques for the
generation of random numbers, there is nothing preventing him
from changing the method used in GPSS-FORTRAN Version 3.

The generation of random numbers in GPSS-FORTRAN Version 3 is
computer-independent.

Random numbers are generated by the function RN(RNUM) according
to the rule:

$$X(I+1) = (DFACT*X(I) + DCONST) \bmod DMODUL$$

The quality of the random numbers generated is only guaranteed if
all the arithmetic operations are performed without rounding.
This means that the result of the operation

$$DFACT*X(I) + DCONST$$

can be exactly represented in the computer.

If the standard random number generator of GPSS-FORTRAN Version 3
is used on a computer which does not satisfy this requirement,
then the following results:

* As a result of the rounding error, the iterative technique
produces a sequence of random numbers which does not agree with
the correct random numbers. It may follow that the results of
examples disagree slightly with the results in this book.

* The quality of the random numbers is no longer guaranteed.
There are two solutions to this which are described below:

A 5.1 The Double Word Random Number Generator

The operation

$$DFACT*X(i)+DCONST$$

is partitioned so that it can be executed without rounding on the
computer to be used. This is done by splitting DFACT, X(i) and
DCONST and processing each part separatly.

In this case, the subroutines INIT1 and RN must be replaced by
INIT1X and RNX. The listing of INIT1X and RNX is given below. The
common area COMMON/DRN/ must be replaced. The call of RN must be
replaced by a call of RNX in the subroutines ERLANG, GAUSS,
BOXEP, and UNIFRM.

This technique is recommended when a small increase in the
computer time is acceptable. The results obtained must agree
exactly with the results in the book.

Note:

* It is to be noted that the common area COMMON/DRN/ must be
replaced.

```
      SUBROUTINE INIT1X
C     =================
C     CALL INIT1X
C
C     FUNKTION: INITIALISATION OF RANDOM NUMBER GENERATORS
C
      INTEGER, DRN, DFACT, DMODUL, DCONST
      COMMON/DRN/ DRN(30), DFACT(30,2), DMODUL(2), DCONST(30,2)
C
C     SPECIFY THE MULTIPLIERS
C     =======================
      DFACT( 1,1)=      74125
      DFACT( 2,1)=     163549
      DFACT( 3,1)=     207253
      DFACT( 4,1)=     224685
      DFACT( 5,1)=     288373
      DFACT( 6,1)=     314685
      DFACT( 7,1)=     324349
      DFACT( 8,1)=     337997
      DFACT( 9,1)=     343917
      DFACT(10,1)=     484997
      DFACT(11,1)=     520061
      DFACT(12,1)=     526981
      DFACT(13,1)=     530197
      DFACT(14,1)=     531493
      DFACT(15,1)=     557749
      DFACT(16,1)=     628861
      DFACT(17,1)=     635149
      DFACT(18,1)=     651237
      DFACT(19,1)=     725925
      DFACT(20,1)=     861221
      DFACT(21,1)=     931725
      DFACT(22,1)=     982525
      DFACT(23,1)=    1085653
      DFACT(24,1)=    1168277
      DFACT(25,1)=    1377333
      DFACT(26,1)=    1455669
      DFACT(27,1)=    1493629
      DFACT(28,1)=    1534917
      DFACT(29,1)=    1548757
      DFACT(30,1)=    1635469
```

```
C
C         Specify the modulus
C         ===================
          DMODUL(1) = 2**30
          DMODUL(2) = 2**15
C
C         Specify both parts of DFACT
C         ===========================
          DO 10 I = 1,30
          DFACT(I,2) = MOD(DFACT(I,1),DMODUL(2))
10        DFACT(I,1) = (DFACT(I,1)-DFACT(I,2))/DMODUL(2)
C
C         Specify the address constants
C         =============================
          DO 20 I = 1,30
          DCONST(I,2) = 16739
20        DCONST(I,1) = 6946
C
C         Specify the initial values
C         ==========================
          DO 30 I = 1,30
30        DRN(I) = 1
          RETURN
          END




          FUNCTION RNX(RNUM)
C         ==================
C         FUNCTION: Generate a random number in the interval (0,1)
C
C         PARAMETER: RNUM = index of the random number generator
C
          INTEGER RNUM
          INTEGER DRN, DFACT, DMODUL, DCONST
          INTEGER DRNH, DRNL, DPRODH, DPRODL
          COMMON/DRN/ DRN(30),DFACT(30,2)MDMODUL(2),DCONST(30,2)
C
C         Divide DRN
C         =========
          DRNL = MOD(DRN(RNUM),DMODUL(2))
          DRNH = (DRN(RNUM)-DRNL)/DMODUL(2)
C
C         Compute the two partial products
C         ================================
          DPRODL = DRNL*DFACT(RNUM,2)+DCONST(RNUM,2)
          DPRODH = DRNL*DFACT(RNUM,1)+DRNH*DFACT(RNUM,2)+
         +DCONST(RNUM,1)
C
C         Compute the new random number
C         =============================
          DPRODH = MOD(DPRODH,DMODUL(2))
          DRN(RNUM) = MOD(DPRODH*DMODUL(2)+DPRODL,DMODUL(1))
          RNX = FLOAT(DRN(RNUM)/FLOAT(DMODUL(1)-1)
          RETURN
          END
```

A 5.2 The Version with Small Multipliers

A smaller value of the multiplier DFACT can be used. This
prevents the expression (DFACT*X(I)) + DCONST from becoming too
large. The subroutine INIT11 shown on the following pages
contains multipliers suitable for a 16-bit Computer. All random
number generators have been thoroughly tested.

Notes:

   * These random number generators produce different random numbers. As a consequence, the results of the examples will be
   slightly different.

   * In subroutine INIT11, DMODUL has the value 4096. This means
   that the length of the cycle is not greater than 4096.

```
      SUBROUTINE INIT11
C     =================
C
C     CALL INIT11
C
C     FUNKTION: Initialisation of random number generators
C
      INTEGER DRN, DFACT, DMODUL, DCONST
      COMMON/DRN/ DRN(30), DFACT(30), DMODUL, DCONST(30)
C
C     Initialisation of multipliers
C     =============================
      DFACT( 1) =  469
      DFACT( 2) =  597
      DFACT( 3) =  733
      DFACT( 4) =  757
      DFACT( 5) =  805
      DFACT( 6) =  893
      DFACT( 7) =  901
      DFACT( 8) =  941
      DFACT( 9) = 1141
      DFACT(10) = 1221
      DFACT(11) = 1541
      DFACT(12) = 1621
      DFACT(13) = 1805
      DFACT(14) = 1853
      DFACT(15) = 1997
      DFACT(16) = 2165
      DFACT(17) = 2173
      DFACT(18) = 2285
      DFACT(19) = 2373
      DFACT(20) = 2397
      DFACT(21) = 2429
      DFACT(22) = 2445
      DFACT(23) = 2517
      DFACT(24) = 2549
      DFACT(25) = 2749
      DFACT(26) = 2813
      DFACT(27) = 2973
      DFACT(28) = 3157
      DFACT(29) = 3285
      DFACT(30) = 3405
```

```
C
C         Initialisation of the additive constant and the module
C         ==========================================================
          DMODUL = 4096
          DO 10 I=1,30
10        DCONST(I) = 865
C
C         Initialisation of the random numbers
C         ====================================
          DO 20 I=1,30
20        DRN(I)=1
          RETURN
          END
```

A 5.3 The Version with Large Multipliers

In the multiplicative congruence method for generating random numbers, the factor DFACT should be as large as possible.
The subroutine INIT12 contains large values for the multipliers.

Note:

  * It is possible to combine the large multipliers with the splitting of the operands described in A 5.1.

```
          SUBROUTINE INIT12
C         =================
C         CALL INIT12
C         ===========
C         FUNKTION: Initialisation of random number generators
C
          INTEGER DRN, DFACT, DMODUL, DCONST
          COMMON/DRN/ DRN(30), DFACT(30), DMODUL, DCONST(30)
C
C         Initialisation of the multipliers
C         =================================
          DFACT( 1) =  10753813
          DFACT( 2) = 228181237
          DFACT( 3) = 348984893
          DFACT( 4) = 590634277
          DFACT( 5) =  10841757
          DFACT( 6) = 107408213
          DFACT( 7) = 469770781
          DFACT( 8) = 832159853
          DFACT( 9) =  10842045
          DFACT(10) = 228244373
          DFACT(11) = 348969437
          DFACT(12) =  10763125
          DFACT(13) = 107452989
          DFACT(14) = 469773661
          DFACT(15) = 590648085
          DFACT(16) =  10784189
          DFACT(17) = 228206429
          DFACT(18) = 469793853
          DFACT(19) = 832230813
          DFACT(20) = 107464661
          DFACT(21) = 469808301
```

```
          DFACT(22) = 590585901
          DFACT(23) = 228178005
          DFACT(24) = 349045949
          DFACT(25) =  10845149
          DFACT(26) = 107441485
          DFACT(27) = 469795933
          DFACT(28) = 349062285
          DFACT(29) = 107380645
          DFACT(30) =  10767581
C
C         Initialisation of the additive constants and the base
C         ========================================================
          DMODUL = 2**30
          DO 10 I = 1,30
10        DCONST(I) = 227623267
C
C         Initialisation of the random numbers
C         ====================================
          DO 20 I = 1,30
20        DRN(I) = 1
          RETURN
          END
```

A 6 User Programs

Appendix 6 contains the user programs which are necessary for producing the model. These are the main FORTRAN program and the subroutines written by the user AKTIV, CHECK, DETECT, DYNPR, EVENT, STATE and TEST.

The user programs also include certain subroutines which are provided for particular situations. They are included in the simulator as dummy routines.

```
C******************************************************************
C
C 1. MAIN PROGRAM AND SUBPROGRAMS
C
C******************************************************************
C     *** GPSS  FORTRAN  SIMULATION PROGRAM VERSION 3
C     ***
C     *** MODELL  **
C     ***
C     *** ISSUED  **. **. **
C     ***
C
C
C
C
C     1. GENERAL FORTRAN DECLARATIONS
C     =================================
      CHARACTER*4 PLOMA3, TXT
      CHARACTER*8 VNAMEI,VNAMER
      INTEGER SVIN, XFORM,SVOUT,UNIT1,UNIT2,XUNIT3,XUNIT4
      INTEGER UNIT5,UNIT6,UNIT7,UNIT8
      INTEGER XGO,XEND,XNEW,XOUT,XMODUS,YMODUS,ZASM,ZBIN
      INTEGER ZEVT,ZFAC,ZFAM,ZGATE,ZGATF,ZGATT,ZLDVAR,ZMATCH
      INTEGER ZMFAC,ZNCOND,ZNCRO,ZNDVAR,ZNPLO,ZNSET,ZNTAB,ZNV
      INTEGER ZPOL,ZPOOL,ZSE,ZSM,ZSRC,ZSTAT,ZSTO,ZTAB,ZTX1
      INTEGER ZTX2,ZUCHF,ZUCHT,ZVAR,ZVERZ,ZVON
      INTEGER CHAINC,CHAINE,CHAINV,CHAINM,CHAINS,CHAINA,SOURCI
      INTEGER TXI,FAC,FAM,ASM,GATHT,GATHF,SE,PLAMA,POL,POOL
      INTEGER SBM, SM, STRAMA, TYPE, BHEAD, USERCT, USERCF
      INTEGER ANROUT,ANSECT,ANSEGM,ANSTA,ANVERZ,BLOCVE
      INTEGER COURMA,DIRECT,FROMTO,ROUTMA,SEGMA,TOFROM
      INTEGER DRN, DFACT, DMODUL, DCONST
      REAL NTXC, INTMA,INTSTA, MONITL,NETSTA
      COMMON /BIN/ BIN(10,8), BINSTA(10,5)
      COMMON /CON/ CONFL(10,5), CHAINC(10), CON(10,500), CLEV
      COMMON /DEL/ IDELAY, NCOMP(2), DEVAR(2,2,100), IDEMA(2,2)
      COMMON /DEL/ IDPNTR(2,2), TAUMAX(2), TCLEAR(2), TDELA(3)
      COMMON /DRN/ DRN(30), DFACT(30,2), DMODUL, DCONST(30,2)
      COMMON /EQU/ EQUL(3,4), CHAINE(3)
      COMMON /EQU/ INTMA(3,8), INTSTA(3,4)
      COMMON /EQU/ IFLAG(3,50), IFLAGP(3,50), JFLAG(3,50),
      COMMON /EQU/ JFLAGL(3,50)
      COMMON /EQU/ SV(3,100), SVLAST(3,100)
      COMMON /EQU/ DV(3,100), DVLAST(3,100), ICONT
```

```
      COMMON /EVT/ EVENTL(50), CHAINV(50)
      COMMON /FAC/ FAC(10,3)
      COMMON /FAM/ FAM(200,2), ASM(200,1)
      COMMON /FIL/ UNIT1,UNIT2,XUNIT3,XUNIT4,NUNIT1,NUNIT2,XFORM
      COMMON /FIL/ UNIT5,UNIT6,UNIT7,UNIT8
      COMMON /GAT/ GATHT(5), GATHF(200,1)
      COMMON /INP/ ITXT, JEPS, NDELAY
      COMMON /MFA/ MFAC(2,2), MBV(2), SE(20,3), LSE
      COMMON /MOD/ XMODUS, YMODUS, SVIN, SVOUT, NSTEP
      COMMON /NET/ ANROUT,ANSECT,ANSEGM,ANSTA,ANVERZ
      COMMON /NET/ BLOCVE(100,2),COORDS(20,2),COORDV(30,2)
      COMMON /NET/ COORDP(200,2),COORMA(20,3),SECTMA(100,6)
      COMMON /NET/ NETSTA(50,6), ROUTMA(20,20),SEGMA(50,20)
      COMMON /NET/ DIRECT(50,50),TOTLEN(50,50)
      COMMON /NET/ FROMTO(50,4,2),TOFROM(50,4,2)
      COMMON /PLA/ PLAMA(2,2)
      COMMON /PLO/ MONITL(10), CHAINM(10)
      COMMON /PLO/ PLOMA1(10,16), PLOMA2(10,5)
      COMMON /PLC/ PLOMA3(10,18)
      COMMON /POL/ POL(10,3)
      COMMON /POO/ POOL(5,2)
      COMMON /RAS/ RASTL(10)
      COMMON /SRC/ SOURCL(10,3), CHAINS(10), SOURCI(10)
      COMMON /SRC/ NTXC, LSL, TXMAX
      COMMON /STO/ SBM(5,2), SM(1024,2), LSM
      COMMON /STR/ STRAMA(5,2)
      COMMON /TAB/ TAB(100,4,7)
      COMMON /TIM/ T, RT, TBUSY, TEND, TCOND(150), EPS, IPRINT
      COMMON /TIM/ JPRINT(25)
      COMMON /TRA/ TXADD(200,4),CARMA(100,10),TARMA(100,7)
      COMMON /TRA/ LOGMA(200,5),LOGPTR(2),STATIS(100,10)
      COMMON /TRA/ STATST(20,4),PARKST(20,4),BLOCST(100,4)
      COMMON /TXS/ TX(200,16), TXC(200), TXI(200), ACTIVL(200,2)
      COMMON /TXS/ CHAINA(200,2), LTX
      COMMON /TXT/ TXT(3,19)
      COMMON /TYP/ TYPE(15), BHEAD(796), THEAD(6), LHEAD(6)
      COMMON /TYP/ TTEST
      COMMON /UCH/ USERCT(2,2), USERCF(200,1,2)
      COMMON /VAR/ IV(50), RV(50)
      COMMON /SYM/ VNAMEI(50),VNAMER(50)
      COMMON /SYS/ ZASM,ZBIN,ZEVT,ZFAC,ZFAM,ZGATE,ZGATF,ZGATT
      COMMON /SYS/ ZLDVAR,ZMFAC,ZNCOND,ZNCRO,ZNDVAR,ZNPLO,ZNSET
      COMMON /SYS/ ZNTAB,ZNV,ZPOL,ZPOOL,ZSE,ZSM,ZSRC,ZSTAT,ZSTO
      COMMON /SYS/ ZTAB,ZTX1,ZTX2,ZUCHF,ZUCHT,ZVAR,ZVERZ,ZVON
C
C
C     SPECIFY COMMON /PRIV/
C     =====================
      COMMON /PRIV/ DUMMY
C
C
C     SPECIFY OPERATIONAL MODE
C     ========================
      XMODUS = 1
      YMODUS = 0
C
```

```
C
C       SPECIFY CHANNEL NUMBERS FOR INPUT AND OUTPUT
C       ============================================
C
C       INPUT FILE: DATAIN
C       ------------------
        UNIT1  = 14
C
C       OUTPUT FILE: DATAOUT
        --------------------
        UNIT2  = 15
C
C       INTERACTIVE INPUT FROM TERMINAL
        -------------------------------
        XUNIT3 =  5
C
C       INTERACTIVE OUTPUT TO TERMINAL
C       ------------------------------
        XUNIT4 =  6
C
C       GRAPHICS FILE FOR SAVING PICTURE DESCRIPTION:  GRAPHDAT
C       ------------------------------------------------------
        UNIT5 = 7
C
C       SCRATCH FILE FOR PLOTTING PHASE DIAGRAMS:  SCRAT2
C       -------------------------------------------------
        UNIT6 = 11
C
C       FILE FOR SAVING MODEL:  SAVED
C       -----------------------------
        UNIT7 = 12
C
C       SCRATCH FILE FOR PLOTTING(ANAR,REPRT5,XINPUT):  SCRAT3
C       ------------------------------------------------------
        UNIT8 = 20
C
C
C       OPEN INPUT AND OUTPUT FILES
C       ===========================
        OPEN(UNIT1,FILE='DATAIN',ACCESS='SEQUENTIAL',FORM=
     +        'FORMATTED')
        OPEN(UNIT2,FILE='DATAOUT',ACCESS='SEQUENTIAL',FORM=
     +        'FORMATTED')
        OPEN(XUNIT3,FILE='INPUT')
        OPEN(XUNIT4,FILE='OUTPUT')
C
C
C       OPEN SCRATCH AND SAVE FILES
C       ===========================
        OPEN(UNIT5,FILE='GRADAT',ACCESS='SEQUENTIAL',FORM='FORMAT
     +        TED')
        OPEN(UNIT6,FILE='SCRAT2',ACCESS='DIRECT',FORM='UNFORMATTED'
     +        ,RECL=101)
        OPEN(UNIT7,FILE='SAVE',ACCESS='SEQUENTIAL',FORM='UNFORMAT
     +        TED')
        OPEN(UNIT8,FILE='SCRAT3',ACCESS='SEQUENTIAL',FORM='UNFOR
     +        MATTED')
C
```

```
C
C       OPEN PLOT FILES
C       ===============
        OPEN(21,FILE='PLOT1',ACCESS='SEQUENTIAL',FORM='UNFORMAT
     +        TED')
        OPEN(22,FILE='PLOT2',ACCESS='SEQUENTIAL',FORM='UNFORMAT
     +        TED')
C
C
C       2. CLEAR DATA AREAS AND ASSIGN DEFAULT VALUES
C       =============================================
C
C       ASSIGN VARIABLES WHICH DEFINE ARRAY SIZES
C       =========================================
        CALL SYSVAR
C
C       CLEAR DATA AREAS
C       ================
        CALL RESET
C
C       ASSIGN DEFAULT VALUES
C       =====================
        CALL PRESET
C
C       ASSIGN DEFAULT VALUES TO USER VARIABLES
C       =======================================
C
C
C
C       3. READ AND ASSIGN DEFAULT VALUES
C       =================================
C
C       DECLARE NAMES OF INTEGER VARIABLES
C       ==================================
        VNAMEI(1) = 'IPRINT  '
        VNAMEI(2) = 'ICONT   '
        VNAMEI(3) = 'SVIN    '
        VNAMEI(4) = 'SVOUT   '
C
C       DECLARE NAMES OF REAL VARIABLES
C       ===============================
        VNAMER(1) = 'TEND    '
        VNAMER(2) = 'TXMAX   '
        VNAMER(3) = 'EPS     '
C
C
C       ASSIGN DEFAULT VALUES FOR FREE FORMAT INPUT
C       ===========================================
1000    IV(1) = IPRINT
        IV(2) = ICONT
        IV(3) = SVIN
        IV(4) = SVOUT
        RV(1) = TEND
        RV(2) = TXMAX
        RV(3) = EPS
C
C
C
```

```
C
C        INPUT
C        =====
         CALL XINPUT(XEND,XGO,XNEW,XOUT,*9999)
         CALL YINPUT(XEND,XGO,XNEW,XOUT,*9999)
C
C        ASSIGN VALUES FOR UNFORMATTED INPUT
C        ===================================
         IPRINT = IV(1)
         ICONT  = IV(2)
         SVIN   = IV(3)
         SVOUT  = IV(4)
         TEND   = RV(1)
         TXMAX  = RV(2)
         EPS    = RV(3)
C
C
         IF(XMODUS.EQ.1) CALL XBEGIN(XEND,XGO,XNEW,XOUT,*6000,*7000)
         IF(SVIN.NE.0) GOTO 5500
C
C
C        4. ASSIGN VALUES OF CONSTANTS AND INITIALISE MODEL
C        ==================================================
C           VARIABLES
C        ============
C
C
C        ASSIGN SOURCE MATRIX
C        ====================
C
C        ASSIGN POLICY, STRATEGY AND PLAN ARRAYS
C        =======================================
C
C        DEFINE CAPACITIES OF POOLS AND STORAGES
C        =======================================
C
C        DEFINE SIZE OF MULTIFACILITIES
C        ==============================
C
C        INITIALISE DATA AREAS
C        =====================
         CALL INIT1
         CALL INIT2(*9999)
         CALL INIT3(*9999)
         CALL INIT4
C
C        INITIALISE NETTOPOLOGY
C        ======================
         CALL ININET(*9999)
C
C
C        5. START MODEL
C        ==============
C
C        SCHEDULE THE FIRST EVENT
C        ========================
```

```
C
C       START SOURCES
C       =============
C
C       PROCEED WITH SIMULATION RUN
C       ===========================
5500    IF(SVIN.NE.0) CALL SAVIN(*9999)
C
C
C
C       6. MODEL
C       ========
6000    CALL FLOWC(*7000)
        IF(XMODUS.EQ.1) GOTO 1000
C
C
C
C       7. TERMINATING SECTION
C       ======================
7000    CONTINUE
C
C
C       FINAL COMPUTATION FOR BINS AND DETERMINATION OF THE
C       ===================================================
C       CONFIDENCE INTERVALS
C       ====================
        CALL ENDBIN
C
C       FINAL COMPUTATION OF USER QUANTIITES
C       ====================================
C
C
C
C       8. OUTPUT OF RESULTS
C       ====================
C
C       OUTPUT OF PLOTS
C       ===============
        IF(ICONT.NE.0) CALL ENDPLO(0)
C
C       OUTPUT OF USER QUANTITIES
C       =========================
C
C
        IF(XOUT.EQ.1) GOTO 1000
C
C       SAVE THE STATE OF THE SYSTEM
C       ============================
        IF(SVOUT.NE.0) CALL SAVOUT
C
C
C
9999    CLOSE(UNIT1,STATUS='KEEP')
        CLOSE(UNIT2,STATUS='KEEP')
        CLOSE(UNIT5,STATUS='KEEP')
        CLOSE(UNIT6,STATUS='DELETE')
        CLOSE(UNIT7,STATUS='KEEP')
        CLOSE(UNIT8,STATUS='DELETE')
        CLOSE(21,STATUS='DELETE')
        CLOSE(22,STATUS='DELETE')
C
```

```
C
      STOP
      END
```

```
      SUBROUTINE ACTIV(*)
C     ***
C     *** CALL ACTIV(EXIT1)
C     ***
C     *** PURPOSE  : MODEL FOR TASKS
C     *** PARAMETER: EXIT1 = EXIT TO TERMINATING SECTION
C     ***
      INTEGER CHAINC, CHAINV, CHAINS, CHAINA, SOURCI, TXI
      INTEGER FAC, FAM, ASM, GATHT, GATHF, SE,PLAMA,POL,POOL
      INTEGER SBM, SM, STRAMA, TYPE, BHEAD, USERCT, USERCF
      INTEGER UNIT1, XFORM, UNIT2, XUNIT3, XUNIT4
      INTEGER UNIT5, UNIT6, UNIT7, UNIT8
      REAL NTXC, LOGMA
      LOGICAL CHECK
      COMMON /BIN/ BIN(10,8), BINSTA(10,5)
      COMMON /CON/ CONFL(10,5), CHAINC(10), CON(10,500), CLEV
      COMMON /EVT/ EVENTL(50), CHAINV(50)
      COMMON /FAC/ FAC(10,3)
      COMMON /FAM/ FAM(200,2), ASM(200,1)
      COMMON /GAT/ GATHT(5), GATHF(200,1)
      COMMON /FIL/ UNIT1,UNIT2,XUNIT3,XUNIT4,NUNIT1,NUNIT2,XFORM
      COMMON /FIL/ UNIT5,UNIT6,UNIT7,UNIT8
      COMMON /MFA/ MFAC(2,2), MBV(2), SE(20,3), LSE
      COMMON /PLA/ PLAMA(2,2)
      COMMON /POL/ POL(10,3)
      COMMON /POO/ POOL(5,2)
      COMMON /RAS/ RASTL(10)
      COMMON /SRC/ SOURCL(10,3), CHAINS(10), SOURCI(10)
      COMMON /SRC/ NTXC, LSL, TXMAX
      COMMON /STO/ SBM(5,2), SM(1024,2), LSM
      COMMON /STR/ STRAMA(5,2)
      COMMON /TAB/ TAB(100,4,7)
      COMMON /TIM/ T, RT, TEND, TCOND(150), EPS, IPRINT
      COMMON /TIM/ JPRINT(25)
      COMMON /TRA/ TXADD(200,4),CARMA(100,10),TARMA(100,7)
      COMMON /TRA/ LOGMA(200,5),LOGPTR(2),STATIS(100,10)
      COMMON /TRA/ STATST(20,4),PARKST(20,4),BLOCST(100,4)
      COMMON /TXS/ TX(200,16), TXI(200),ACTIVL(200,2)
      COMMON /TXS/ CHAINA(200,2), LTX
      COMMON /TYP/ TYPE(15), BHEAD(796), THEAD(6), LHEAD(6)
      COMMON /TYP/ TTEST
      COMMON /UCH/ USERCT(2,2), USERCF(200,1,2)
C
C     SPECIFY COMMON /PRIV/
C     =====================
      COMMON /PRIV/ DUMMY
C
C     DETERMINE LABEL
C     ===============
      IF(LSL.GT.0) NADDR = NINT(SOURCL(LSL,2)
      IF(LTX.GT.0) NADDR = NINT(ACTIVL(LTX,2)
C
C     TRANSFER CONTROL TO LABEL
C     =========================
C
      GOTO (1), NADDR
C
      WRITE(NUNIT2,3000) T,NADDR
3000  FORMAT(1H0,5(1H+),10H ACTIV: T=,F12.4,
     +' ERROR IN LABEL SELECTOR NADDR = ',I3)
      GOTO 9999
```

```
C
C
C      MODEL
C      =====
C
1      CONTINUE
C
C
C      EXIT TO FLOW CONTROL
C      ====================
9000   RETURN
C
C      EXIT TO TERMINATING SECTION
C      ===========================
9999   RETURN 1
       END
```

```
        LOGICAL FUNCTION CHECK(NCOND)
C       ***
C       *** PURPOSE  : TEST LOGICAL CONDITION
C       *** PARAMETER: NCOND = INDEX OF LOGICAL CONDITION
C       ***
        CHARACTER*4 PLOMA3
        INTEGER CHAINC, CHAINE, CHAINV, CHAINM, CHAINS, CHAINA
        INTEGER FAC, FAM, ASM, GATHT, GATHF, SE,PLAMA,POL,POOL,SBM
        INTEGER SM,STRAMA,TYPE,BHEAD,USERCT,USERCF,SOURCI,TXI
        INTEGER UNIT1,XFORM,UNIT2,XUNIT3,XUNIT4
        INTEGER UNIT5, UNIT6, UNIT7, UNIT8
        REAL NTXC, INTMA, INTSTA, MONITL
        COMMON /BIN/ BIN(10,8), BINSTA(10,5)
        COMMON /CON/ CONFL(10,5), CHAINC(10), CON(10,500), CLEV
        COMMON /EQU/ EQUL(3,4), CHAINE(3)
        COMMON /EQU/ INTMA(3,8), INTSTA(3,4)
        COMMON /EQU/ IFLAG(3,50), IFLAGP(3,50), JFLAG(3,50),
        COMMON /EQU/ JFLAGL(3,50)
        COMMON /EQU/ SV(3,100), SVLAST(3,100)
        COMMON /EQU/ DV(3,100), DVLAST(3,100), ICONT
        COMMON /EVT/ EVENTL(50), CHAINV(50)
        COMMON /FAC/ FAC(10,3)
        COMMON /FAM/ FAM(200,2), ASM(200,1)
        COMMON /GAT/ GATHT(5), GATHF(200,1)
        COMMON /FIL/ UNIT1,UNIT2,XUNIT3,XUNIT4,NUNIT1,NUNIT2,XFORM
        COMMON /FIL/ UNIT5,UNIT6,UNIT7,UNIT8
        COMMON /MFA/ MFAC(2,2), MBV(2), SE(20,3), LSE
        COMMON /PLA/ PLAMA(2,2)
        COMMON /PLO/ MONITL(10), CHAINM(10)
        COMMON /PLO/ PLOMA1(10,16), PLOMA2(10,5)
        COMMON /PLC/ PLOMA3(10,18)
        COMMON /POL/ POL(10,3)
        COMMON /POO/ POOL(5,2)
        COMMON /RAS/ RASTL(10)
        COMMON /SRC/ SOURCL(10,3), CHAINS(10), SOURCI(10)
        COMMOM /SRC/ NTXC, LSL, TXMAX
        COMMON /STO/ SBM(5,2), SM(1024,2), LSM
        COMMON /STR/ STRAMA(5,2)
        COMMON /TAB/ TAB(100,4,7)
        COMMON /TIM/ T, RT, TEND, TCOND(150), EPS, IPRINT
        COMMON /TIM/ JPRINT(25)
        COMMON /TXS/ TX(200,16), TXI(200)
        COMMOM /TXS/ ACTIVL(200,2), CHAINA(200,2), LTX
        COMMON /TYP/ TYPE(15), BHEAD(796), THEAD(6), LHEAD(6)
        COMMON /TYP/ TTEST
        COMMON /UCH/ USERCT(2,2), USERCF(200,1,2)
C
C       SPECIFY COMMON /PRIV/
C       ====================
        COMMON /PRIV/ DUMMY
C
C
C       EXCLUDE REPEATED CHECKS
C       =======================
        CHECK = .FALSE.
        IF (TCOND(NCOND) .EQ. T) RETURN
C
```

```
C       LABEL SELECTOR
C       ==============
C
        GOTO (1), NCOND
C
        WRITE(NUNIT2,3000) T,NCOND
3000    FORMAT(1H0,5(1H+),10H CHECK: T=,F12.4,
       +' ERROR IN LABEL SELECTOR NCOND = ',I3)
        GOTO 9999
C
C       CONDITIONS
C       ==========
C
1       CONTINUE
        GOTO 100
C
C
C       SET INDICATOR FOR SATISFIED CONDITION
C       =====================================
100     IF (CHECK) TCOND(NCOND) = T
        RETURN
9999    RETURN
        END
```

```
      SUBROUTINE DETECT(NSET,*,*)
C     ***
C     *** CALL DETECT(NSET,*1000,*9999)
C     ***
C     *** PURPOSE  : CHECK ALL CROSSINGS WHICH CAN OCCUR IN A
C     ***             SET WITH INDEX NSET
C     *** PARAMETERS: NSET = INDEX OF SET FOR WHICH CROSSING
C     ***                    IS TO BE CHECKED
C     ***             EXIT1 = EXIT TO EQUAT WHEN IFLAG WAS SET
C     ***                     TO 2 IN SUBROUTINE CROSS
C     ***             EXIT2 = ERROR EXIT
C     ***
      INTEGER CHAINE
      INTEGER UNIT1,XFORM,UNIT2,XUNIT3,XUNIT4
      INTEGER UNIT5, UNIT6, UNIT7, UNIT8
      REAL INTMA, INTSTA
      LOGICAL CHECK
      COMMON /EQU/ EQUL(3,4), CHAINE(3)
      COMMON /EQU/ INTMA(3,8), INTSTA(3,4)
      COMMON /EQU/ IFLAG(3,50), IFLAGP(3,50), JFLAG(3,50),
      COMMON /EQU/ JFLAGL(3,50)
      COMMON /EQU/ SV(3,100), SVLAST(3,100)
      COMMON /EQU/ DV(3,100), DVLAST(3,100), ICONT
      COMMON /FIL/ UNIT1,UNIT2,XUNIT3,XUNIT4,NUNIT1,NUNIT2,XFORM
      COMMON /FIL/ UNIT5,UNIT6,UNIT7,UNIT8
      COMMON /TIM/ T, RT, TBUSY, TEND, TCOND(150) , EPS, IPRINT
      COMMON /TIM/ JPRINT(25)
C
C     SPECIFY COMMON /PRIV/
C     =====================
      COMMON /PRIV/ DUMMY
C
C     LABEL SELECTOR
C     ==============
      GOTO(1,2,3), NSET
      WRITE(NUNIT2,3000) T,NSET
3000  FORMAT(1H0,5(1H+),11H DETECT: T=,F12.4,
     +33H ERROR IN LABEL SELECTOR NSET=,I3)
      GOTO 9999
C
C     CALL SUBROUTINE CROSS FOR SET1
C     ==============================
1     CONTINUE
      RETURN
C
C     CALL SUBROUTINE CROSS FOR SET2
C     ==============================
2     CONTINUE
      RETURN
C
C     CALL SUBROUTINE CROSS FOR SET3
C     ==============================
3     CONTINUE
      RETURN
C
C     RETURN TO EQUAT
C     ===============
977   RETURN 1
9999  RETURN 2
      END
```

```
          SUBROUTINE EVENT(NE,*)
C         ***
C         *** CALL EVENT(NE,*120)
C         ***
C         *** FUNCTION  :  PERFORM EVENTS AND SCHEDULE NEXT EVENT
C         *** PARAMETER:  NE = INDEX OF EVENT
C         ***
          CHARACTER*4 PLOMA3
          INTEGER CHAINC, CHAINE, CHAINV, CHAINM, CHAINS, CHAINA
          INTEGER FAC, FAM, ASM, GATHT, GATHF, SE,PLAMA,POL,POOL,SBM
          INTEGER SM,STRAMA,TYPE,BHEAD,USERCT,USERCF,SOURCI,TXI
          INTEGER UNIT1,XFORM,UNIT2,XUNIT3,XUNIT4,NUNIT1,NUNIT2
          INTEGER UNIT5, UNIT6, UNIT7, UNIT8
          REAL NTXC, INTMA, INTSTA, MONITL, LOGMA
          LOGICAL CHECK
          COMMON /BIN/ BIN(10,8), BINSTA(10,5)
          COMMON /CON/ CONFL(10,5), CHAINC(10), CON(10,500), CLEV
          COMMON /EQU/ EQUL(3,4), CHAINE(3)
          COMMON /EQU/ INTMA(3,8), INTSTA(3,4)
          COMMON /EQU/ IFLAG(3,50), IFLAGP(3,50), JFLAG(3,50),
          COMMON /EQU/ JFLAGL(3,50)
          COMMON /EQU/ SV(3,100), SVLAST(3,100)
          COMMON /EQU/ DV(3,100), DVLAST(3,100), ICONT
          COMMON /EVT/ EVENTL(50), CHAINV(50)
          COMMON /FAC/ FAC(10,3)
          COMMON /FAM/ FAM(200,2), ASM(200,1)
          COMMON /GAT/ GATHT(5), GATHF(200,1)
          COMMON /FIL/ UNIT1,UNIT2,XUNIT3,XUNIT4,NUNIT1,NUNIT2,XFORM
          COMMON /FIL/ UNIT5,UNIT6,UNIT7,UNIT8
          COMMON /MFA/ MFAC(2,2), MBV(2), SE(20,3), LSE
          COMMON /PLA/ PLAMA(2,2)
          COMMON /PLO/ MONITL(10), CHAINM(10)
          COMMON /PLO/ PLOMA1(10,16), PLOMA2(10,5)
          COMMON /PLC/ PLOMA3(10,18)
          COMMON /POL/ POL(10,3)
          COMMON /POO/ POOL(5,2)
          COMMON /RAS/ RASTL(10)
          COMMON /SRC/ SOURCL(10,3), CHAINS(10), SOURCI(10)
          COMMON /SRC/ NTXC, LSL, TXMAX
          COMMON /STO/ SBM(5,2), SM(1024,2), LSM
          COMMON /STR/ STRAMA(5,2)
          COMMON /TAB/ TAB(100,4,7)
          COMMON /TIM/ T, RT, TEND, TCOND(150), EPS, IPRINT
          COMMON /TIM/ JPRINT(25)
          COMMON /TRA/ TXADD(200,4), CARMA(100,10), TARMA(100,7)
          COMMON /TRA/ LOGMA(200,5), LOGPTR(2), STATIS(100,10)
          COMMON /TRA/ STATST(20,4), PARKST(20,4), BLOCST(100,4)
          COMMON /TXS/ TX(200,16), ACTIVL(200,2), TXI(200)
          COMMON /TXS/ CHAINA(200,2), LTX
          COMMON /TYP/ TYPE(15), BHEAD(796), THEAD(6), LHEAD(6)
          COMMON /TYP/ TTEST
          COMMON /UCH/ USERCT(2,2), USERCF(200,1,2)
C
C         SPECIFY COMMON /PRIV/
C         ====================
          COMMON /PRIV/ DUMMY
C
C
          IF(IPRINT.EQ.0.AND.JPRINT(19).EQ.0.OR.JPRINT(19).EQ.-1)
         +GOTO 100
          WRITE(NUNIT2,3000) T,NE
```

```
3000  FORMAT(12H EVENT:   T =,F12.4,2X,'EVENT ',I3,
     +' PERFORMED')
C
100   CONTINUE
C
C     LABEL SELECTOR
C     ==============
C
      GOTO (1), NE
C
      WRITE(NUNIT2,3010) T,NE
3010  FORMAT(1H0,5(1H+),10H EVENT: T=,F12.4,
     +' ERROR IN LABEL SELECTOR  NE=',I3)
      GOTO 9999
C
C
C     PROCESS EVENTS
C     ==============
C
1     CONTINUE
C
      RETURN
C
C     EXIT TO TERMINATING SECTION
C     ===========================
9999  RETURN 1
      END
```

```
      FUNCTION DYNPR(LTX1)
C     ***
C     *** PURPOSE  : RECOMPUTE THE PRIORITY OF A TRANSACTION
C     ***  PARAMETER: LTX1 = ROW INDEX OF THE TRANSACTION WHOSE
C     ***                    PRIORITY IS TO BE RECOMPUTED
C     ***
      INTEGER CHAINA
      INTEGER UNIT1,TXI,XFORM,UNIT2,XUNIT3,XUNIT4
      INTEGER UNIT5, UNIT6, UNIT7, UNIT8
      COMMON /FIL/ UNIT1,UNIT2,XUNIT3,XUNIT4,NUNIT1,NUNIT2,XFORM
      COMMON /FIL/ UNIT5,UNIT6,UNIT7,UNIT8
      COMMON /TXS/ TX(200,16), TXI(200)
      COMMON /TXS/ ACTIVL(200,2), CHAINA(200,2), LTX
C
C     DETERMINE THE PRIORITY
C     ======================
      DYNPR = TX(LTX1,4)
      RETURN
      END
```

```
      SUBROUTINE STATE(NSET,*)
C     ***
C     *** CALL STATE(NSET,*9999)
C     ***
C     *** PURPOSE  :  CONTAINS CODE OF DIFFERENTIAL EQUATIONS
C     ***                FOR CONTINUOUS VARIABLES
C     *** PARAMETERS: NSET  = INDEX OF SET
C     ***             EXIT1 = ERROR EXIT
C     ***
      INTEGER CHAINE
      INTEGER UNIT1,UNIT2,XUNIT3,XUNIT4,XFORM
      INTEGER UNIT5, UNIT6, UNIT7, UNIT8
      REAL INTMA, INTSTA
      LOGICAL CHECK
      COMMON /EQU/ EQUL(3,4), CHAINE(3)
      COMMON /EQU/ INTMA(3,8), INTSTA(3,4)
      COMMON /EQU/ IFLAG(3,50), IFLAGP(3,50), JFLAG(3,50),
      COMMON /EQU/ JFLAGL(3,50)
      COMMON /EQU/ SV(3,100), SVLAST(3,100)
      COMMON /EQU/ DV(3,100), DVLAST(3,100), ICONT
      COMMON /FIL/ UNIT1,UNIT2,XUNIT3,XUNIT4,NUNIT1,NUNIT2,XFORM
      COMMON /FIL/ UNIT5,UNIT6,UNIT7,UNIT8
      COMMON /TIM/ T, RT, TBUSY, TEND, TCOND(150), EPS, IPRINT
      COMMON /TIM/ JPRINT(25)
C
C     SPECIFY COMMON /PRIV/
C     =====================
      COMMON /PRIV/ DUMMY
C
C     LABEL SELECTOR
C     ==============
C
      GOTO (1,2,3),NSET
C
      WRITE(NUNIT2,3000) T,NSET
3000  FORMAT(1H0,5(1H+),10H STATE: T=,F12.4,
     +' ERROR IN LABEL SELECTOR  NSET=',I3)
      GOTO 9999
C
C     *** EQUATIONS FOR SET 1 ***
1     CONTINUE
      RETURN
C
C     *** EQUATIONS FOR SET 2 ***
2     CONTINUE
      RETURN
C
C     *** EQUATIONS FOR SET 3 ***
3     CONTINUE
      RETURN
C
9999  RETURN 1
      END
```

```
          SUBROUTINE TEST(*)
C         ***
C         *** CALL TEST(*710)
C         ***
C         *** PURPOSE  :  AUTOMATIC TESTING OF ALL CONDITIONS   WHICH
C         ***             CONTAIN CROSSINGS
C         *** PARAMETERS: EXIT1 = EXIT TO TERMINATING SECTION
C         ***
          CHARACTER*4 PLOMA3
          INTEGER CHAINC, CHAINE, CHAINV, CHAINM, CHAINS, CHAINA
          INTEGER FAC, FAM, ASM, GATHT, GATHF, SE,PLAMA,POL,POOL,SBM
          INTEGER SM, STRAMA, TYPE, BHEAD, USERCT, USERCF
          INTEGER UNIT1,XFORM,UNIT2,XUNIT3,XUNIT4
          INTEGER UNIT5, UNIT6, UNIT7, UNIT8
          REAL NTXC, INTMA, INTSTA, MONITL
          LOGICAL CHECK
          COMMON /BIN/ BIN(10,8), BINSTA(10,5)
          COMMON /CON/ CONFL(10,5), CHAINC(10), CON(10,500), CLEV
          COMMON /EQU/ EQUL(3,4), CHAINE(3)
          COMMON /EQU/ INTMA(3,8), INTSTA(3,4)
          COMMON /EQU/ IFLAG(3,50), IFLAGP(3,50), JFLAG(3,50),
          COMMON /EQU/ JFLAGL(3,50)
          COMMON /EQU/ SV(3,100), SVLAST(3,100)
          COMMON /EQU/ DV(3,100), DVLAST(3,100), ICONT
          COMMON /EVT/ EVENTL(50), CHAINV(50)
          COMMON /FAC/ FAC(10,3)
          COMMON /FAM/ FAM(200,2), ASM(200,1)
          COMMON /GAT/ GATHT(5), GATHF(200,1)
          COMMON /FIL/ UNIT1,UNIT2,XUNIT3,XUNIT4,NUNIT1,NUNIT2,XFORM
          COMMON /FIL/ UNIT5,UNIT6,UNIT7,UNIT8
          COMMON /MFA/ MFAC(2,2), MBV(2), SE(20,3), LSE
          COMMON /PLA/ PLAMA(2,2)
          COMMON /PLO/ MONITL(10), CHAINM(10)
          COMMON /PLO/ PLOMA1(10,16), PLOMA2(10,5)
          COMMON /PLC/ PLOMA3(10,18)
          COMMON /POL/ POL(10,3)
          COMMON /POO/ POOL(5,2)
          COMMON /RAS/ RASTL(10)
          COMMON /SRC/ SOURCL(10,3), SOURCI(10)
          COMMON /SRC/ CHAINS(10), NTXC, LSL, TXMAX
          COMMON /STO/ SBM(5,2), SM(1024,2), LSM
          COMMON /STR/ STRAMA(5,2)
          COMMON /TAB/ TAB(100,4,7)
          COMMON /TIM/ T, RT, TEND, TCOND(150), EPS, IPRINT
          COMMON /TIM/ JPRINT(25)
          COMMON /TXS/ TX(200,16), ACTIVL(200,2), CHAINA(200,2), LTX
          COMMON /TYP/ TYPE(15), BHEAD(796), THEAD(6), LHEAD(6)
          COMMON /TYP/ TTEST
          COMMON /UCH/ USERCT(2,2), USERCF(200,1,2)
C
C         SPECIFY COMMON /PRIV/
C         =====================
          COMMON /PRIV/ DUMMY
C
C
C         TEST THE CONDITIONS
C         ===================
1         CONTINUE
C
C
          RETURN
```

```
C
C      EXIT TO TERMINATING SECTION
C      ===========================
9999   RETURN 1
       END
```

Dummy subroutines for occupation and freeing plans, policies, occupation and freeing strategies, and integration methods

```
SUBROUTINE PLANI2(MFA)
RETURN
END

SUBROUTINE PLANI3(MFA)
RETURN
END

SUBROUTINE PLANI4(MFA)
RETURN
END

SUBROUTINE PLANI5(MFA)
RETURN
END

SUBROUTINE PLANO2(MFA)
RETURN
END

SUBROUTINE PLANO3(MFA)
RETURN
END

SUBROUTINE PLANO4(MFA)
RETURN
END

SUBROUTINE PLANO5(MFA)
RETURN
END

SUBROUTINE POLI3
RETURN
END

SUBROUTINE POLI4
RETURN
END

SUBROUTINE POLI5
RETURN
END

SUBROUTINE STRAA3(NST,NE)
RETURN
END

SUBROUTINE STRAA4(NST,NE)
RETURN
END

SUBROUTINE STRAA5(NST,NE)
RETURN
END
```

```
SUBROUTINE STRAF1(NST,KEY)
RETURN
END

SUBROUTINE STRAF2(NST,KEY)
RETURN
END

SUBROUTINE STRAF3(NST,KEY)
RETURN
END

SUBROUTINE STRAF4(NST,KEY)
RETURN
END

SUBROUTINE STRAF5(NST,KEY)
RETURN
END

SUBROUTINE INTE5
RETURN
END
```

A 7 Subroutines

Appendix A 7 contains the call and the list of parameters of all
subroutines of GPSS-FORTRAN Version 3.

Notes:

   * The user should make certain that the expressions in the
   subroutine calls have the same type as the corresponding parameter. Otherwise errors occur which may lead to errors in
   another part of the program.

   * The type of variable in the parameter is determined by the
   inital letter in its name. The names are chosen in accordance
   with the FORTRAN conversion: names which begin with I, J, K, L,
   M, N are of type integer.


```
      SUBROUTINE ACTIV(*)
***
*** CALL ACTIV(EXIT1)
***
*** PURPOSE  : MODEL
*** PARAMETER: EXIT1 = EXIT TO TERMINATING SECTION
***


      SUBROUTINE ADVANC(AT,IDN,*)
***
*** CALL ADVANC(AT,IDN,*9000)
***
*** PURPOSE   : SCHEDULE A TRANSACTION
*** PARAMETERS: AT = TIME UNTIL REACTIVATION
***             IDN = LABEL AT WHICH REACTIVATED


      SUBROUTINE ALLOC(NST,NE,MARK,IBLOCK,LINE,ID,*)
***
*** CALL ALLOC(NST,NE,MARK,IBLOCK,LINE,ID,*9000)
***
*** PURPOSE  : OCCUPY A STORAGE
*** PARAMETER: NST    = INDEX OF STORAGE
***            NE     = NUMBER OF LOCATIONS TO BE OCCUPIED
***            MARK   = LOCATION INDICATOR
***            IBLOCK = BLOCKING PARAMETER
***                   = 0: STORGE REQUIREMENT IS TESTED
***                        ON ARRIVAL OF TRANSACTION
***                   = 1: TRANSACTION IS BLOCKED ON
***                        ARRIVAL
***            LINE   = LOCATION
***            ID     = LABEL OF SUBROUTINE CALL
```

```
    SUBROUTINE ANAR(X,IDIM,ICNUM,CLEV,RMEAN,HALFW,JMIN,KMIN,
    +IP,IPRIN,*)
***
*** CALL ANAR(X,IDIM,ICNUM,CLEV,RMEAN,HALFW,JMIN,KMIN,
*** +IP,IPRIN,EXIT1)
***
*** PURPOSE  : DETERMINE A CONFIDENCE INTERVAL
***             (FISHMAN: PRINCIPLES OF DISCRETE EVENT
***              SIMULATION, 1978)
*** PARAMETERS: X     = ARRAY CONTAINING COLLECT. VALUES
***             IDIM  = NUMBER OF VALUES
***             ICNUM = INDEX OF CONFIDENCE INTERVAL
***             CLEV  = CONFIDENCE LEVEL
***             RMEAN = COMPUTED MEAN VALUE
***             HALFW = COMPUTED HALF INTERVAL WIDTH
***             JMIN  = END OF SETTLING PHASE
***             KMIN  = DISTANCE BETWEEN INDEPENDENT
***                     SAMPLES
***             IP    = ORDER
***             IPRIN = OUTPUT PARAMETER
***                     =0 NO OUTPUT
***                     =1 OUTPUT OF AUTOCOVARIANCE
***                     =2 ADDITIONAL OUTPUT OF INTERVAL
***                        MEANS AND VALUE OF CMEAN
***             EXIT1 = ERROR EXIT
***


    SUBROUTINE ANNOUN(NE,TE,*)
***
*** CALL ANNOUN(NE,TE,EXIT1)
***
*** PURPOSE  : SCHEDULE, ALTER, OR UNSCHEDULE AN EVENT
*** PARAMETERS: NE    = EVENT INDEX
***             TE    = TIME OF ACTIVATION
***                     >= 0: SCHEDULE OR CHANGE
***                     <  0: UNSCHEDULE
***             EXIT1 = ERROR EXIT
***


    SUBROUTINE ARRIVE(NBN,NT)
***
*** CALL ARRIVE(NBN,NT)
***
*** PURPOSE   : ENTER A BIN
*** PARAMETERS: NBN = INDEX OF BIN
***             NT  = NUMBER OF TOKENS
***
```

```
      SUBROUTINE ASSEMB(NASS,NTX,*)
***
*** CALL ASSEMB(NASS,NTX,*9000)
***
*** PURPOSE   : COMBINE TRANSACTIONS OF A FAMILY
*** PARAMETERS: NASS = INDEX OF ASSEMBLY STATION
***             NTX  = NUMBER OF TRANSACTIONS TO
***                    BE COMBINED
***


      SUBROUTINE BEGIN(NSET,*)
***
*** CALL BEGIN(NSET,*9999)
***
*** PURPOSE   : COMPUTE DERIVATIVE AFTER DISCRETE
***             STATE TRANSITION
***             START INTEGRATION
***             REGISTER POSSIBLE CROSSINGS
***             RECORD DELAYED VARIABLES
*** PARAMETERS: NSET  = INDEX OF SET
***             EXIT1 = ERROR EXIT
***


      SUBROUTINE BFIT(NST,NE)
***
*** CALL BFIT(NST,NE)
***
*** PURPOSE   : SEARCH FOR FREE STORAGE REGION USING BEST
***             FIT STRATEGY
*** PARAMETERS: NST = INDEX OF STORAGE
***             NE  = NUMBER OF LOCATIONS TO BE OCCUPIED
***


      SUBROUTINE BLOCK(NT,NS,LFAM,IFTX)
***
*** CALL BLOCK(NT,NS,LFAM,IFTX)
***
*** PURPOSE   : INSERT A TRANSACTION INTO BLOCKED CHAIN BEHIND
***             TRANSACTION WITH ROW INDEX IFTX
*** PARAMETERS: NT   = STATION TYPE
***             NS   = INDEX IN TYPE
***             LFAM = ROW INDEX IN FAM ARRAY FOR GATHER STATIONS
***                    FOR FAMILIES, USER CHAINS FOR FAMILIES,
***                    TRIGGER STATIONS FOR FAMILIES
***             IFTX = ROW INDEX OF PRECEDING TRANSACTION
***
```

```
      SUBROUTINE BOXEXP(RMIN,RMAX1,RMAX2,RATIO,IRNUM,RANDOM)
***
*** CALL BOXEXP(RMIN,RMAX1,RMAX2,RATIO,IRNUM,RANDOM)
***
*** PURPOSE   : GENERATE A RANDOM NUMBER FROM A DISTRIBUTION WITH
***             UNIFORM AND EXPONENTIAL COMPONENTS
*** PARAMETERS: RMIN    = LOWER BOUND OF UNIFORM DISTRIBUTION
***             RMAX1   = UPPER BOUND OF UNIFORM DISTRIBUTION
***             RMAX2   = UPPER BOUND OF EXPONENTIAL DISTRIBUTION
***             RATIO   = PROBABILITY THAT RANDOM NUMBER BELONGS
***                       TO UNIFORM DISTRIBUTION
***             IRNUM   = INDEX OF RANDOM NUMBER GENERATOR
***             RANDOM  = RANDOM NUMBER COMPUTED
***
```

```
      LOGICAL FUNCTION CHECK(NCOND)
***
*** PURPOSE   : CHECK LOGICAL CONDITION
*** PARAMETER : NCOND = INDEX OF LOGICAL CONDITION
***
```

```
      SUBROUTINE CLEAR(NFA,*,*)
***
*** CALL CLEAR(NFA,EXIT1,*9999)
***
*** PURPOSE   : FREE A FACILITY
*** PARAMETERS: NFA    = INDEX OF FACILITY
***             EXIT1  = EXIT FOR PREEMPTION
***
```

```
      SUBROUTINE CONF(NBN)
***
*** CALL CONF(NBN)
***
*** PURPOSE   : SUM WAITING TIMES
*** PARAMETER : NBN   = INDEX OF BIN
***




      SUBROUTINE CONFI(NBN)
***
*** CALL CONFI(NBN)
***
*** PURPOSE   : AUTOMATIC DETERMINATION OF INTERVAL LENGTHS
*** PARAMETER : NBN = INDEX OF BIN
***




      SUBROUTINE CROSS(NSET,NCR,NX,NY,CMULT,CADD,LDIR,TOL,*,*)
***
*** CALL CROSS(NSET,NCR,NX,NY,CMULT,CADD,LDIR,TOL,*977,*9999)
***
*** PURPOSE   : RECOGNISE AND LOCATE CROSSINGS, SET IFLAG
***             AND JFLAG
*** PARAMETERS: NSET  = INDEX OF SET
***             NCR   = INDEX OF CROSSING
***             NX    = INDEX OF CROSSING VARIABLE 'X'
***                     WITHIN THE SETS 'NSET'
***                     NX > 0 : VARIABLE IS SV
***                     NX < 0 : VARIABLE IS DV
***             NY    = INDEX OF CROSSED VARIABLE 'Y'
***                     NY > 0 : VARIABLE IS SV
***                     NY < 0 : VARIABLE IS DV
***                     NY = 0 : CROSSED VALUE = CADD
***             CMULT = MULTIPLIER OF Y
***             CADD  = ADDED TO CMULT*Y
***                     CROSSED VALUE IF NY = 0
***             LDIR  = DIRECTION IN WHICH CROSSING IS TO BE
***                     LOCALISED
***                     0 : CROSSING FROM ABOVE OR BELOW
***                     +1: CROSSING FROM ABOVE
***                     -1: CROSSING FROM BELOW
***             TOL   = TOLERANCE
***             EXIT1 = EXIT IF IFLAG = 2
***             EXIT2 = ERROR EXIT
***
```

```
      SUBROUTINE DBLOCK(NT,NS,LFAM,MAX)
***
*** CALL DBLOCK(NT,NS,LFAM,MAX)
***
*** PURPOSE   : UNBLOCK TRANSACTIONS AT A STATION
*** PARAMETERS: NT   = STATION TYPE
***             NS   = INDEX IN STATION
***             LFAM = ROW INDEX IN FAMILY ARRAY
***             MAX  = NUMBER OF TRANSACTIONS TO BE UNBLOCKED
***                    > 0 : MAXIMUM NUMBER
***                    = 0 : ALL TRANSACTIONS BLOCKED AT
***                              STATION
***
```

```
      SUBROUTINE DEFILL(NSET, NVAR, X, IDIM, *)
***
***  CALL DEFILL(NSET,NVAR,X,IDIM,*9999)
***
***  PURPOSE   : STORE VALUES OF DELAYED VARIABLE
***  PARAMETERS: NSET = INDEX OF SET
***              NVAR = INDEX OF DELAYED VARIABLE
***                     > 0 : CONTINUOUS VARIABLE
***                     < 0 : DERIVATIVE
***              X    = ARRAY OF BASE POINTS OF DELAYED
***                     VARIABLE
***              IDIM = NUMBER OF POINTS IN X
***              EXIT1= ERROR EXIT
```

```
      SUBROUTINE DELAY(NSET, NVAR, TAU, DVALUE, *)
***
*** CALL DELAY(NSET,NVAR,TAU,DVALUE,*9999)
***
*** PURPOSE   : DETERMINE VALUE OF DELAYED VARIABLE
*** PARAMETERS: NSET = INDEX OF SET
***             NVAR = INDEX OF DELAYED VARIABLE
***                    > 0 : CONTINUOUS VARIABLE
***                    < 0 : DERIVATIVE
***              TAU = DELAY
***            DVALUE= COMPUTED VALUE OF DELAYED VARIABLE
***             EXIT1 = ERROR EXIT
```

```
      SUBROUTINE DEPART(NBN,NT,VL,*)
***
*** CALL DEPART(NBN,NT,VL,*9999)
***
*** PURPOSE   : LEAVE A BIN
*** PARAMETERS: NBN  = INDEX OF BIN
***             NT   = NUMBER OF TOKENS
***             VL   = LENGTH OF INTERVAL
***                  = 0: AUTOMATIC DETERMINATION
***                  › 0: PROVIDED BY USER
***
```

```
      SUBROUTINE DETECT(NSET,*,*)
***
*** CALL DETECT(NSET,*1000,*9999)
***
*** PURPOSE   : CHECK ALL CROSSINGS IN A SET
*** PARAMETERS: NSET  = INDEX OF SET
***             EXIT1 = EXIT TO EQUAT WHEN IFLAG WAS NOT SET
***                     EQUAL TO 2
***             EXIT2 = ERROR EXIT
***
```

```
      FUNCTION DYNPR(LTX1)
***
*** PURPOSE   : RECOMPUTE THE PRIORITY OF A TRANSACTION
*** PARAMETER : LTX1 = ROW INDEX OF TRANSACTION
***
```

```
      SUBROUTINE DYNVAL(NT,NS,LFAM,ICOUNT)
***
*** CALL DYNVAL(NT,NS,LFAM,ICOUNT)
***
*** PURPOSE   : RECOMPUTE THE PRIORITY OF ALL TRANSACTIONS
***             BLOCKED AT A STATION
*** PARAMETERS: NT     = TYPE OF STATION
***             NS     = INDEX OF STATION IN TYPE
***             LFAM   = ROW INDEX IN FAMILY ARRAY
***             ICOUNT = NUMBER OF PRIORITIES RECOMPUTED
***
```

```
      SUBROUTINE ENDBIN
***
*** CALL ENDBIN
***
*** PURPOSE   : FINAL COMPUTATION FOR BINS AND DETERMINATION
***              OF THE CONFIDENCE INTERVALS
***



      SUBROUTINE ENDPLO(ISTAT)
***
*** CALL ENDPLO(ISTAT)
***
*** PURPOSE   : OUTPUT OF ALL PLOTS
***
*** PARAMETER : ISTAT = COMPUTATION OF STATISTICAL QUANTITIES
***                      =0 NO
***                      =1 YES



      SUBROUTINE ENDTAB(NTAB,IGRAPH,YLL,YUL)
***
*** CALL ENDTAB(NTAB,IGRAPH,YLL,YUL)
***
*** PURPOSE   : COMPUTE, PRINT, AND PLOT A HISTOGRAM
*** PARAMETERS: NTAB    = INDEX OF HISTOGRAM
***                     = 0 PROCESS ALL HISTOGRAMS
***             IGRAPH  = PLOT MODE
***                     = 0 NO PLOT
***                     = 1 ABSOLUTE FREQUENCIES
***                     = 2 RELATIVE FREQUENCIES
***                     = 3 ABSOLUTE CUMULATIVE FREQUENCIES
***                     = 4 RELATIVE CUMULATIVE FREQUENCIES
***             YLL     = LOWER BOUND OF PLOT
***             YUL     = UPPER BOUND OF PLOT
                          YLL=0. und YUL=0. : AUTOMATIC SCALING
```

```
      SUBROUTINE ENTER(NPL,NE,IBLOCK,ID,*)
***
*** CALL ENTER(NPL,NE,IBLOCK,ID,*9000)
***
*** PURPOSE   : OCCUPY A POOL
*** PARAMETERS: NPL    = INDEX OF POOL
***             NE     = NUMBER OF POOL ELEMENTS TO BE OCCUPIED
***             IBLOCK = BLOCKING INDICATOR
***                    = 0: THE REQUIRMENT IS TESTED ON ARRIVAL
***                         OF THE TRANSACTION
***                    = 1: THE TRANSACTION IS BLOCKED ON
***                         ARRIVAL
***             ID     = LABEL OF SUBROUTINE CALL



      SUBROUTINE EQUAT(NSET,*)
***
*** CALL EQUAT(NSET,*720)
***
*** PURPOSE   : PERFORM AN INTEGRATION STEP FOR A SET,
***             ADJUST THE STEP SIZE TO THE RELATIVE
***             ERROR
***             LOCATE A CROSSING
***             DEAL WITH EFFECT OF CROSSING ON OTHER SETS
*** PARAMETER : NSET = INDEX OF SET
***



      SUBROUTINE ERLANG(RMEAN,K,RNIM,RMAX,IRNUM,RANDOM,*)
***
*** CALL ERLANG(RMEAN,K,RMIN,RMAX,IRNUM,RANDOM,*9999)
***
*** PURPOSE   : GENERATE A RANDOM NUMBER WITH ERLANG DISTRIBUTION
*** PARAMETERS: RMEAN   = MEAN
***             K       = DEGREE
***             RMIN    = MINIMUM
***             RMAX    = MAXIMUM
***             IRNUM   = INDEX OF RANDOM NUMBER GENERATOR
***             RANDOM  = COMPUTED RANDOM NUMBER
***
```

```
      SUBROUTINE EVENT(NE,*)
 ***
 *** CALL EVENT(NE,*9999)
 ***
 *** PURPOSE   : PROCESS AN EVENT AND SCHEDULE THE NEXT EVENT
 *** PARAMETER : NE = INDEX OF EVENT
 ***


      SUBROUTINE EXTPOL(NSET,TSTEP,RERR,*)
 ***
 *** CALL EXTPOL(NSET,TSTEP,RERR,*9999)
 ***
 *** PURPOSE   : PERFORM AN INTEGRATION STEP USING EXTRAPOLATION
 *** PARAMETERS: NSET  = INDEX OF SET
 ***             TSTEP = STEP SIZE
 ***             RERR  = RELATIVE ERROR OF INTEGRATION
 ***             EXIT1 = ERROR EXIT



      SUBROUTINE FFIT(NST,NE)
 ***
 *** CALL FFIT(NST,NE)
 ***
 *** PURPOSE   : SEARCH FOR FREE STORAGE REGION USING FIRST
 ***             FIT STRATEGY
 *** PARAMETERS: NST = INDEX OF STORAGE
 ***             NE  = NUMBER OF LOCATIONS TO BE OCCUPIED
 ***



      SUBROUTINE FIFO(K,IFTX,NP)
 ***
 *** CALL FIFO(K,IFTX,NP)
 ***
 *** PURPOSE   : SEARCH FOR POSITION IN QUEUE ACCORDING TO FIFO
 *** PARAMETERS: K    = INDEX OF STATION
 ***             IFTX = LAST TRANSACTION
 ***             NP   = POSITION OF TRANSACTION TO BE INSERTED IN
 ***                    QUEUE


      SUBROUTINE FLOWC(*)
 ***
 *** CALL FLOWC(*7000)
 ***
 *** PURPOSE   : FLOW CONTROL
 *** PARAMETER : EXIT1 = ERROR EXIT
```

```
      SUBROUTINE FREE(NST,NE,KEY,LINE,*)
***
*** CALL FREE(NST,NE,KEY,LINE,EXIT1)
***
*** PURPOSE   : FREE STORAGE REGION USING FREEING INDICATOR
*** PARAMETERS: NST   = INDEX OF STORAGE
***             NE    = NUMBER OF LOCATIONS TO BE FREED
***             KEY   = FREEING INDICATOR
***             LINE  = START OF REMAINDING REGION
***             EXIT1 = EXIT IF LOCATIONS CANNOT BE FREED
***
```

```
      SUBROUTINE FREEFO(XFILE,NSCR,FIELD,FIELDC,INDIC,IELEM,*)
***
*** CALL FREEFO(XFILE,FIELD,FIELDC,INDIC,IELEM,EXIT1)
***
*** PURPOSE   : INPUT A FREE FORMAT DATA RECORD
*** PARAMETERS: XFILE  = INPUT/ OUTPUT INDICATOR
***             FIELD  = CONTAINS DECODED INPUT ELEMENT OF
***                      TYPE INTEGER OR REAL
***             FIELDC = CONTAINS DECODED INPUT ELEMENT OF
***                      TYPE CHARACTER
***             INDIC  = TYPE INDICATOR OF INPUT
***             IELEM  = INDEX OF FIRST SYNTACTICALLY WRONG
***                      CHARACTER
***             EXIT1  = ERROR EXIT
***
```

```
      SUBROUTINE FUNCT(VFUNCT,IDIM,X,Y,IND,*)
***
***   CALL FUNCT(VFUNCT,IDIM,X,Y,IND,*9999)
***
***   PURPOSE   :   LINEAR INTERPOLATION
***   PARAMETERS:   VFUNCT = ARRAY OF BASE POINTS ARRANGED IN
***                          INCREASING ORDER OF THE INPEPENDENT
***                          VARIABLES
***                 IDIM   = NUMBER OF BASE POINTS
***                 X      = VALUE OF INDEPENDENT VARIABLE FOR
***                          WHICH THE VALUE OF Y IS TO BE
***                          COMPUTED
***                 Y      = COMPUTED VALUE OF Y
***                 IND    = RANGE INDICATOR
***                        = 0: INTERPOLATION
***                        = 1: LINEAR EXTRAPOLATION
***                        = 2: ERROR INDICATOR



      SUBROUTINE GATE(NG,NCOND,IGLOBL,IBLOCK,ID,*)
***
***   CALL GATE(NG,NCOND,IGLOBL,IBLOCK,ID,*9000)
***
***   PURPOSE   : BLOCK A TRANSACTION OR ALLOW IT TO PROCEED
***               ACCORDING TO THE LOGICAL VALUE OF AN EXPRESSION
***   PARAMETERS: NG     = INDEX OF GATE
***               NCOND  = INDEX OF LOGICAL CONDITION IN FUNCTION
***                        CHECK
***               IGLOBL = PARAMETER INDICATOR
***                      = 0: THE LOGICAL EXPRESSION CONTAINS
***                           USER VARIABLES
***                      = 1: THE LOGICAL EXPRESSION CONTAINS
***                           ONLY GLOBAL PARAMETERS
***               IBLOCK = BLOCKING PARAMETER
***                      = 0: THE TRANSACTION CHECKS THE
***                           CONDITION ON ARRIVAL
***                      = 1: THE TRANSACTION IS BLOCKED ON
***                           ARRIVAL
***               ID     = LABEL OF STATEMENT CALL
***
```

```
      SUBROUTINE GATHR1(NG,NTX,ID,*)
***
*** CALL GATHR1(NG,NTX,ID,*9000)
***
*** PURPOSE   : COLLECT A QUEUE OF TRANSACTIONS
*** PARAMETERS: NG  = INDEX OF GATHER STATION FOR TRANSACTIONS
***             NTX = NUMBER OF TRANSACTIONS TO BE COLLECTED
***             ID  = LABEL OF SUBRROUTINE CALL
***




      SUBROUTINE GATHR2(NG,NTX,ID,*)
***
*** CALL GATHR2(NG,NTX,ID,*9000)
***
*** PURPOSE   : COLLECT QUEUES OF TRANSACTIONS ACCORDING
***             TO FAMILY MEMBERSHIP
*** PARAMETERS: NG  = INDEX OF GATHER STATION FOR FAMILIES
***             NTX = NUMBER OF TRANSACTIONS TO BE COLLECTED
***             ID  = LABEL OF SUBROUTINE CALL
***




      SUBROUTINE GAUSS(RMEAN,SIGMA,RMIN,RMAX,IRNUM,RANDOM)
***
*** CALL GAUSS(RMEAN,SIGMA,RMIN,RMAX,IRNUM,RANDOM)
***
*** PURPOSE   : GENERATE A RANDOM NUMBER WITH NORMAL DISTRIBUTION
*** PARAMETERS: RMEAN   = MEAN
***             SIGMA   = STANDARD DEVIATION
***             RMIN    = MINIMUM
***             RMAX    = MAXIMUM
***             IRNUM   = INDEX OF RANDOM NUMBER GENERATOR
***             RANDOM  = RANDOM NUMBER COMPUTED
***




      SUBROUTINE GENERA(ET,PR,*)
***
*** CALL GENERA(ET,PR,*9999)
***
*** PURPOSE   : GENERATE A TRANSACTION
*** PARAMETERS: ET = TIME UNTIL NEXT GENERATION
***             PR = PRIORITY OF TRANSACTION GENERATED
***
```

```
      SUBROUTINE GRAPH(VFUNC,IDIM,YLL,YUL,TEXT)
***
*** CALL GRAPH(VFUNC,IDIM,YLL,YUL,TEXT)
***
*** PURPOSE   :  OUTPUT A BAR CHART
*** PARAMETERS:  VFUNC = ARRAY CONTAINING VALUES TO BE
***                      PLOTTED
***              IDIM  = DIMENSION OF VFUNC
***              YLL   = LOWER BOUND OF COLUMN
***              YUL   = UPPER BOUND OF COLUMN
***                      YLL=0. und YUL=0.: AUTOMATIC SCALING
***              TEXT  = HEADING
***


      SUBROUTINE INIT1
***
*** CALL INIT1
***
*** PURPOSE   : INITIALISE RANDOM NUMBER GENERATORS
***


      SUBROUTINE INIT2(*)
***
*** CALL INIT2(*9999)
***
*** PURPOSE   : DEFINE DATA AREAS FOR MULTIFACILITIES
***


      SUBROUTINE INIT3(*)
***
*** CALL INIT3(*9999)
***
*** PURPOSE   : DEFINE DATA AREAS FOR STORAGES
***


      SUBROUTINE INIT4
***
*** CALL INIT4
***
*** PURPOSE   : INITIALISE THE TYPE ARRAY
***
```

```
      SUBROUTINE INPUT(XFILE,*)
***
*** CALL INPUT (XFILE,*9999)
***
*** PURPOSE   : READ FREE FORMAT DATA FROM INPUT FILE
*** PARAMETERS: XFILE = INPUT/OUTPUT INDICATOR
***             EXIT1 = ERROR EXIT
***


      SUBROUTINE INTEG(NSET,TSTEP,RERR,IERR,*)
***
*** CALL INTEG(NSET,TSTEP,RERR, IERR,*9999)
***
*** PURPOSE   : SELECT INTEGRATION METHOD FOR A SET
*** PARAMETERS: NSET  = INDEX OF SET
***             TSTEP = STEP SIZE
***             RERR  = RELATIVE ERROR OF INTEGRATION
***             IERR  = INDICATOR FOR ESTIMATION OF ERROR
***             EXIT1 = ERROR EXIT
***


      SUBROUTINE KNOCKD(NFA,RKT,IDN,*,*)
***
*** CALL KNOCKD(NFA,RKT,IDN,*9000,*9999)
***
*** PURPOSE   : CLOSE DOWN FACILITY
*** PARAMETERS: NFA = INDEX OF FACILITY
***             RKT = CLOSING DOWN TIME
***             IDN = LABEL AT WHICH TRANSACTION IS TO BE
***                   REACTIVATED


      SUBROUTINE LEAVE(NPL,NE,*)
***
*** CALL LEAVE(NPL,NE,EXIT1)
***
*** PURPOSE   : FREE POOL ELEMENTS
*** PARAMETERS: NPL   = INDEX OF POOL
***             NE    = NUMBER OF ELEMENTS TO BE FREED
***             EXIT1 = EXIT IF FREEING NOT POSSIBLE
***
```

```
      SUBROUTINE LFIRST(MFA)
***
*** CALL LFIRST(MFA)
***
*** PURPOSE   : SEARCH FOR THE FIRST FREE ELEMENT OF A MULTI-
***             FACILITY
*** PARAMETER : MFA  = INDEX OF MULTIFACILITY
***


      SUBROUTINE LINK1(NUC,ID,*)
***
*** CALL LINK1(NUC,ID,*9000)
***
*** PURPOSE   : BLOCK TRANSACTIONS IN A USER CHAIN
*** PARAMETERS: NUC = INDEX OF USER CHAIN FOR TRANSACTIONS
***             ID  = LABEL OF SUBROUTINE CALL
***


      SUBROUTINE LINK2(NUC,ID,*)
***
*** CALL LINK2(NUC,ID,*9000)
***
*** PURPOSE   : BLOCK TRANSACTIONS OF A FAMILY IN A
***             USER CHAIN
*** PARAMETERS: NUC = INDEX OF USER CHAIN FOR FAMILIES
***             ID  = LABEL OF SUBROUTINE CALL
***


      SUBROUTINE LOGNOR(RMEAN,SIGMA,RMIN,RMAX,IRNUM,RANDOM)
***
*** CALL LOGNOR(RMEAN,SIGMA,RMIN,RMAX,IRNUM,RANDOM)
***
*** PURPOSE   : GENERATE A RANDOM NUMBER WITH LOGNORMAL
***             DISTRIBUTION
*** PARAMETERS: RMEAN   = MEAN VALUE
***             SIGMA   = STANDARD DEVIATION
***             RMIN    = MINIMUM
***             RMAX    = MAXIMUM
***             IRNUM   = INDEX OF RANDOM NUMBER GENERATOR
***             RANDOM  = RANDOM NUMBER COMPUTED
***
```

```
      SUBROUTINE MATCH(NM,ID,*)
***
*** CALL MATCH(NM,ID,*9000)
***
*** PURPOSE   : BUFFER A TRANSACTION
*** PARAMETERS: NM = INDEX OF MATCH STATION
***             ID = LABEL OF SUBROUTINE CALL
***




      SUBROUTINE MCLEAR(MFA,*,*)
***
*** CALL MCLEAR(MFA,EXIT1,*9999)
***
*** PURPOSE   : FREE AN ELEMENT OF A MULTIFACILITY
*** PARAMETERS: MFA   = INDEX OF MULTIFACILITY
***             EXIT1 = EXIT FOR PREEMPTED TRANSACTIONSTRS




      SUBROUTINE MKNOCK(MFA,RKT,IDN,*,*)
***
*** CALL MKNOCK(MFA,RKT,IDN,*9000,*9999)
***
*** PURPOSE   : CLOSE DOWN AN ELEMENT OF A MULTIFACILITY
*** PARAMETERS: MFA = INDEX OF MULTIFACILITY
***             RKT = CLOSING DOWN TIME
***             IDN = LABEL AT WHICH TRANSACTION IS TO
***                   REACTIVATED




      SUBROUTINE MONITR(NPLOT)
***
*** CALL MONITR(NPLOT)
***
*** PURPOSE   : RECORD CONTINUOUS VARIABLES
*** PARAMETER : NPLOT = INDEX OF PLOT
***                   = 0   record for all plots
***
```

```
      SUBROUTINE MPREEM(MFA,ID,*)
***
*** CALL MPREEM(MFA,ID,*9000)
***
*** PURPOSE   : OCCUPY AND POSSIBLY PREEMPT AN ELEMENT OF A
***             MULTIFACILITY
*** PARAMETERS: MFA = INDEX OF MULTIFACILITY
***             ID  = LABEL OF SUBROUTINE CALL
***


      SUBROUTINE MSEIZE(MFA,ID,*)
***
*** CALL MSEIZE(MFA,ID,*9000)
***
*** PURPOSE   : OCCUPY AN ELEMENT OF A MULTIFACILITY
*** PARAMETERS: MFA = INDEX OF MULTIFACILITY
***             ID  = LABEL OF SUBROUTINE CALL


      SUBROUTINE MSETUP(MFA,ST,IDN,*,*)
***
*** CALL MSETUP(MFA,ST,IDN,*9000,*9999)
***
*** PURPOSE   : SET UP AN ELEMENT OF A MULTIFACILITY
*** PARAMETERS: MFA = INDEX OF MULTIFACILITY
***             ST  = SETTING UP TIME
***             IDN = LABEL AT WHICH TRANSACTION IS TO BE
***                   REACTIVATED


      SUBROUTINE MWORK(MFA,WT,IEX,IDN,*,*)
***
*** CALL MWORK(MFA,WT,IEX,IDN,*9000,*9999)
***
*** PURPOSE   : PROCESS A TRANSACTION IN AN ELEMENT OF A
***             MULTIFACILITY
*** PARAMETERS: MFA = INDEX OF MULTIFACILITY
***             WT  = PROCESSING TIME
***             IEX = PREEMPTION INDICATOR
***                 = 0: THE TRANSACTION CAN BE PREEMPTED
***                 = 1: THE TRANSACTION CANNOT BE PREEMPTED
***             IDN = LABEL AT WHICH TRANSACTION IS TO BE
***                   REACTIVATED
```

```
      SUBROUTINE NCHAIN(LIST,LINE,*)
***
*** CALL NCHAIN(LIST,LINE,EXIT1)
***
*** PURPOSE   : REMOVE AN ELEMENT OF A SCHEDULE
*** PARAMETERS: LIST  = INDEX OF SCHEDULE
***                   = 1: EVENT SCHEDULE
***                   = 2: SOURCE SCHEDULE
***                   = 3: TRANSACTION SCHEDULE
***                   = 4: BIN SCHEDULE
***                   = 5: MONITOR SCHEDULE
***                   = 6: SET SCHEDULE
***             LINE  = INDEX OF ELEMENT TO BE REMOVED
***             EXIT1 = ERROR EXIT
***


      SUBROUTINE PFIFO(K,IFTX,NP)
***
*** CALL PFIFO(K,IFTX,NP)
***
*** PURPOSE   : SEARCH FOR POSITION IN QUEUE ACCORDING TO PFIFO
*** PARAMETERS: K    = INDEX OF STATION
***             IFTX = ROW INDEX OF TRANSACTIONS AFTER WHICH
***                    TRANSACTION IS TO BE INSERTED
***             NP   = INDEX OF POSITION
***


      SUBROUTINE PLANI(MFA)
***
*** CALL PLANI(MFA)
***
*** PURPOSE   : DETERMINE PLAN ACCORDING TO WHICH AN ELEMENT OF A
***             MULTIFACILITY IS TO BE OCCUPIED
*** PARAMETER : MFA   = INDEX OF MULTIFACILITY
***


      SUBROUTINE PLANO(MFA)
***
*** CALL PLANO(MFA)
***
*** PURPOSE   : DETERMINE PLAN ACCORDING TO WHICH A TRANSACTION
***             IS TO BE PREEMPTED FROM A FACILITY
*** PARAMETER : MFA   = INDEX OF MULTIFACILITY
***
```

```
      SUBROUTINE PLOT(IPLOT, IFILE, OFILE, RTIMSC, IPLOTA, ISCAL,
     +RYMIN, RYMAX, XPLOT, ISTAT, RVNAME)
***
*** CALL PLOT(IPLOT,IFILE,OFILE,RTIMSC,IPLOTA,ISCAL,RYMIN,RYMAX,
***           XPLOT,ISTAT,RVNAME)
***
*** PURPOSE   : OUTPUT OF PLOTS, TABLES OF VALUES, AND
***             AND PHASE DIAGRAMS
***
*** PARAMETERS:
***             IPLOT = INDEX OF PLOT
***             IFILE = NUMBER OF PLOT FILE
***             OFILE = NUMBER OF OUTPUT FILE
***             RTIMSC= TIME STEP
***             IPLOTA= TYPE OF OUTPUT
***                     =1 PLOT
***                     =2 PLOT AND TABLE OF VALUES (DEFAULT)
***                     =3 PLOT, TABLE OF VALUES, AND PHASE
***                        DIAGRAM
***             ISCAL = TYPE OF SCALING OF Y AXSIS
***                     =0 INDIVIDUAL SCALING FOR EACH VARIABLE
***                        WITH ROUNDED SCALING FACTOR
***                     =1 INDIVIDUAL SCALING FOR EACH VARIABLE
***                        FROM MINIMUM TO MAXIMUM VALUE
***                     =2 SAME SCALING FOR ALL VARIABLES.
***                        MINIMUM AND MAXIMUM VALUES OF Y
***                        ARE PROVIDED BY RYMIN AND RYMAX
***                     =3 SAME SCALING FOR ALL VARIABLES
***                        FROM SMALLEST MINIMUM TO LARGEST
***                        MAXIMUM WITH ROUNDED SCALING FACTOR
***                     =4 LOGARTHMIC SCALING
***             RYMIN =  MINIMUM VALUE OF Y
***                      (ONLY FOR ISCAL=2)
***             RYMAX =  MAXIMUM VALUE OF Y
***                      (ONLY FOR ISCAL=2)
***             XPLOT =  PLOT INDICATOR
***                      =0 OUTPUT TO PRINTER
***                         (132 CHARACTER PER LINE)
***                      =1 OUTPUT TO TERMINAL
***                         (80 CHARACTER PER LINE)
***             ISTAT =  CALCULATE STATISTICAL QUANTITIES
***                      =0: NO; =1: YES
***             RVNAME = SYMBOLS AND IDENTIFIERS USED
***
```

```
      SUBROUTINE POLICY(NT,NS,LFAM,IFTX,NP)
***
*** CALL POLICY(NT,NS,LFAM,IFTX,NP)
***
*** PURPOSE   : DETERMINE POLICY ACCORDING TO WHICH A
***             TRANSACTION IS TO OCCUPY A FACILITY
*** PARAMETERS: NT   = TYPE OF STATION
***             NS   = INDEX IN TYPE
***             LFAM = ROW INDEX IN FAMILY ARRAY
***             IFTX = ROW INDEX OF PROCEEDING TRANSACTION
***             NP   = POSITION INDICATOR
```

```
      SUBROUTINE PREEMP(NFA,ID,*)
***
*** CALL PREEMP(NFA,ID,*9000)
***
*** PURPOSE   : OCCUPY AND POSSIBLY PREEMPT A FACILITY
*** PARAMETERS: NFA = INDEX OF FACILITY
***             ID  = LABEL OF SUBROUTINE CALL
***
```

```
      SUBROUTINE PRESET
***
***  CALL PRESET
***
*** PURPOSE   : ASSIGN DEFAULT VALUES
***
```

```
      SUBROUTINE PRIOR(MFA)
***
*** CALL PRIOR(MFA)
***
*** PURPOSE   : SELECT TRANSACTION WITH LOWEST PRIORITY
***             IN A MULTIFACILITY
*** PARAMETERS: MFA ‹ INDEX OF MULTIFACILITY
***
```

```
    SUBROUTINE RBLOCK(NT,NS,LFAM,MAX)
***
*** CALL RBLOCK(NT,NS,LFAM,MAX)
***
*** PURPOSE    : REBLOCK UNBLOCKED TRANSACTION
*** PARAMETER : NT   = TYPE OF STATION
***              NS   = INDEX WITHIN TYPE
***              LFAM = ROW INDEX IN FAM ARRAY
***              MAX  = NUMBER OF TRANSACTIONS TO BE BLOCKED
***                   = 0: BLOCK ALL TRANSACTIONS
***


    SUBROUTINE REPRT1(NT)
***
*** CALL REPRT1(NT)
***
*** PURPOSE    : PRINT STATE OF STATIONS OF TYPE NT
*** PARAMETER : NT = TYPE OF STATION;
***                  TYPES 8 AND 9 OR 10 AND 11 ARE ALWAYS
***                  PRINTED TOGETHER
***


    SUBROUTINE REPRT2
***
*** CALL REPRT2
***
*** PURPOSE    : PRINT TRANSACTION ARRAY AND THE FAMILY ARRAY
***


    SUBROUTINE REPRT3
***
*** CALL REPRT3
***
*** PURPOSE    : PRINT THE ARRAYS USED BY THE FLOW CONTROL
***


    SUBROUTINE REPRT4
***
*** CALL REPRT4
***
*** PURPOSE    : PRINT THE BIN AND BINSTA ARRAYS
***
```

```
      SUBROUTINE REPRT5(NBIN1,NBIN2,NBIN3,NBIN4,NBIN5,NBIN6)
***
*** CALL REPRT5(NBIN1,NBIN2,NBIN3,NBIN4,NBIN5,NBIN6)
***
*** PURPOSE    : PLOT THE DYNAMIC BEHAVIOUR OF THE QUEUE LENGTHS
***               OF UP TO 6 BINS
*** PARAMETERS: NBIN1 = INDEX OF 1'ST BIN
***             NBIN2 = INDEX OF 2'ND BIN
***             NBIN3 = INDEX OF 3'RD BIN
***             NBIN4 = INDEX OF 4'TH BIN
***             NBIN5 = INDEX OF 5'TH BIN
***             NBIN6 = INDEX OF 6'TH BIN
***



      SUBROUTINE REPRT6
***
*** CALL REPRT6
***
*** PURPOSE    : PRINT THE INTEGRATION STATISTICS ARRAY
***



      SUBROUTINE REPRT7
***
*** CALL REPRT7
***
*** PURPOSE    : PRINT PAST VALUES OF DELAYED VARIABLES



      SUBROUTINE RESET
***
*** CALL RESET
***
*** PURPOSE    : RESET DATA AREAS
***
```

```
      SUBROUTINE RKF(NSET,TSTEP,RERR,IERR,*)
***
***  CALL RKF(NSET,TSTEP,RERR,IERR,*9999)
***
***  PURPOSE   : PERFORM ONE INTEGRATION STEP USING RUNGE KUTTA
***               FEHLBERG METHOD
***  PARAMETERS: NSET  = INDEX OF SET TO BE INTEGRATED
***               TSTEP = STEP SIZE
***               RERR  = RELATIVE ERROR
***               IERR  = INDICATOR FOR ERROR COMPUTATION
***               EXIT1 = ERROR EXIT
***
```

```
       SUBROUTINE RKIMP(NSET,TSTEP,RERR,IERR,*)
***
***   CALL RKIMP(NSET,TSTEP,RERR,IERR,*9999)
***
***  PURPOSE   : PERFORM ONE INTEGRATION STEP USING IMPLICIT
***               GAUSSIAN RUNGE KUTTA METHOD
***  PARAMETERS: NSET  = INDEX OF SET TO BE INTEGRATED
***               TSTEP = STEP SIZE
***               RERR  = RELATIVE ERROR
***               IERR  = INDICATOR FOR ERROR COMPUTATION
***               EXIT1 = ERROR EXIT
***
```

```
      FUNCTION RN(IRNUM)
***
***  PURPOSE   : GENERATE A RANDOM NUMBER IN THE INTERVAL (0.1)
***  PARAMETER : IRNUM = INDEX OF RANDOM NUMBER GENERATOR
***
```

```
      SUBROUTINE SAVIN
***
***  CALL SAVIN
***
***  PURPOSE   : INPUT THE STATE OF THE MODEL FROM FILE WITH
***               LOGICAL NUMBER = 12
***
```

```
      SUBROUTINE SAVOUT
***
*** CALL SAVOUT
***
*** PURPOSE   : SAVE STATE OF MODEL IN FILE WITH LOGICAL
***             NUMBER = 12


      SUBROUTINE SEIZE(NFA,ID,*)
***
*** CALL SEIZE(NFA,ID,*9000)
***
*** PURPOSE   : OCCUPY A FACILITY
*** PARAMETERS: NFA = INDEX OF FACILITY
***             ID  = LABEL OF SUBROUTINE CALL
***



      SUBROUTINE SETUP(NFA,ST,IDN,*,*)
***
*** CALL SETUP(NFA,ST,IDN,*9000,*9999)
***
*** PURPOSE   : SET UP A FACILITY
*** PARAMETERS: NFA = INDEX OF FACILITY
***             ST  = SETTING UP TIME
***             IDN = LABEL AT WHICH TRANSACTION IS
***                   REACTIVATED
***


      SUBROUTINE SIMEND(NBN,NDP,P)
***
*** CALL SIMEND(NBN,NDP,P)
***
*** PURPOSE   : TEST FOR THE END OF THE SIMULATION RUN USING
***             THE MEAN OCCUPATION TIME OF A BIN
*** PARAMETERS: NBN    = INDEX OF BIN TO BE TESTED
***             NDP    = NUMBER OF CALLS OF DEPART BETWEEN 2
***                      CALLS
***             P      = PERMISSIBLE DEVIATION OF MEAN IN PER
***                      CENT


      SUBROUTINE SPLIT(NDUP,IDN,*)
***
*** CALL SPLIT(NDUP,IDN,*9999)
***
*** PURPOSE   : DUPLICATE A TRANSACTION
*** PARAMETERS: NDUP = NUMBER OF DUPLICATES
***             IDN  = LABEL AT WHICH DUPLICATES ARE TO BE
***                    REACTIVATED
```

```
      SUBROUTINE START(NSC,TSC,IDG,*)
***
*** CALL START(NSC,TSC,IDG,EXIT1)
***
*** PURPOSE     : SCHEDULE, ALTER OR CLOSE A SOURCE
*** PARAMETERS: NSC   = INDEX OF SOURCE
***             TSC   = TIME OF ACTIVATION
***                     >= 0: SCHEDULE OR ALTER
***                     <  0: UNSCHEDULE
***             IDG   = LABEL OF CORRESPONDING CALL OF GENERA
***             EXIT1 = ERROR EXIT




      SUBROUTINE STATE(NSET,*)
***
*** CALL STATE(NSET,*9999)
***
*** PURPOSE     : CONTAINS CODE FOR DIFFERENTIAL EQUATIONS AND
***               COMPUTATION OF CONTINUOUS VARIABLES
*** PARAMETERS: NSET  = INDEX OF SET
***             EXIT1 = ERROR EXIT
***


      SUBROUTINE STRATA(NST,NE)
***
*** CALL STRATA(NST,NE)
***
*** PURPOSE     : DETERMINE STRATEGY FOR OCCUPING STORAGE
*** PARAMETERS: NST    = INDEX OF STORAGE
***             NE     = NUMBER OF LOCATIONS TO BE OCCUPIED
***


      SUBROUTINE STRATF(NST,KEY,*)
***
*** CALL STRATF(NST,KEY,EXIT1)
***
*** PURPOSE     : DETERMINE STRATEGY FOR FREEING STORAGES
*** PARAMETERS: NST    = INDEX OF STORAGE
***             KEY    = FREEING INDICATOR
***             EXIT1  = ERROR EXIT
```

```
      SUBROUTINE SYSVAR
***
*** CALL SYSVAR
***
*** PURPOSE    : ASSIGN VARIABLES FOR ARRAY BOUNDS
***



      SUBROUTINE TABULA(NTAB,NG,X,Y,OG1,GBR)
***
*** CALL TABULA(NTAB,NG,X,Y,OG1,GBR)
***
*** PURPOSE    : INSERT PAIR OF VALUES IN FREQUENCY TABLE
*** PARAMETERS: NTAB = INDEX OF FREQUENCY TABLE
***              NG   = NUMBER OF INTERVALS
***              X    = INDEPENDENT VARIABLE
***              Y    = DEPENDENT VARIABLE
***              OG1  = UPPER BOUND OF FIRST INTERVAL
***              GBR  = WIDTH OF INTERVAL



      SUBROUTINE TCHAIN(LIST,LINE,*)
***
*** CALL TCHAIN(LIST,LINE,EXIT1)
***
*** PURPOSE    : INSERT AN ENTRY IN A SCHEDULE
*** PARAMETERS: LIST  = INDEX OF SCHEDULE
***                   = 1: EVENT SCHEDULE
***                   = 2: SOURCE SCHEDULE
***                   = 3: TRANSACTION SCHEDULE
***                   = 4: BIN SCHEDULE
***                   = 5: MONITOR SCHEDULE
***                   = 6: SET SCHEDULE
***              LINE  = INDEX OF ROW TO BE INSERTED
***              EXIT1 = ERROR EXIT



      SUBROUTINE TERMIN(*)
***
*** CALL TERMIN(*9000)
***
*** PURPOSE    : ELIMINATE A TRANSACTION
***
```

```
      SUBROUTINE TEST(*)
***
*** CALL TEST(*710)
***
*** PURPOSE   : TEST ALL CONDITIONS
*** PARAMETER : EXIT1 = EXIT TO TERMINATING SECTION
***


      SUBROUTINE TRANSF(RATIO,IRNUM,*)

***
*** CALL TRANSF(RATIO,IRNUM,EXIT1)
***
*** PURPOSE   : STOCHASTIC SPLITTING OF A STREAM OF TRANSACTIONS
*** PARAMETERS: RATIO = PROBABILITY OF SELECTION OF TRANSACTION
***             IRNUM = INDEX OF RANDOM NUMBER GENERATOR
***             EXIT1 = LABEL TO WHICH CONTROL IS TRANSFERRED FOR
***                     SELECTED TRANSACTIONS


      SUBROUTINE UNIFRM(A,B,IRNUM,RANDOM)
***
*** CALL UNIFRM(A,B,IRNUM,RANDOM)
***
*** PURPOSE   : GENERATE A RANDOM NUMBER WITH UNIFORM
***             DISTRIBUTION IN RANGE (A,B)
*** PARAMETERS: A      = MAXIMUM
***             B      = MINIMUM
***             IRNUM  = INDEX OF RANDOM NUMBER GENERATOR
***             RANDOM = RANDOM NUMBER COMPUTED


      SUBROUTINE UNLIN1(NUC,MIN,MAX,ID,*)
***
*** CALL UNLIN1(NUC,MIN,MAX,ID,*9000)
***
*** PURPOSE   : FETCH A BLOCK OF TRANSACTIONS FROM A USER
***             CHAIN FOR TRANSACTIONS
*** PARAMETERS: NUC = INDEX OF USER CHAIN FOR TRANSACTIONS
***             MIN = MINIMUM
***             MAX = MAXIMUM
***             ID  = LABEL OF THE SUBROUTINE CALL
***
```

```
      SUBROUTINE UNLIN2(NUC,MIN,MAX,ID,*)
***
*** CALL UNLIN2(NUC,MIN,MAX,ID,*9000)
***
*** PURPOSE   : FETCH A BLOCK OF TRANSACTIONS FROM A USER
***               CHAIN FOR FAMILIES
*** PARAMETERS: NUC = INDEX OF USER CHAIN FOR FAMILIES
***             MIN = MINIMUM
***             MAX = MAXIMUM
***             ID  = LABEL OF SUBROUTINE CALL
***


      SUBROUTINE WORK(NFA,WT,IEX,IDN,*,*)
***
*** CALL WORK(NFA,WT,IEX,IDN,*9000,*9999)
***
*** PURPOSE   : PROCESS A TRANSACTION IN A FACILITY
*** PARAMETERS: NFA = INDEX OF FACILITY
***             WT  = PROCESSING TIME
***             IEX = PREEMPTION INDICATOR
***                 = 0: PREEMPTION ALLOWED
***                 = 1: PREEMPTION FORBIDDEN
***             IDN = LABEL AT WHICH TRANSACTION WILL BE
***                   REACTIVATED
***


      SUBROUTINE XBEGIN (XENDA,XGO,XNEW,XOUT),*,*)
***
*** CALL XBEGIN(XEND,XGO,XNEW,XOUT,*6000,*7000)
***
*** PURPOSE   : CALLED OF BEGIN AFTER "NEW" COMMAND,
***               PROCESS COMMAND INDICATOR
*** PARAMETERS: XEND  = END INDICATOR
***             XGO   = GO INDICATOR
***             XNEW  = NEW INDICATOR
***             XOUT  = OUT INDICATOR
***             EXIT1 = EXIT TO FLOWC
***             EXIT2 = EXIT TO TERMINATING SECTION
***
```

```
         SUBROUTINE XINPUT (XEND,XGO,XNEW,XOUT,*)
***
***      CALL XINPUT (XEND,XGO,XNEW,XOUT,*9999)
***
***      PURPOSE   : INTERACTIVE INPUT
***      PARAMETERS: XEND  = END INDICATOR
***                  XGO   = GO INDICATOR
***                  XNEW  = NEW INDICATOR
***                  XOUT  = OUT INDICATOR
***                  EXIT1 = ERROR EXIT
***


         SUBROUTINE YCLOCK (*,*)
***
***      CALL YCLOCK (*10,*9999)
***
***      PURPOSE   : ADMINISTRATION OF CLOCK IN REAL TIME
***
***      PARAMETERS: EXIT1 = INITIATE ACTIVITY TRIGGERED BY REAL
***                          SYSTEM
***                  EXIT2 = ERROR EXIT
***
```

Index

A

ACTIV 21,38,41,42,45,58,59,70
ADVANC 44,59
ALLOC 106
ANNOUN 3,16
ARRIVE 52,78
Activating transactions 123
Amount of rain 184
Amplitude of the force 177
Animals, carnivorous 155
Animals, herbivorous 155
Array bounds 224
Arrays, multidimensional 211
Average time 44
Averages 69

B

BEGIN 3,18,26,61
BIN table 52
BINSTA 105
BINSTA table 52
Barrel 38
Best fit 110
Bin 52,71,123
Block, unoccupied 106
Brewery model I 37
Brewery model II 37
Brewery model II 51
Brewery model III 37,58

C

CHECK 21,24,25,39,40,59,62,134,135,148
CLEAR 70,72
COMMON/PRIV/ 21,22
CROSS 27,147
Capacity 99
Car telephone 112,124
Cash register 161
Cedar bog lake model 155,157
Characters, treatment of 195
Combination 155
Combined simulation models 28
Command name 6
Computer model I 96
Computer model II 96
Computer model II 106
Conditions 24,25,59,72,134,148
Conditions, checking the 26,27
Conditions, definition of 1
Conditions, initial 14
Conditions, testing of 1

Conditions, testing the 136
Confidence interval 9,57,69,158
Consulting rooms 90
Crossing 27,60,136
Crossings 25

D

DBLOCK 40,46,61,97,106
DEFILL 185
DELA 185
DELAY 185
DEPART 52,77
DETECT 21,60,147
DT 168
DYNVAL 82,85,86
Damping constant 173
Data areas 200
Data areas, combining the 186
Deactivate 45
Decrease, rates of 168
Delay 166,170,184
Delay of second order 170
Delay, maximum 185
Description, short 6
Differential equations 173,157,168
Duplicate symbols 10
Dynamic alteration 32

E

ENDBIN 52
ENDPLO 9
ENDTAB 84
ENTER 97
EQUAT 24
ERLANG 51,57,70
EVENT 3,21,26
Emergencies 90
Ending, criterion for 76,101
Energy, loss of 155
Energy, units of 155
Error 6
Error, relative 8
Event 30
Events 1,3,15,18,24,25,30,123

F

FORTRAN features 194
FREE 106
Facility 69,78

Factor, multiplicative 28
Family 41
File handling   194
First fit 106,107
Flag 130,147
Flow control 45,46,50,72
Framework 139
Frequency distribution 117
GASP IV 128
GATE 38,45,46
GATHR1 112
GAUSS 57
GENERA 38,41,45,51,70
GOTO, computed 195
GRAPH 84,101
Gap 106,110
Gate 115,122
Graphical representation 155
Gravity, center of 173
Group practice 69
Group practice model 90
Growth curve, exponential 34
Growth curve, logistic 33

H

Host parasite model 184
Host parasite model I 1
Host parasite model II 1,15
Host parasite model III 1,24
Host parasite model IV 1,32
Host parasite model V 144
Host parasite model VI 155,184

I

IBLOCK 43
IFLAG 25,27,60,135,147
INTI 5
INTSTA array 4
IPRINT 18,46
IV 20
Impulse 183
Increase, rates of 168
Increased brightness 24
Incubation, period of 184
Influence 184
Initial conditions 34
Initial setting 24
Input 20
Input data 4,139,148
Input data record 43
Input strategies 96
Integration algorithm 6

Integration statistic 9
Integration step size 8,168
Integration steps, maximum number of 6
Job administration 69
Job administration model 82

K

KEY 106

L

LEAVE 97
LFIRST 91
Labels 46
Lamp 24
Level 166
Level of water 184
Logical value 26
Logistic growth function 32

M

MCLEAR 91
MKNOCK 91
MONITR 3,10,18,61
MSEIZE 91
MSETUP 91
Main program 63,79,84,101
Mass 173
Match station 124
Material 155
Mean time 77
Mean waiting time 42
Memory requirements 105
Memory usage 105
Memory, administration of the 96
Memory, secondary 96,97
Mobile model component 37
Model components 155,161
Model components, stationary 37
Model, combined 1
Model, description of 1
Model, structure of the 32,58
Models, continuous 1
Models, combined discrete and continuous 15
Models, complex 63
Models, queued 37,69
Monitor, step size of 6
Multifacility 69,90
Multifacility, elements of a 90
Multipliers, large 232
Multipliers, small 232

N

Normal distribution   179
Notes   227

O

Occupation   96
Output   170
Output strategies   96

P

PLAMA   91
PLOT   5
PRESET   73
PRIOR   91
Parallel branches   121
Parallel processing   117
Parasite model VI   184
Parcel transport   112
Patients, normal   90
Patients, urgent   90
Plan array   91
Plants   155
Plot   7,10,123
Plot symbol   6
Plot, number of   6,7
Pool   96,99
Pool array   99
Pools of resources   96
Practice   90
Preemption   69,81
Print indicator   7
Priorities, dynamic assignment of   69,85
Priorities, reassignment of   82
Priority   77,82,105,124
Priority assignment   84
Priority, initial   82
Processor   96
Production, rate of   184
Pump   38

R

RANDOM   51
REPRT1   47
REPRT2   47
REPRT3   47
REPRT4   52,105
REPRT6   4,8

RESET 73
RV 20
Random number generators 51,57,73
Random number generator, double word 229
Random numbers 51,229
Random numbers, generation of 37,183
Random variations 57
Rate at which the barrel is filled 58
Rate of change 184
Recalculate 82
Record 20
Repair workshop 69,77,162
Report subroutines 46

S

SEIZE 70
SIMEND 84,101
SOURCE 41
START 41,119
STATE 2,21,24,59
STRAMA 106,110
STRATA 106
Scaling 7
Scenic mountain 112,117
Service time 44
Set concept 144
Set, number of the 6
Setting up time 77
Settling phase 9,105,158
Simulation, combined 128
Simulation, repetition of 73
Simulator, handling the 197
Sine function 177
Single branch 112
Snow tire model 170
Snowtire supply model 155
Source array 70
Sources 119
Spring 173
Spring constant 173
Squirrel 69
Starting sources 123
State transition 50
State variable 122,130
State, previous 185
Station 37
Station type 123
Station, general type of 115
Station, index of the 123
Statistical data 52
Statistical information
Step size 168
Step size, initial 6
Step size, maximum integration 6

Step size, minimum integration 6
Stochastic systems 51
Stock of capital goods 184
Stock of cars 170
Storage 110
Storage tank 128
Strategy 106
Strategy matrix 106
Structure, modular 63
Submodels 144
Submodels, coupled 144,146
Subroutines 255
Subroutines, multiple exits from 196
Supermarket 161
Supermarket model 155
System dynamics models 155,166
Systems, continuous stochastic 155,179

T

TABULA 117,118
TAU 184
TAUMAX 187
TERMIN 39,99
TEST 21,27,40,61
TEXT 5
TRANSF 77
TTEST 24,27,40,136
Tanker 128
Tanker fleet model 128
Test flag 24,27
Test indicator 136
Test track 183
Time interval 124
Time of completion 44
Time step, size of 7
Time slice, size of the 101
Token 52,71
Total time 77
Trace 46
Trace of the execution 18
Transaction 38,41,78,121,123
Transaction array 45
Transaction, time spent by a 53
Transactions, blocked 112
Transactions, simultanious 112
Trigger station 117

U

UNIFRM 51
UNLIN1 117
User attributes 44,45
User chain 117

User programs   235

V

VARI   5,20
Value   26
Values, assignment of   20
Values, new   3
Values, table of   10
Variable which effects the crossing   27
Variable, identifier of
Variables   200,228

W

WORK   70
Wheel suspension model I   155,173
Wheel suspension model II   155,179,183

X

XINPUT   20